THE GRAMMAR OF POLITICS

Also by CRESSIDA J. HEYES
Line Drawings: Defining Women through Feminist Practice

THE GRAMMAR OF POLITICS

Wittgenstein and Political Philosophy

EDITED BY

Cressida J. Heyes

Cornell University Press

ITHACA AND LONDON

Copyright © 2003 by Cornell University

All rights reserved. Except for brief quotations in a review, this book, or parts thereof, must not be reproduced in any form without permission in writing from the publisher. For information, address Cornell University Press, Sage House, 512 East State Street, Ithaca, New York 14850.

First published 2003 by Cornell University Press
First printing, Cornell Paperbacks, 2003

Printed in the United States of America

Library of Congress Cataloging-in-Publication Data

The grammar of politics : Wittgenstein and political philosophy / edited by Cressida J. Heyes.
    p. cm.
Includes bibliographical references and index.
  ISBN 0-8014-4056-4 (cloth : alk. paper) — ISBN 0-8014-8838-9 (pbk. : alk. paper)
  1. Political science—Philosophy. 2. Wittgenstein, Ludwig, 1889–1951. I. Heyes, Cressida J. II. Title
  JA71 .G695 2003
  320'.01—dc21
                                                    2002015020

Cornell University Press strives to use environmentally responsible suppliers and materials to the fullest extent possible in the publishing of its books. Such materials include vegetable-based, low-VOC inks and acid-free papers that are recycled, totally chlorine-free, or partly composed of nonwood fibers. For further information, visit our website at www.cornellpress.cornell.edu.

Cloth printing   10 9 8 7 6 5 4 3 2 1
Paperback printing   10 9 8 7 6 5 4 3 2 1

*In memory of Karen Lee Pilkington
1959–2000*

Contents

Acknowledgments — ix

Abbreviations — xi

    Introduction — 1
    Cressida J. Heyes

Part I. Wittgenstein and Method

1. **Wittgenstein and Political Philosophy: Understanding Practices of Critical Reflection** — 17
   James Tully

2. **The Limits of Conservatism: Wittgenstein on "Our Life" and "Our Concepts"** — 43
   David R. Cerbone

3. **Wittgenstein, Fetishism, and Nonsense in Practice** — 63
   Denis McManus

4. **Genealogy as Perspicuous Representation** — 82
   David Owen

Part II. A Wittgensteinian Politics

5. **Notes on the Natural History of Politics** — 99
   Allan Janik

6. **Wittgenstein and the Conversation of Justice** — 117
   Richard Eldridge

7. **Doing without Knowing: Feminism's Politics of the Ordinary** — 129
   Linda M. G. Zerilli

8. **On Seeing Liberty As** — 149
   Jonathan Havercroft

Part III. Wittgenstein Applied

9. "But One Day Man Opens His Seeing Eye":
   The Politics of Anthropomorphizing Language — 167
   Wendy Lynne Lee

10. Does Your Patient Have a Beetle in His Box?
    Language-Games and the Spread of Psychopathology — 186
    Carl Elliott

11. Wittgenstein on Bodily Feelings:
    Explanation and Melioration in Philosophy of Mind, Art, and Politics — 202
    Richard Shusterman

Notes — 221

Bibliography — 247

About the Contributors — 253

Index — 257

Acknowledgments

I'd like to thank, first, all the contributors to this volume for their hard work and good humor. I've often heard editors lamenting the drudgery and frustrations of compiling a book like this one, but my experience has been entirely positive. In particular I thank Jim Tully, who first introduced me to the study of Wittgenstein and political philosophy, and who has done so much to create scholarly interest in this field. The idea for this volume came from Alison Shonkwiler, then my editor at Cornell University Press. Her suggestion turned out to be a good one, and I thank her for it; thanks are also due to Catherine Rice at Cornell University Press, who actually did the work! I'm also grateful to Bernie Linsky, chair of the Philosophy Department at the University of Alberta, for the opportunity to teach a graduate seminar on Wittgenstein and political philosophy, shortly followed by a term blessedly free from teaching commitments—the ideal combination for producing a book like this one. Thanks, finally, to Leah Armontrout Spencer, who compiled an excellent index.

This book is dedicated to Karen Pilkington, a wonderful philosopher and friend, who died much too soon and too suddenly when this volume was in its early stages. We talked about the project in her hospital room as she underwent treatment for leukemia, and her intellectual acumen and commitment to excellence in scholarship helped me do a better job. She is very much missed.

Two chapters in this volume are reprinted by permission of Sage Publications. An earlier version of James Tully's chapter appeared as "Wittgenstein and Political Philosophy: Understanding Practices of Critical Reflection," *Political Theory* 17, no. 2 (1989): 172–204, copyright © 1989 by Sage Publications, Inc. Linda M. G. Zerilli's chapter, "Doing without Knowing: Feminism's Politics of the Ordinary," first appeared in *Political Theory* 26, no. 4 (1998): 435–458, copyright © 1998 by Sage Publications, Inc.

C.J.H.

Abbreviations

All references to Wittgenstein's works appear in the text in parentheses using the following abbreviations and a page or section number, except where otherwise stated.

BB *The Blue and Brown Books* (Oxford: Blackwell, 1964).
CV *Culture and Value,* ed. G. H. von Wright with Heikki Nyman, trans. Peter Winch (Chicago: University of Chicago Press, 1980).
RCV Revised edition of *Culture and Value,* ed. G. H. von Wright with Heikki Nyman, revised by Alois Pichler, trans. Peter Winch (Oxford: Blackwell, 1998).
LWPPI *Last Writings on the Philosophy of Psychology,* vol. 1, *Preliminary Studies for Part II of "Philosophical Investigations,"* ed. G. H. von Wright and Heikki Nyman, trans. C. G. Luckhardt and Maximilian A. E. Aue (Oxford: Blackwell, 1982).
LWPPII *Last Writings on the Philosophy of Psychology,* vol. 2, *The Inner and the Outer, 1949–1951,* ed. G. H. von Wright and Heikki Nyman, trans. C. G. Luckhardt and Maximillian A. E. Aue (Oxford: Blackwell, 1992).
N *Notebooks 1914–1916,* ed. G. H. von Wright and G. E. M. Anscombe, trans. G. E. M. Anscombe (Oxford: Blackwell, 1961).
OC *On Certainty,* ed. G. E. M. Anscombe and G. H. von Wright, trans. Denis Paul and G. E. M. Anscombe (Oxford: Blackwell, 1969).
PI *Philosophical Investigations,* trans. G. E. M. Anscombe, 2d ed. (Oxford: Blackwell, 1958).
PR *Philosophical Remarks,* ed. Rush Rhees, trans. Raymond Hargreaves and Roger White (Oxford: Blackwell, 1975).
RC *Remarks on Colour,* ed. G. E. M. Anscombe (Berkeley: University of California Press, 1978).

RFM	*Remarks on the Foundations of Mathematics,* ed. G. H. von Wright, R. Rhees, and G. E. M. Anscombe, trans. G. E. M. Anscombe (Oxford: Blackwell, 1956).
RPPI	*Remarks on the Philosophy of Psychology,* vol. 1, ed. G. E. M. Anscombe and G. H. von Wright, trans. G. E. M. Anscombe (Chicago: University of Chicago Press, 1980).
RPPII	*Remarks on the Philosophy of Psychology,* vol. 2, ed. G. E. M. Anscombe and G. H. von Wright, trans. G. E. M. Anscombe (Chicago: University of Chicago Press, 1980).
Z	*Zettel,* ed. G. E. M. Anscombe and G. H. von Wright, trans. G. E. M. Anscombe (Berkeley: University of California Press, 1967).

Introduction

Cressida J. Heyes

> The sickness of a time is cured by an alteration in the mode of life of human beings, and it was possible for the sickness of philosophical problems to get cured only through a changed mode of thought and of life, not through a medicine invented by an individual.
> —Ludwig Wittgenstein, *Remarks on the Foundation of Mathematics*

It's not hard to imagine Ludwig Wittgenstein's first reaction to a book entitled *The Grammar of Politics*. He definitely did not want to be imitated, and he considered professional philosophy—perhaps especially when sanctimoniously *applied* to "real life" problems—to be "a kind of living death."[1] Besides, he wrote next to nothing that might now be labeled "political philosophy" and was deeply skeptical about the possibility of social change through the application of programmatic political thought. He disdained the activist efforts of contemporaries like Bertrand Russell, and in 1946 he wrote in his notebooks:

> The hysterical fear of the atom bomb the public now has, or at least expresses, is almost a sign that here for once a really salutary discovery has been made. . . . I cannot rid myself of the thought: if there were not something good here, the *philistines* would not be making an outcry. . . . The people now making speeches against the production of the bomb are undoubtedly the *dregs* [*Auswurf*] of the intelligentsia, but even that does not prove beyond question that what they abominate is to be welcomed. (*RCV* 55–56)

Maurice Drury reports a conversation in which he mentioned to Wittgenstein an acquaintance who was "working on a thesis as to why the League of Nations had failed." Wittgenstein's reply reveals his belief in the futility of political analysis of human action: "Tell him to find out first why wolves eat lambs!"[2] Much later in his life Wittgenstein reiterated his skepticism: "Who knows the laws according to which society unfolds? I am sure even the cleverest has no idea" (RCV 69).[3]

Wittgenstein's attitude to politics was not only characterized by skepticism about what philosophy can do. He sometimes appeared insensitive to social injustices in his own milieu. Ray Monk cites a story told by Paul Engelmann: "When, in the 'twenties, Russell wanted to establish, or join, a 'World Organization for Peace and Freedom,' or something similar, Wittgenstein rebuked him so severely, that Russell said to him, 'Well, I suppose you would rather establish a World Organization for War and Slavery,' to which Wittgenstein passionately assented: 'Yes, rather that, rather that!' "[4]

He was no supporter of women's rights, and in an argument with David Pinsent about suffrage was reportedly "very much against it . . . for no particular reason except that 'all the women he knows are such idiots.' "[5] Although tormented by the demands of personal relationships in general, especially sexual relationships, there is little evidence that Wittgenstein's homosexuality caused him any unique torment, let alone that it had any political significance for him.[6] Finally, as a number of commentators have discovered, it's difficult to know exactly what to make of Wittgenstein's high regard for Otto Weininger's manifestly misogynist, homophobic, and anti-Semitic book *Sex and Character;* whatever the conclusion, it's hardly evidence of Wittgenstein's political acumen.[7]

Somewhat against the current of these views, Wittgenstein was supportive of socialism to the point of visiting the Soviet Union in 1935 with the idea of gaining work as a laborer (he was disappointed and frustrated that only academic positions in philosophy were offered).[8] A great believer in the value of manual work, Wittgenstein often set himself up in situations where meeting his own basic needs required considerable physical effort, and he seems to have believed that such labor was morally enriching. More sanguine interpreters see in this preoccupation vestiges of a political analysis that informs Wittgenstein's larger philosophy; critical biographers have suggested that it was more the result of Wittgenstein's romantic attitude toward the working class (his own family was, of course, one of the wealthiest in *fin-de-siècle* Vienna) rather than any particularly insightful analysis of capitalism.[9]

Whatever we make of this ambiguous biographical evidence,[10] Wittgenstein's writings themselves show a much greater concern with the ethical integrity of the individual than with any larger political ambit. His seeming conservatism on social issues perhaps led Russell to write to Ottoline Morrell: "I feel his lack of civilization & suffer from it. . . . He has not a sufficiently wide curiosity or a sufficient wish for a broad survey of the world. It won't spoil his work on logic, but it will make him always a very narrow specialist."[11] This is a rather harsh evaluation, but Wittgenstein's approach to ethics was undoubtedly solipsistic—as he put it, "just improve yourself—that is all you can do to improve the world."[12] Thus at first pass it's hard even to imagine any direct connections between his life and a broader political vision, and not only because they would risk anachronism.

This book thus poses a complicated hermeneutical challenge: how to make "political philosophy" out of such meager and enigmatic fare? While Wittgenstein's own political views remain of interest to historians of ideas, they are not the primary material from which this volume draws its inspiration. Nor is it the case that Wittgenstein's philosophy leads naturally or inexorably toward any particular political position (although I'll examine below some attempts to force his thought in this direction). One might therefore choose, reasonably enough, to make a solely negative argument: that Wittgenstein's work cannot appropriately be used to support any particular political approach.[13] The mandate of this collection, however, is to assemble essays that *show* the relevance to political thought of the methods Wittgenstein outlines. This mandate is complicated by the fact that these methods are developed in his later work (especially his *Philosophical Investigations*) primarily in the context of debates in philosophy of language and logic. The contributors to this volume must therefore transpose Wittgenstein's arguments into very different areas of philosophy. As I'll show, certain general currents in the recent history of political thought make this task more congenial than it would have been for Wittgenstein's contemporaries, who were writing at a moment when "political philosophy" was uniquely moribund. All the contributors take their lead from Wittgenstein's attempts to break the hold of certain *pictures* that tacitly direct our language and thus our forms of life. Making these pictures visible *as* pictures reveals the hitherto concealed structure and the contingency of certain ways of thinking about politics. Thus the contributors place less emphasis on interpreting (while remaining loyal to) Wittgenstein than on moving out into the world of politics to reveal the structure and complexity of particular grammars, some of which Wittgenstein could never have anticipated. This move is itself plausibly Wittgensteinian, in the spirit of his much-quoted remark in the preface to the *Philosophical Investigations*: "I should not like my writing to spare someone the trouble of thinking. But, if possible, to stimulate someone to thoughts of his own."

Wittgenstein, Conservatives, and Relativists

It's therefore quite clear that any analysis of Wittgenstein and political philosophy will not start from his own political writings or reported views. Despite the opacity and polyvocality of his written remarks, however, he has been placed in a political camp—in my view, and as I hope this volume will show, quite mistakenly. Many philosophers, Wittgenstein experts and dilettantes alike, believe that Wittgenstein's later thought loosely endorses a form of quietism, in particular with regard to what the philosopher (and philosophy) can achieve. This view circulates as much as an impression as an argument; however, to the extent that it finds articulate support, it's in the view that the Wittgenstein of the *Philosophical Investigations* is a distinctively conservative thinker, a precursor and underwriter of contemporary conservative philosophers such as Michael Oakeshott. A flurry of articles in the 1980s took up the articulation, defense, and critical evaluation of this view, which has become something of an orthodoxy in Wittgenstein scholarship.

The best-known representative of this position, J. C. Nyíri, argues: "The specific tone of Wittgenstein's analyses, the content of many of his remarks and reflections, and the historical circumstances in which this philosophy came into being definitely invite an interpretation in the light of which there indeed emerge family resemblances between Wittgenstein on the one hand and some important representatives of conservatism on the other."[14] Nyíri's analysis of Wittgenstein's relation to his time, and his suggestion that we can infer from his social circle and intellectual predilections some tacit commitment to a conservative worldview, have been contested by Terry Eagleton, among others.[15] Here I'll set aside the historical assessment of Wittgenstein and his milieu—which has in any case already been ably undertaken by Allan Janik and Stephen Toulmin in their *Wittgenstein's Vienna*—to look instead at the philosophical substance of Nyíri's argument and those of his opponents.[16]

Nyíri suggests that Wittgenstein's remarks on rule-following and forms of life in the *Philosophical Investigations* incorporate a "new framework" whose basic concepts are "training and behaviour, use, custom, institution, practice, technique, agreement": "The following of a rule is a custom, an institution, embedded in the agreements, in the correspondences of behaviour within society. The question concerning the interpretation of any rule can be raised—though it need not be—and it should be answered by referring to agreements in behaviour. Rule-following is, in the last analysis, blind: it cannot be explained or justified."[17] From this interpretation of Wittgenstein's later work, it's a small step for Nyíri to conclude that "although any given form of life, mode of thought and behaviour, can be superseded by or have superimposed upon itself other forms of life, it cannot actually be criticized. All criticism presupposes a form of life, a language, that is, a tradition of agreements; every judgment is necessarily embedded in traditions. That is why traditions cannot be judged."[18]

This interpretation is also found—voiced in a far more critical tenor—in the work of Ernest Gellner, who states baldly of Wittgenstein's later work: "nothing was or could be either explained or justified: it could only be described and accepted. It could only be accepted as custom and example, as a 'form of life.' *Gemeinschaft* is self-justifying."[19] And David Bloor similarly comments that "Wittgenstein's texts show how, time and again, he develops the characteristic themes of conservative thinkers."[20]

There is a paradoxical connection here with another well-known approach to Wittgensteinian social theory, first articulated by Peter Winch. In a classic article Winch argued that "understanding a primitive society" requires one to accept the worldview adopted by the members of that society, a worldview incommensurable with that of the Western anthropological observer.[21] This incommensurability entails that no cross-cultural judgments about which group has the "better" beliefs are possible—in particular, one cannot judge Western scientific beliefs to be more rational than the "primitive" belief in witchcraft. Winch cites Wittgenstein as his philosophical inspiration for this position—perhaps unsurprisingly, when in *On Certainty* the latter remarks: "Supposing . . . instead of the physicist, [people] consult an oracle. (And for that we consider them primitive.) Is it wrong for them to consult an oracle and be guided by it?—If we call this 'wrong' aren't we using our language-game as a base from which to *combat* theirs?" (OC § 609). Winch builds upon Wittgenstein's suggestion that there is no reality to which language can correspond, but rather a variety of different uses of language, none of which can be taken to ground an assessment of language itself: "Reality is not what gives language sense. What is real and what is unreal shows itself in the sense that language has. Further, both the distinction between the real and the unreal and the concept of agreement with reality themselves belong to our language."[22] Thus, for Winch, Wittgenstein's notions of rule-following and form of life effectively endorse cultural relativism.

Winch wants to put this endorsement to political use by positioning himself against a certain kind of anthropological arrogance, rather than by supporting conservatism. He nonetheless paints a picture of Wittgenstein remarkably similar to Nyíri's. What Nyíri, Gellner, and Winch share—their political differences notwithstanding—is the assumption that a form of life is self-justifying and cannot be criticized except from some transcendental standpoint that Wittgenstein renders unavailable. These interpretations are certainly tempting, especially when Wittgenstein makes such much-quoted remarks as "What has to be accepted, the given, is—so one could say—*forms of life*" (PI p. 226). Or: "The point here is not that our sense-impressions can lie, but that we understand their language. (And this language like any other is founded on convention)" (PI § 355). Later commentators have pointed out, however, that nothing in Wittgenstein's writings precludes the possibility of change within a language-game;[23] indeed, he explicitly imagines very different language-games coexisting and evolving:

> But how many kinds of sentence are there? . . . There are *countless* kinds. . . . And this multiplicity is not something fixed, given once and for all; but new types of language, new language-games, as we may say, come into existence, and others become obsolete and get forgotten. . . . Here the term "language-

game" is meant to bring into prominence the fact that the *speaking* of language is part of an activity, or of a form of life. (PI § 23)

Furthermore, the necessity of working from within particular language-games to inspire critical reflection or effect social change does not obviate critique; indeed, this insight provides a starting point for a number of the chapters in this volume.

This Is Not a School

This volume's first theme, then, is "Wittgenstein and Method." The four chapters in part I share an emphasis on undercutting readings of Wittgenstein as a skeptical conservative or hapless relativist, thus setting the stage for later, more specific and constructive appropriations of Wittgenstein's philosophy. In "The Limits of Conservatism: Wittgenstein on 'Our Life' and 'Our Concepts,' " David Cerbone aims to move beyond the frustratingly persistent interpretive struggle over Wittgenstein's alleged conservatism. Cerbone suggests that such allegations arise through mistaken readings of Wittgenstein's concept of "our form of life." Such readings construe this concept as a *limit,* but in so doing they offer explanations of those limits that are independent of the concepts within them. This move fails to recognize that "limits" are for Wittgenstein one candidate for the philosophical treatment he recommends in the *Philosophical Investigations* and in *Remarks on the Philosophy of Psychology.* Cerbone concludes by arguing that this deflationary interpretation does not imply political helplessness: drawing on James Baldwin's critique of *Uncle Tom's Cabin,* he argues that liberatory political analyses need not rely only on the possibility of transcendence of existing social conditions but should be rooted in what Wittgenstein refers to as "the fixed point of our real need."

Here, contained in this repudiation of the charge of conservatism, is the first opening to a Wittgensteinian political philosophy. At the heart of political thought after Rawls is the question of the extent to which some extracultural, value-neutral standpoint is both possible and necessary for adjudicating conflict and reaching agreement. The post-Kantian tradition, of which Jürgen Habermas is probably the best-known exponent, vies with the countercurrents of communitarianism and poststructuralism to generate many of the most intractable and engaging debates in political philosophy. For most analysts Wittgenstein's work lines up against the inheritances of Descartes and Kant (although others prefer to say that he dispels the terms of these dichotomies and stubbornly resists assimilation into any extant tradition: "The philosopher is not a citizen of any community of ideas. That is what makes him into a philosopher" [Z § 455]).

A number of contributors to this volume argue that it is precisely Wittgenstein's insistence on working on our practices from within a language-game that provides the basis for efforts to motivate social change. In his "Wittgenstein, Fetishism, and Nonsense in Practice," for example, Denis McManus describes and rejects the view that Wittgenstein simply contributes to the undercutting of foundations on which political critique might be grounded. He outlines a "test of meaningfulness" dominant in the social sciences, founded on the assumption that reality gives language sense, before arguing that in showing this test to be incoherent Wittgenstein gives nothing useful away. Wittgenstein certainly stressed the need for those agreements in judgment that enable a form of life to continue, as Winch rightly recognized. However, McManus argues, we sometimes come to fetishize such agreements as "reality" or "truth" in ways that evacuate meaning from our activities rather than justifying them. Politically speaking, McManus sees this "slow, almost invisible leaching away of sense from our practices" exposed in Weber's critique of the Protestant work ethic, Foucault's work on psychiatry, or Nietzsche's analysis of the last man.

This book thus moves away from the rather inward-looking discussions of Wittgenstein's conservatism and relation to his times, to ask how his philosophy informs a broadly linguistic turn in contemporary political thought, and a growing preoccupation with questions of method. A tenacious existing scholarship provides a fertile ground for this new growth. Best known is Hanna Pitkin's germinal book, *Wittgenstein and Justice: On the Significance of Ludwig Wittgenstein for Social and Political Thought,* in which Pitkin argues in a very wide-ranging way for the importance of Wittgensteinian philosophy to political thinking. Toward the end of the book, she contemplates a Wittgensteinian political theory, and concludes that it would "share [Wittgenstein's] suspicion of broad, systematic generalization, his therapeutic stress on the particular case, on the investigating and speaking self, and on the acceptance of plurality and contradiction."[24] This part of *Wittgenstein and Justice* is both self-consciously speculative and remarkably prescient, and these admonitions have been taken up by a number of later commentators, including in this volume by Jonathan Havercroft and Linda Zerilli.[25]

Pitkin's work is linked in many respects to the work of Stanley Cavell, another vital progenitor of this field. In his arguments for a "return to the ordinary" Cavell confronts the question of how invoking "what we do" can permit critical reflection. Cavell's "conversation of justice" affirms the heterogeneity of the "we" (rather than insisting on its unity), and this move reveals spaces for political dissent from any society that does not allow for the intelligibility of all of its members.[26] Thus a Cavellian tradition in political philosophy has emerged, whose exponents include, among others, Cora Diamond, Sabina Lovibond, Stephen Mulhall, and Naomi Scheman. These philosophers share a commitment to what Lovibond calls "moral imagination," for creating and sustaining immanent yet sometimes oppositional political languages.

As this initial marshaling of Wittgenstein interpreters suggests, any attempt to impose unity on political thought after Cavell will surely be forced.[27] Over the last fifteen years or so, Wittgenstein has been taken up by a striking diversity of theorists, all to some extent preoccupied with language-related approaches in political philosophy. Wittgenstein has been held aloft as a representative for every school of thought from critical theory, feminism, and democratic theory to pragmatism, poststructuralism, and psychoanalysis. This book cannot manage to review all that has gone before, and the moment has passed when one might reasonably expect to represent every extant approach to Wittgenstein and the political. In this context, a central difficulty in assembling these essays has been the editorial imperative to find unity in diversity. As I've already mentioned, it was far from Wittgenstein's intention that he should inspire faithful mimicry in his students, or that anyone should strike camp on his ideas: "It is not by any means clear to me, that I wish for a continuation of my work by others, more than a change in the way we live, making all these questions superfluous. (For this reason I could never found a school.)" (RCV 70).

Thus in structuring the introduction to this volume, I've thought of myself less as neatly arraying a set of essays that simply share common characteristics than as pointing to philosophical fibers that run through a twined thread. ("And the strength of the thread does not reside in the fact that some one fibre runs through its whole length, but in the overlapping of many fibres" [PI § 67].) I've already identified some of these fibers: a refusal to be held captive by pictures that set some concepts outside our language-games; a concomitant desire to imagine forms of political critique from within our forms of life; and emphases on the particular case and plurality among speaking subjects.

Adding to these themes, James Tully suggests that Wittgenstein's post-1930 method of perspicuous representation provides a touchstone for a broad contextual and historical approach to political philosophy, an approach associated with Quentin Skinner and Charles Taylor and represented in this volume by Jonathan Havercroft and David Owen. This approach starts from the rough ground of practice rather than theory: from political language-games that are experienced as problematic and are called into question to become the site of struggle. The aim is not to generate a particular theoretical solution but rather to provide a perspicuous survey of the languages in which the problem is expressed and disputed in practice and in theory. To this end, genealogies of the languages in question are employed in the same way as Wittgenstein employed alternative language-games. These historical investigations are used as objects of comparison, which, by means of similarities and dissimilarities, put the problem under another description and so in a different light, thereby freeing us from the hegemonic ways of conceptualizing the problem and its solutions that are often deeply sedimented and assumed to be necessary or universal. This method thus engenders the kind of critical and reflective understanding that Wittgenstein's later philosophy is explicitly designed to achieve: to change our conventional way of looking at the problems in which we are entangled and to enable us to think differently about them.[28]

Tully instantiates this approach in his chapter for this volume. Revising and expanding a pivotal argument he first made in the journal *Political Theory* in 1989, Tully argues that political thought needs to free itself from the mistaken belief that our political life, in order to be free and rational, must be founded on a particular form of critical reflection. Tully surveys the justificational foundation advanced by Jürgen Habermas's project of critical theory and contrasts it with Charles Taylor's defense of hermeneutics. He attempts to dissolve the problem around which this debate revolves by drawing on Wittgenstein's remarks in the *Philosophical Investigations* to the effect that we need to assemble reminders in order to make visible to ourselves the picture offered by our language. Tully concludes that since "any practice of critical reflection is itself already founded in the popular sovereignty of our multiplicity of humdrum ways of acting with words," our free and critical political life is best assured by a refusal to accept any single form of critical reflection as a foundation.

The injunction "political, not metaphysical" comes together with an emphasis on self-government and critical reflection in David Owen's rich contribution, "Genealogy as Perspicuous Representation." Owen argues that certain pictures of politics "hold us captive" in ways that limit our capacity for self-government, understood (more broadly than its narrow Kantian connotation) as the capacity to make and acts on one's own judgments. The kind of limit a picture imposes contrasts with the more familiar *ideological* captivity of the Marxist tradition; it cannot be overcome simply by refuting false beliefs but rather requires a novel kind of philosophical therapy. Owen argues that such a therapy can be found in Wittgenstein's notion of "perspicuous representation" and suggests that genealogy in its Nietzschean and Foucauldian forms can be productively understood in light of this Wittgensteinian approach.

Both Tully and Owen implicitly challenge an understanding of politics as seeking permanent answers to Socratic inquiries. Pursuing this theme, the four chapters in part II are deeply concerned with the question "What is political?" although they approach it from different directions. In "Notes on the Natural History of Politics," Allan Janik argues that the task of the philosopher is to explain how politics forms a part of our human "natural history," and he appeals to Wittgenstein's famous dictum that philosophy "leaves everything as it is" to elaborate this claim. Janik argues, with

Wittgenstein, that rule-following is an a priori feature of language, and that practical rules make action possible. Thus our capacity to act is "bound to the discipline which facilitates that action at the same time that it constrains"; for Janik, there is an identity between Aristotle's visions of *zoon politikon* and *zoon logon echon*. Drawing on the work of William Connolly, Janik points to the essential contestability of concepts (and its connection to family resemblances) that underlies political conflict. He suggests that the necessity of arguing from within rule-governed action limits the possibility of finding acontextual criteria for political arbitration, while both broadening the field of politics to all human action and making disagreement intelligible.

Richard Eldridge's chapter, again resonating with Tully's model and with Cavell's idiom, distinguishes three approaches to politics. *Classical political theory*, exemplified for Eldridge by Plato's *Republic*, is primarily concerned with the full realization of our rational humanity. Concerned with theoretical ideals, it disdains investigation of everyday political practice. In contrast, *political science* aims to describe empirical limits on political life, as Hobbes does in his account of human nature. *Political judgment*—as exemplified by Ronald Dworkin's legal theory—presents itself as a third method that is founded in quotidian practice yet is not immune to normative considerations. Eldridge argues that the intellectual idealism of classical political theory removes us from our roles as human speakers and citizens who are embedded in practices; political science exhibits an empiricist naturalism that neglects our human potential and powers of self-improvement; interpretivism tends to be arbitrary and insensitive to the legitimate roles in judgment of both theory and empirical research. Turning to Wittgenstein and Cavell, Eldridge suggests a way of understanding ourselves as always both alienated from and engaged with ordinary practice. He surveys Wittgenstein's accounts of ordinary language and practice as necessary homes for human judgment, which at the same time inevitably seek to escape them. From this survey, he elaborates Cavell's accounts of "the argument of the ordinary" and "the conversation of justice" in order to develop a picture of more mature citizenship and political judgment.

What this "return to the ordinary" would mean in particular political contexts is a question taken up by Linda Zerilli's "Doing without Knowing: Feminism's Politics of the Ordinary." Zerilli sees Wittgenstein as disrupting the "idling" conversation between the skeptic and the foundationalist, and here she applies Wittgenstein's epistemological response to the skeptic to contemporary feminist debates about gender, arguing that they are trapped by the same misguided assumptions about foundations that Wittgenstein identifies in skepticism. The questioning of foundations in feminism itself depends on taking for granted a series of what Wittgenstein calls "hinge propositions" that stand fast. In particular, the suggestion that the term "women" be used "strategically" is, Zerilli comments, a "curiously Humean solution to a distinctly philosophical sort of problem." Further, these suggestions are captured by the picture they claim to reject: an impossible vision of politics without exclusion. Instead, Zerilli concludes, political action brings a subject into existence, and the game of politics necessarily consists in testing the limits of that subject.

Finally, Owen's earlier emphasis on perspicuous representation is mirrored in Jonathan Havercroft's "On Seeing Liberty As." Havercroft turns to the later sections of the *Philosophical Investigations*, which are less often taken up by political theorists, and specifically to Wittgenstein's remarks on changes of aspect.[29] Starting from Wittgenstein's suggestion that "the discovery of a new aspect in an image is akin to experiencing the meaning of a word in a new way," Havercroft argues that *liberty* should be understood aspectivally. Surveying four different accounts of the meaning of the word—in the writing of Berlin, Taylor, Skinner, and Rawls—Havercroft concludes that political philosophers who seek a comprehensive explanation of liberty will necessarily be disappointed and that a better approach to the study of political thought will aim for a perspicuous representation of the uses of the term.

Wittgenstein Further Afield

The three final chapters in the volume move further afield, taking Wittgenstein at his word when he says: "I ought always to hope only for the most indirect of influences" (RCV 71). Wendy Lynne Lee continues an ongoing Wittgensteinian project of unraveling the linguistic politics of anthropomorphism. In her chapter she aims to capture the connections between anthropomorphizing language and the maintenance of sexist, heterosexist, and racist practices and institutions. She uses Wittgenstein's critique of the ontological pictures created by grammar, starting from his remarkable comment in the *Philosophical Investigations*: "The evolution of the higher animals and of man, and the awakening of consciousness at a particular level. The picture is something like this: Though the ether is filled with vibrations the world is dark. But one day man opens his seeing eye, and there is light" (PI p. 184). Lee analyzes the anthropocentrism *and* androcentrism implicit in the pictures Wittgenstein himself conjures up. Given the ubiquity of anthropomorphizing Wittgenstein evinces, does it necessarily carry with it anthropocentrism, heterosexism, and racism? Lee argues that this link can and must be ruptured, and she reads bell hooks's *Wounds of Passion*—an autobiographical account of growing up as a black female writer—as a successful example of this rupture.

Carl Elliott reminds us of Wittgenstein's famous analogy in section 293 of the *Philosophical Investigations*: "suppose everyone had a box with something in it: we call it a 'beetle.' No one can look into anyone else's box, and everyone says he knows what a beetle is only by looking at *his* beetle." This language-game might perversely continue to posit the existence of beetles, yet "the thing in the box has no place in the language-game at all." Elliott suggests that our picture of mental illness tends to operate as if such illnesses were beetles: ontologically real and consistent entities enclosed in the box of the mind. And indeed, the language-games of *diagnosis* and *treatment*, as well as the process of defining (new) disorders, conspire to endorse this understanding. Yet Wittgenstein shows this view to be a kind of nonsense. The attempt to explain meaning by pointing to the mental or to mental processes is unintelligible; rather, meaning is a consequence of the application of language. If we accept this conclusion, Elliott argues, we see that mental illnesses can be understood only as embedded in particular forms of life, themselves political sites where different interests battle not only for profit and accolades but also for conceptual domination. He separates out some of the strategies used by patients, psychiatrists, and drug companies, in order to provide a perspicuous representation of an area of our lives previously very much in thrall to a picture from which Wittgenstein helps us break free.

Finally, Owen's allusions to self-government, and the demands of several other contributors that we learn a better kind of political imagination, point to another strand in Wittgensteinian political thought, less obviously connected to any of the themes discussed so far. "Working on oneself" was for Wittgenstein a central goal of philosophy: "Work on philosophy—like work in architecture in many respects—is really more work on oneself. On one's own conception. On how one sees things. (And what one expects of them.)" (RCV 24). Thus a political reading of Wittgenstein might look to his ethical vision of a good life. One might, indeed, take Wittgenstein's life itself as a model, and in fact Richard Shusterman does just this in his book *Practicing Philosophy*.[30] Where some commentators see in Wittgenstein's manifest alienation from "the prevailing European and American civilization" a disdain for social engineering and a kind of nostalgia for healthier, more organic forms of life, others interpret this distance as illuminating for the contemporary radical.[31]

Shusterman echoes this approach in his chapter for this volume, in which he argues that Wittgenstein's elliptical comments on bodily feelings in fact suggest a fuller role for somaesthetics—an understanding of the body as a locus of sensory-aesthetic appreciation and self-development. Shusterman examines the actual and potential significance of bodily feelings to a Wittgensteinian philosophy of mind, aesthetics, ethics, and politics. Elaborating many of Wittgenstein's more cryptic remarks in *Culture and Value*, Shusterman shows that Wittgenstein's refutation of William

James's philosophy of psychology—which takes bodily feelings as the cause or explanation of mental concepts such as emotion or will—need not imply an indiscriminate rejection of the significance of the kinaesthetic. Attention to bodily feelings may lead to information about our emotions that was previously tacit, or even to means of controlling undesirable emotional states. Further, Wittgenstein's suggestion that the body forms a condition of possibility for our aesthetic appreciation implies that somatic feelings may be understood as having their own aesthetic use and value. Finally, Shusterman argues that our sense of the body grounds our concept of the human, and thus our form of life. This foundation can be a unifying force, but too often it fragments community, as when political enmities (particularly racism and anti-Semitism) are unconsciously founded in protection of the body's supposed integrity and purity. Thus Shusterman concludes that somaesthetics has a crucial yet neglected role in political education.

This volume concludes with a bibliography, the compilation of which has itself been a task requiring the application of some Wittgensteinian methods. It aims to include all secondary literature with political themes that makes explicit reference to Wittgenstein while putting his ideas to use in a more than token way. It thus excludes those numerous texts that open with an enticing aphorism or two but never follow up with any substantive discussion of how Wittgenstein's ideas fit with the author's project. With a few exceptions, I've also omitted works that dwell on Wittgenstein's milieu (from which politics can hardly be absent) or that set themselves exclusively interpretive tasks in the history of ideas ("What did Wittgenstein really think about *x*?"). The question of what exactly counts as a political theme has been more difficult to rule on, and here I've tried to be generous and included work in, for example, ethics, legal theory, and philosophy of social science. Finally, I've been sparing with texts primarily concerned with discussion of the work of a philosopher closely associated with Wittgenstein. The most striking example here is Stanley Cavell: while almost all critical commentators on Cavell's oeuvre make reference to (Cavell's) Wittgenstein, the risk of infinite regress led me to exclude all but those that undertake some original commentary on Wittgenstein himself.

At the end of all this, I still think Wittgenstein would have been horrified by the idea of his work being incorporated into political projects. Too bad for him: his ideas have long since escaped his governance (if they were ever in his thrall); they have grown up, moved out, and created families of their own. Nonetheless, even if there aren't more or less *authentic* ways of being a Wittgensteinian, there are, I would argue, *better and worse* ways. I hope that the essays collected in this book exemplify the better ways, and thus that they will indeed inspire the reader to thoughts of her own.

Part I

Wittgenstein and Method

1

Wittgenstein and Political Philosophy

Understanding Practices of Critical Reflection

James Tully

My aim is to draw our attention to, and so enable us to free ourselves from, a widespread but mistaken convention of contemporary political thought: that our way of political life is free and rational only if it is founded on some form or other of critical reflection. I do this by means of a survey of two well-known practices of critical reflection that have been presented as candidates for this foundational role: the justificational or validational form advanced by Jürgen Habermas and the interpretive or hermeneutical form advanced by Charles Taylor. It is our engagement in the discussion itself—the discussion in the philosophy of social science between critical theory and hermeneutics, among others, about which sort of critical reflection is essential to political freedom and reason—that tends to hold in place, beyond question, and thereby render conventional, the rule that *some* form must be foundational. In surveying and clarifying language-games of critical reflection we can see that *no* form of critical reflection can (or need) play the role presupposed for it in this discussion.

Before proceeding to the types of critical reflection presented by Habermas and Taylor, consider two other examples just to recollect the widespread acceptance of this convention and its concurrent discussion. One fashionable example is what might be called representational critical reflection. This is the view—the ethos—that our political way of life is free and rational insofar as it is based on a form of critical reflection that aims at objective representations. Such a "Cartesian" type of reflexivity has come in for sustained criticism in recent years, and there is no need to rehearse the arguments here.[1] A second formulation of the sovereignty of some form of critical reflection is Heidegger's proposal that humans are beings whose being is in question.[2] Here the general activity of posing reflexive questions about our being is suggested to be our fundamental way of being in the world. Again, there have been many criticisms of, for example, the voluntaristic way Sartre took this in *Being and Nothingness*, where, by a critically reflective activity of calling into question one's customary way of life, a person might disengage from it and, in a godlike fashion, find a free and rational life in an "autonomous choice" or free act of will.[3] Nonetheless, the more modest and situated versions of critical reflection that have followed in the wake of these criticisms still tend to be based on the prevailing custom that the only free and rational way of thought and action is one governed by a canonical type of critical reflection.

The ubiquity of these and other examples illustrates the irony of our situation: a misunderstanding of the very activity that is supposed to free us from the blind adherence to convention (critical reflection) has itself become conventional. Therefore, if we wish to conserve the traditions of critical political thought, it is necessary to call into question this captivating and Faustian convention and, at the same time, avoid the equally dangerous error of embracing the abdication of critical thought that various schools of conservatism claim follows from abandoning the convention.

One way to pursue this double strategy is to use the methods developed by Ludwig Wittgenstein in the *Philosophical Investigations* to free us from captivity to mistaken ways of thinking (PI §§ 127–33).[4] That is, we can "survey" the language-games of critical freedom proffered by Habermas and Taylor and show, by means of "objects of comparison," that neither validation nor interpretation grounds our motley of free and reasonable ways of being in the world.[5] The key here is to realize that validation and interpretation are activities or *practices* of thought and they therefore share features common to other practices. As participants in various practices of validation and interpretation, we take it as a matter of course that they are foundational to our freedom and reason. This is precisely the convention that playing the language-games holds in place. The use of the languages of validation and interpretation tends both to generate what Wittgenstein calls a captivating "picture" of their foundational roles and to repeat the picture "inexorably" (PI § 115). The survey thus frees us from the convention or picture and accounts for its hold. This enables us to set it aside and, with a clearer understanding of the nonfoundational role of critical reflection, to get on with the common task of using our countless techniques of critical reflection to assess the pressing political issues of our age.

1. Habermas's Picture of Critical Reflection

Habermas's attempt to work out a satisfactory form of critical reflection seems to be guided by the following picture. First, we live a free and rational way of political life insofar as the rules in accordance with which we act are based on our agreement. Second, the activity of "coming to an agreement" must be some form of critical reflection that ensures that the agreement is free and rational. I think it is fair to say that this general picture informs much of our political thinking, from theories of contract, consent, and civic participation to theories of rational choice.

The importance of Habermas's solution to this problem is the thought-provoking way he has attempted to work out the requirements of the activity of "coming to an agreement." For him, the activity must combine two types of critical reflection. In the first, transcendental and reconstructive in form, reason must turn back on itself and determine the conditions of possibility of a rational agreement. In the second, emancipatory in form, everyone affected by the agreement must in principle engage in critical discussion to justify the rules governing their political life. The critical discussion—"practical discourse" or "discourse ethics"—must conform to the conditions of possibility discovered by the transcendental reflection and usher in an agreement based on the force of the better argument. This ideal model is used to evaluate the legitimacy of actual processes of deliberation and agreement. It thus represents a powerful expression of the demands of reason and freedom that underlie the activity of "reaching agreement" in our public rhetoric about the legitimacy of constitutional democracy, in some of our most cherished political institutions, such as parliament and the public sphere, and in many political theories, such as recent theories of deliberative democracy. Moreover, he claims that his specific form of critical discussion is inherent in the very activity of communication these institutions and theories presuppose.[6]

I now want to lay out the steps Habermas takes in constructing the activity of "coming to an agreement" so we will be in a position to see a misunderstanding it involves. His move from the earlier critical theory assumption, that relations of productions are basic, to the view that relations of communication are as basic is put in the following way: "If we assume that the human species maintains itself through socially coordinated activities of its members and that this coordination has to be established through communication—and in central spheres through communication aimed at reaching agreement—then the reproduction of the species also requires satisfying the conditions of a rationality that is inherent in communicative action."[7] "These conditions," he continues, "have become perceptible in the modern period with the decentration of our understanding of the world and the differentiation of various universal validity claims." Thus we should study communicative action, and the form of rationality inherent in it, because it is "fundamental" relative to other types of action: for example, teleological, strategic-instrumental, dramaturgical, and norm-regulative.[8]

In "communicative action" actors seek "to reach understanding" about their "action situation" and "plans of action" with the aim of coordinating their actions by way of "agreement."[9] Why is communication "oriented to reaching understanding" the "paradigm" or "standard" form of communication, and other forms, such as conflict, deception, manipulation, irony, and so on, "derivative"? He says that this form is the "original mode" of using language because "the telos of reaching understanding is inherent in the concept of speech."[10] The phrase "reaching understanding" translates the German word *Verständigung*, which also can be, and often is, translated as "reaching agreement." It can be translated as "reaching *an* understanding" or "*an* agreement." So we should really say, "reaching [an] understanding/agreement."

Given that reaching understanding/agreement is fundamental, Habermas goes on to engage in the first form of critical reflection: to reconstruct the conditions under which reaching understanding/agreement is achieved. "We can reconstruct," he writes, "the normative content of possible understanding by stating which universal presuppositions have to be met for understanding to be achieved in an actual case."[11] This reconstructive turn assumes that the multiplicity of activities of "reaching understanding" must rest on some underlying structure or set of "conditions of possibility" that is repeated (inexorably) in every instance. For Habermas, the conditions of reaching understanding are those that make a speech-act acceptable. "We understand/agree to a speech-act," he states, "when we know what makes it acceptable."[12] Again, it is difficult for an English reader to believe that he means to say that we understand a speech-act only when we know what would make it acceptable as opposed to simply intelligible; and so we must bear in mind his polysemic phrase "reaching understanding/agreement" and the different uses of it.

The final step is his claim that the conditions of possibility of a comprehensible speech-act oriented to reaching understanding/agreement are "precisely" three criticizable claims of validity. These are claims that the speech-act is "right," that its propositional content is "true," and that the speaker is "sincere" or "truthful." As he sums up:

> It belongs to the communicative intent of the speaker (a) that he perform a speech act that is *right* in respect to the given normative context, so that between him and the hearer an intersubjective relation will come about which is recognized as legitimate; (b) that he make a *true* statement (or correct existential presuppositions), so that the hearer will accept and share the knowledge of the speaker; and (c) that he express *truthfully* his beliefs, intentions, feelings, desires, and the like, so that the hearer will give credence to what is said.[13]

The three validity claims relate to three "world-relations": the claim of rightness to interpersonal relations and a norm-conformative attitude (the world of morality and law), the claim of truth to representations of states of affairs and events and an "objectivating" attitude (the world of science), and the claim of sincerity to one's own subjective world and expressive attitude (the world of art and ethics). He concludes:"Communicatively achieved agreement is measured against exactly three criticizable validity claims; in coming to an understanding about something with one another and thus making themselves understandable, actors cannot avoid embedding their speech acts in precisely three world-relations and claiming validity for them under these three aspects."[14]

Habermas draws a sharp distinction between our everyday, customary activities of thinking and acting and the practice of critical reflection. In our everyday communications we do not normally question the validity of speech-acts along the three axes. Our agreement in judgments is based in the force of (pre-reflexive) custom or habit, in the "taken for granted." This is the "lifeworld": "The communicative practice of everyday life is immersed in a sea of cultural 'taken for grantedness,' that is, of consensual certainties. To this lifeworld background of actual processes of reaching understanding, there also belong normative convictions and empathetic identifications with the feeling of others."[15]

However, our customary agreements are reasonable only if the participants could give reasons that justify them; that is, if they could redeem, through argument aimed at validation, the three claims of validity implicit in their speech-acts. And the way agents disengage from their customary practices, suspend their assent, and engage in the activity of reaching an agreement—based not on custom but on the force of the better argument—is by questioning what is taken for granted: to ask for the reasons that justify or validate the rightness, truth, or sincerity of the speech-act. That is, they move, or could move, to a critically reflective language-game of validation of their customary agreements by means of argumentation. "The rationality inherent in this [everyday communicative] practice is seen in the fact that a communicatively achieved agreement must be based *in the end* on reasons. And the rationality of those who participate in this communicative practice is determined by whether, if necessary, they could, *under suitable conditions,* provide reasons for their expressions."[16] The rationality of communication thus rests on the implicit possibility of reflective justification and, he continues, can be assessed by means of actual justification by argumentation as a "court of appeal."

In a practical discourse of validation by argumentation the participants suspend their customary assent to a speech-act and exchange reasons pro and contra its normative rightness, propositional truth, and/or the sincerity of the speaker with the telos of reaching agreement *(Verständigung)* or consensus *(Einverständnis).* The universal rules by which they proceed are of two kinds. The three conventional rules of logical-semantic consistency, mutual recognition, and reciprocity and the three post-conventional rules that every subject with the competence to speak and act is allowed to take part in discourse (the principle of universal moral respect), everyone is allowed to question and introduce any assertion whatever and express his or her attitudes, desires, and needs (the principle of egalitarian reciprocity), and no speaker may be prevented, by internal or external coercion, from exercising these rights (the principle of noncoercion). Two further principles of argumentation, principles D and U, are derived from the two types of rule, conventional and post-conventional respectively. The conjunction of the conventional and post-conventional rules and principles D and U "burst asunder" and "transcend" any taken-for-granted consensus and ensure the "double" universal validity of a norm or proposition agreed upon through argumentation: that is, everyone in the practical discourse should agree that the proposition or norm is valid for everyone. In contrast, argumentation to redeem the third validity claim in the third sphere of aesthetics and ethics is oriented to goodness rather than rightness and so is always context-dependent and non-universal. Thus, a universal norm of action coordination agreed to through the demanding form of argumentation Habermas sets out would not be conditioned by anything but would be grounded in the unforced conviction of a rationally motivated agreement.[17] As he concludes:

> Every agreement . . . is based on (convertible) grounds or reasons. Grounds have a special property: they force us into yes or no positions. Thus, built into the structure of action oriented toward reaching understanding is an element of unconditionality. And it is this unconditional element that makes the validity *(Gültigkeit)* we claim for our views different form the mere de facto acceptance *(Geltung)* of habitual practices. From the perspective of first persons, what we consider justified is not a function of custom but a question of justification or grounding.[18]

There are two final points in this difficult quotation. First, it is precisely the calling into question of the validity claims of truth and rightness that enables the ensuing, reflective agreement to transcend the taken-for-granted horizons of the lifeworld and so be unconditional and universal: "The validity claims that we raise in conversation—that is, when we say something with conviction—transcend this specific conversational context, pointing to something beyond the spatiotemporal ambit of the occasion."[19] Second, the practice of argumentation then serves to validate unconditionally, or invalidate, the "certainties" that are taken for granted and so customarily function as grounds in our everyday communicative practices. This agreement is "unconditional" because, so to speak, the grounds of justifications are themselves justified. Finally, this form of agreement/understanding is distinguished, on the one hand, from the forms of activity in the lifeworld, where agreement is based on the de facto acceptance of habitual practice, and, on the other, from the rationalized forms of activity colonized from the lifeworld by processes of modernization, where action-coordination is the product of the functional integration of the consequences of actions in self-regulating systems (such as the market).[20]

Clearly, a very powerful picture of rationality and freedom informs this project. It is not a picture of standing back from our lifeworld and functionally integrated systems as a whole and justifying them once and for all. Rather, it is a picture of making explicit the *implicit universal rules* for reaching mutual understanding and agreements over disputed norms of cooperation, propositions, and claims of truthfulness in communicative action, and using this ideal set of rules as a standard to judge the degree of validity and legitimacy of actual procedures of understanding and agreement in practice.[21] We would thereby tend to become the self-validating animals we are disposed to become in virtue of being language communicators.

2. Understanding Habermas's Practice of Validation

Let us first notice the specialized nature of the activity of reaching understanding/agreement. We can think of many examples of "understanding" and even of "coming to an understanding" that involve "disagreement" rather than "agreement." There are also many forms of agreement that involve "reasonable disagreement." The toleration of dissent, the right of free speech, the right of review, and the principle of *audi alteram partem* (always listen to the other side), for example, are often justified by reference to the irreducibility of reasonable disagreement.[22] We can also think of many examples of agreement where rightness, truth, and sincerity are not relevant considerations. It is also possible to raise these validity claims in circumstances in which understanding/agreement is not the *telos*, or to raise other validity claims (goodness, concern, respect) where reaching understanding/agreement is the *telos*. These are, as we have seen, "derivative" forms of standard speech activity. For Habermas, we call an activity "reaching understanding/agreement" (*Verständigung*) only when the speakers are oriented to an "agreement" (*Einverständnis*) based on redeeming his three validity claims. Critics have been quick to point out how difficult it would be to establish this as the basic form of speech and how his project looks similar to the old Platonic attempt to legislate "rhetorical" speech to a derivative position in order to found politics on "serious" speech.[23]

I would like to accept Habermas's practice of reaching understanding/agreement as one form of justification and ask if it could ground our everyday speech-acts in reflectively validating reasons unconditionally (rather than conditionally).

Suppose Habermas says, "I am Jürgen Habermas and I believe that the workplace ought to be organized democratically." Instead of questioning the second part of this speech-act, someone raises the issue of sincerity. "I think you are being insincere and untruthful and deceiving us about your name. You are not really Jürgen Habermas." We move into our reflective practice of justification either to redeem this validity claim or to get the respondent to understand/agree that this is an illegitimate use of "sincerity." Let us take up the first option.

2.1. Three Features of Giving Grounds

Habermas replies that he really is Habermas. How do we justify this claim to sincerity (and truth)? One possibility is that we could check his birth certificate, but why should we take this as authoritative? We could then check with government officials, police, and so on, but we could also ask what justifies our taking their statements as authoritative. Or, someone impressed by first-person avowals might suggest that the avowal "I know I am Jürgen Habermas," accompanied with a lie-detector test, is a good reason. But what justifies our confidence in *this* ground? Another speaker who has read some popular commentaries on Wittgenstein might say that the speaker who says he is Habermas is Habermas because the members of the community agree in calling him Habermas. Another speaker would surely respond that we should read Wittgenstein's own refutation of this kind of theory and so ask what justifies taking the community as authoritative.[24] And, if justifications were advanced for any of these three warrants, we could in turn ask what reason we have for accepting them, and so on.

You will say this is a trivial example that barely counts as a question of sincerity at all. This is precisely my point. It would be *unreasonable* in these circumstances to raise recursive doubts that Habermas is being insincere about his name. It would be reasonable to take it for granted and to assume, as a matter of course, that Habermas is being sincere about his name at some point. That is, it is reasonable to accept without further question and justification that Habermas is sincere about his name.

Three distinct features of "reaching agreement" are brought to light by this example. First, it is reasonable to take something for granted, to take it as a matter of course without further justification, even in circumstances of critical reflection. According to Habermas, we are rational only insofar as we could give reasons for what we take for granted in these special conditions. This is a mistaken view that identifies "reasonable" with providing reasons "in the end."[25] As we have seen, it is perfectly reasonable not to ask for reasons in some circumstances; indeed, it is sometimes unreasonable to ask for reasons. And the circumstances in which this can be the case are not always in the "lifeworld" but also in our most critically reflective activities.

This misunderstanding about raising doubts and providing justifications is just the sort of "disguised nonsense" that Wittgenstein is concerned to bring into clear view, and show to be "patent nonsense," as he puts it, in many examples in the *Philosophical Investigations*. A classic example of this is given in section 87 in response to an interlocutor who says she cannot "understand" a claim until she has *the* "final"—non-circumstantial and unconditional—explanation: "As though an explanation as it were hung in the air unless supported by another one. Whereas an explanation may indeed rest on another one that has been given, but none stands in need of another—unless *we* require it to prevent a misunderstanding. One might say: an explanation serves to remove or to avert a misunderstanding—one, that is, that would occur but for the explanation; not every one that I can imagine" (PI § 87).

So, if we raise some doubts about Habermas's sincerity, then a reason is needed to clear it up, but we are not necessarily unreasonable or irrational in not raising the doubt. And, if we raise the doubt and accept his birth certificate as the justification, we are not in turn unreasonable or unreflective for not raising further doubts, for it is precisely our reflection on the role of giving reasons that is our reason for not raising further doubts. As Wittgenstein puts it in his succinctly anti-Cartesian continuation of section 87:

> It may easily look as if every doubt merely *revealed* an existing gap in the foundations; so that secure understanding is only possible if we first doubt everything that *can* be doubted, and then remove all these doubts.
> The sign-post is in order—if, under normal circumstances, it fulfills its purpose.

In section 211 Wittgenstein asks how someone can instruct another about how to obey a rule, to continue a pattern, or use a word (for example, to predicate "sincere" of Habermas's speech-act). He answers, "If that means 'Have I reasons?' the answer is: my reasons will soon give out. And then I shall act, without reasons." In section 217 he says: "If I have exhausted the justifications I have reached bedrock, and my spade is turned. Then I am inclined to say: 'This is simply what I do.' "

He is also at pains to show that the exhaustion of reasons—the inability of reasons to justify the justifications unconditionally—is not in any way irrational or epistemically defective, not in any way an opening for the philosophic skeptic. "To use a word without a justification *(Rechtfertigung)* does not mean to use it without right *(Unrecht)*" (PI § 289). The spatial and temporal phenomenon of using signs reasonably, reflectively, and critically is not ultimately based on, and thus cannot be equated with, the giving of validational reasons. As he puts it in *Zettel*, "He must go on like this *without a reason*. Not, however, because he cannot yet grasp the reason but because—

in *this* system—there is no reason. (The chain of reasons comes to an end.)" (Z § 301).

The second of the three features of "reaching agreement" is simply another aspect of the first. For the activity of reaching understanding/agreement to get underway something must be taken for granted and as a matter of course for us, and so, in these circumstances, to be a ground: namely, that Habermas is sincere about his name, or that one of three justifications (offered above) are authoritative for us, or so on. That we are already in agreement in taking birth certificates as authoritative is the ground for redeeming the claim that Habermas is sincere when he presents his birth certificate as validation. In these circumstances this is where the chain of reasons comes to an end. That is, activities (language-games) of justification, of giving reasons, are themselves grounded in customary or conventional uses of words—that is, in what is not called into question in the course of our activity of asking and answering questions, of offering, rejecting, and accepting reasons. The critical activity that frees us from a customary usage itself rests on other customary uses and cannot justify these in turn, on pain of infinite regress. The critically reflective speakers and hearers are not, as Habermas claims, "out of the context of their pre-interpreted world."[26] Therefore, his view that reaching understanding/agreement is based on reasons or validation is also a mistake. The activity of reaching understanding/agreement involves the giving of reasons in the search for mutual understanding and/or agreements. However, this critical and reflective argumentation is based in a more fundamental form of speech activity in which we are always already in tacit agreement and understand one another in our thoughtful, confident, rational, yet unreflective uses of words that *eo ipso* act as grounds in these circumstances.

This is why it is correct to call Habermas's validational form of critical reflection a "practice." He calls everyday communications in the lifeworld "practices"; but his critically reflective language-game of argumentation he calls an "activity," "practical discourse," or "discourse ethics."[27] As I have sought to bring to light, however, our most sophisticated forms of reflection, including reflection on language-games of reflection, are practices in the sense that participation in them presupposes customary, intersubjective ways of acting with words.

Throughout the *Philosophical Investigations* Wittgenstein is concerned to draw our attention to this feature—"the fact that," as he puts it in section 23, "the *speaking* of language is part of an activity, or of a form of life." He goes on to explicate language-games ("consisting of language and the actions into which it is woven"), such as asking and answering questions and forming and testing a hypothesis, in terms of regular use, custom, and practice, and these in terms of the abilities of "being able to" and "mastery of a technique."[28] In *On Certainty* he crisply sums up this second feature of practices of justification: "If the true is what is grounded, then the ground is not *true*, nor yet false" (OC § 205). The ground is neither the activity of validation nor what is validated but the practice, language-game, or system in which validation takes place: "All testing, all confirmation, and disconfirmation of a hypothesis takes place already within a system. And this system is not a more or less arbitrary and doubtful point of departure for all our arguments: no, it belongs to the essence of what we call an argument. This system is not so much the point of departure, as the element in which arguments have their life" (OC § 105).

It is clear from all his later writings that the "system" or "language-game" is nothing more (or less) than the "loci of linguistic practices"—the congeries of uses of abilities employed as a matter of course in our activities of confirming and disconfirming, of using words in a multiplicity of ways.[29] No matter how deep philosophical questioning goes, it will always rest on uses of language that cannot in the circumstances be in question, and so, as he famously concludes, "philosophy... cannot give it [language use] any foundation" (PI § 124).

We can say, then, that our activities of justification are less discontinuous with everyday conversation than Habermas allows. One reason for his misunderstanding is the overly sharp distinction he draws between the reflective grounding of speech acts in argumentation and the mere de facto acceptance of habitual practices. It is precisely this false dichotomy between the demands of autonomous reason and the force of conditioning that keeps the debate going between the radical defenders of Enlightenment reason and the conservative defenders of the authority of custom. For once we free ourselves from the convention that we are free and rational only if we can justify the grounds of any uses we follow, we can see that there is a multiplicity of ways of being rationally (and thoughtfully) guided by rules of use, short of self-grounding validation, that is not reducible to the behaviorist's causal compulsion of habit. Between the Charybdis of unconditional reflection and the Scylla of the deadweight of custom lies the vast landscape where our critically reflective games of freedom have their home, which Wittgenstein opens up and explores.

In section 172 Wittgenstein strikingly illustrates the vastness and diversity of this landscape of rule-following (being guided).[30] In the following section he warns against being guided by one picture of "being guided," such as the reduction of all forms of rational thought short of the chimera of self-grounding critical reflection to the mechanical compulsion of habit: "But being guided is surely a particular experience!" his interlocutor replies. "The answer to this is: you are now *thinking* of a particular experience of being guided" (PI § 173). (Just as in politics, where there is a diverse world of political thought and action between total revolution and unthinking conformity.)

The third and final feature of "reaching agreement" illuminated by the sincerity example is the role of "the force of the better argument." Let us suppose that someone responds in the following way to the person who doubted Habermas's truthfulness. "No, he really is Habermas. He signed up for this discussion in the proper way last night and I just forgot to give him his name tag, and this has caused the confusion." Suppose we come to agree this answers the doubt for us. If it does, it is not the "force" of this better argument alone that brings about our assent. Rather, it is our being in tacit agreement on the trustworthiness of the conference organizers that gives sufficient "force" to it as a better argument. Our unwillingness to raise doubts about their trustworthiness, our having no reason to doubt, and so taking their word on trust and acting on it in the course of raising other doubts is a circumstantial and conditional ground of the force of the better argument. In *On Certainty* Wittgenstein makes just this sort of point:[31] "Giving grounds, justifying the evidence, comes to an end;—but the end is not certain propositions' striking us immediately as true, i.e. it is not a kind of *seeing* on our part; it is our *acting*, which lies at the bottom of the language-game" (OC § 204). He puts this even more forcefully in response to the query as to what counts as an "adequate test" of a proposition: "As if giving grounds did not come to an end sometime. But the end is not an ungrounded proposition: it is an ungrounded way of acting" (OC § 110).

To guard against the conservative interpretation of this point, which is often mistakenly attributed to Wittgenstein (as Cressida Heyes mentions in the introduction), we need only recall that what holds the conventions of a language-game in place is just our continuing to speak and act in conventional ways. Furthermore, what constitutes "continuing in the conventional way" is itself questioned and interpreted variously and creatively in the course of a language-game (PI § 83–84; Z § 135). In our example, one is free to question the trustworthiness of the organizers. A rumor could spread that the conference had been rigged in some way. Our confidence in the organizers' word would correspondingly dissolve and, consequently, the force of the argument would diminish. One could argue that it is reasonable to raise doubts in light of these circumstances. Another could reply that it is unreasonable to raise doubts on such flimsy evidence. Here, then, we would be calling into question our usages of the word "reasonable" itself: the criteria for its application, its reference, whether there is "reasonable disagreement" over "reasonable" or whether it is always appropriate to act reasonably—whether it may be appropriate to act "non-reasonably" or "unreasonably" in some circumstances in the name of some other value, or so on. When it is reasonable to raise doubts and when it is not is itself not fixed beyond question. Of course, as our questioning moves in this way it does so in the context of a whole repertoire of varying speech acts that are not themselves in question. What is taken for granted and what is explicitly called into question and reflected on are therefore provisional and subject to change and reversal over time—in the historical course of our activities of critical reflection (PI § 23).[32]

2.2. Questioning the Validity Claim of Rightness

Leaving aside the difficulties of coming to an agreement on the use of the word "sincerity" (which Habermas uses interchangeably with "truthfulness" and "authenticity"), let us turn to the second part of the speech-act example—"that the workplace ought to be organized democratically"—and question its validity claim to rightness. First, I think everyone will appreciate that there are several competing and contested uses of the terms "democracy" and "workplace" and no obvious self-justifying reason that could justify one use over the others, or even justify one description of the complex range of uses of these two terms.[33] However, suppose we all came to agree in the use of these terms. Of course, it would have to be agreement in use and not simply agreement on definitions. For if it were only agreement on definitions we would have the problem of how to apply the definitions in the same way, and so on.

Even if we agreed in use, this would not ensure that each one of us continued to use these terms in the same way, or that some future uses could be shown, beyond reasonable doubt, to be correct and others incorrect. As Wittgenstein's examples show, it is not only novitiates being inducted into a language-game who reasonably "go on differently" in continuing a series and so on. Seasoned practitioners, who are all masters of techniques in using these two words, continue to use the words in slightly different ways, and there is no sharp demarcation between normal and abnormal uses or between "same" and "different" (PI §§ 224–25). Indeed, the examples seem set up to show how it is always possible, due to the indeterminacy of use, to unsettle in a reasonable way our most settled and convention-ridden ways of thought. His aim is to expose the mistaken view he once held, that "if anyone utters a sentence and *means* or *understands* it he is operating a calculus according to definite rules" (PI § 81). Rather, the reasonable use and extension of a concept exhibits an element of freedom and indeterminacy precisely because its use is "not everywhere circumscribed by rules" (PI § 68).[34] Moreover, it is always possible to attempt to justify a deviant use of, say, "democracy" by appeal to an intersubjective warrant that is not, in that context, in doubt and so can function as a ground. Quentin Skinner (and Richard Rorty) have shown how much of critically reflective political theory actually proceeds by exploiting this indeterminacy in criteria and application through novel "redescription."[35] Yet, determinacy of use and meaning is laid down as a condition of validational argumentation for Habermas.[36]

If we are to assess Habermas's speech-act in terms of rightness, then we must somehow overcome these disagreements and bring about, by agreement, stable conformity in our use of "democracy" and "workplace" (as well as "ought," "organize," and so on). If we do not have this basic agreement in meaning to constrain us, then the validation activity (where the speakers are restricted to a stance of either yes or no with respect to its rightness) will move to these other disagreements in the course of the free play of questions and answers. Therefore, I do not see how Habermas could achieve the degree of conformity (in judgments) required to get his form of critical reflection going, short of presupposing widespread acceptance of the very type of sedimented practice he claims to oppose.

Let us now survey the validity claim of rightness. First, it would not be unreasonable—on the face of it—to ask why rightness is the claim of validity. A civic humanist or an ecologist would surely want to argue that goodness has priority over rightness in politics and morality.[37] It seems reasonable to discuss this important disagreement and to try to come to an agreement, yet it is impossible to do so within the constraints of Habermas's validational activity because a condition of our being modern, rational agents engaged in reflection is that we take it as beyond question that rightness has priority over goodness in politics and morality and that questions of the good belong in a separate "ethical" sphere with a distinct, non-universal form of argumentation. Rightness is one of the bounds of justificatory argumentation laid down by the transcendental and reconstructive critique. Despite Habermas's complex arguments to identify the priority of rightness with modernity, and this with the development of reason into three spheres, it would surely be reasonable to exercise our right to raise a question about these inconclusive arguments from *within* a practical discourse, and thus reasonably subvert the bounds of reason he has set for us. A practice of critical reflection designed to ground our world of politics, morality, and law that excludes the discussion of these two great claims, as well as others, is a constraint on, rather than a defense of, a free and rational society. It would constrain us to assess our moral and political norms in a deontological or juridical manner and to subordinate other ways of thinking and acting politically. Habermas thus belongs to a line of political thinkers who have sought to promote juridical institutions and forms of thought—based on the priority of right—to a position of sovereignty in our political life.[38] The initial plausibility of the exclusive sway of the rightness claim rests on our being accustomed to assessing our morals and politics predominantly in the juridical terms of "right," "rights," "law," and "universal" and being unused to other political and moral language-games. All the more reason, then, that we should be able to challenge, rather than to reinforce, this convention *in* practical discourses designed to guard our freedom.[39]

Let us look at this limitation on free thought in Habermas's theory from another perspective. Habermas writes from within a Kantian tradition in which it is conventional to employ transcendental arguments to legislate the boundary conditions of discursive rationality (the three validity claims), and to assert that rational speech and action is what takes place within this stage-setting, as we have seen.[40] Even if we did not have the humanist and ecological traditions available to us, we could still show that his universal validity claims do not constitute a universal framework for free and rational argument. We could simply ask for the reason why "rightness" is the validity claim. This is reasonable according to Habermas, since the ability to give reasons is the mark of rationality, yet it is a question that goes beyond the bounds of discursive rationality because it inaugurates a discussion that cannot take place on the ground of the validity claim of rightness (for we cannot justify rightness on the basis of rightness). Habermas will reply that rightness is laid down outside the activity of validation, by the transcendental argument, as the condition of the activity of validation and so does not come up in the activity of validation itself. It would constitute a performative contradiction to question it.[41]

The reader will now be aware that Habermas's theory of communicative action is strikingly similar in this aspect to Hegel's *Philosophy of Right*. Hegel's argument against those who wished to preserve freedom of thought by questioning the limitations of the juridical institutions of free speech, equality before the law, and the universality of its application is that if they reflected on these constitutional arrangements of right they would see that they are the conditions of possibility of free and rational thought, and therefore are not themselves to be questioned. This argument, just as Habermas's theory of communicative action, is backed up by a long historical story about the development and institutionalization of reason and freedom in the various spheres of modernity. Like some of the Young Hegelians, we can afford to be a little skeptical of Habermas's argument and so reassert our right to question the claim of rightness as the ground of political reflection from within the language-game of critical reflection itself. After all, we continually dispute his boundary conditions in our broader current reflective republic of letters and remain untroubled about the lack of fixed boundaries, while drawing conditional (non-transcendental) boundaries for particular purposes.[42] This republic is an open federation of language-games of critical reflection that embodies our freedom and rationality. We are always free within it to call into question the hegemony of any particular language-game. Yet Habermas invites us to subordinate and translate our multiplicity of language-games to his allegedly transcendental framework of precisely three forms of argumentation.

This kind of argument is self-defeating, since our right to call the priority of the claim of rightness (or sincerity) into question is itself grounded in a convention of the language-game; namely, the right in appropriate circumstances to ask for reasons. And it is no response to say now that these circumstances are inappropriate or that questioning the priority of rightness involves a performative contradiction, for these circumstances are by definition the ones in which we radically reflect on and call into question what is taken for granted or presented to us as universal and necessary. Habermas's error at this point is one to which political theorists are occupationally prone, although he was trying to avoid it. He has proffered a form of critical reflection in which we are free to call into question and dissent from the conventions governing our political and legal practices, but we are not free in turn to call into question and to dissent from the conventions governing the practice of critical reflection itself. Habermas's theory thus excludes the very freedom—to question the boundaries of our questioning practices—it is supposed to embody.

This was Michel Foucault's main concern about the direction of Habermas's theory. It tends to freeze certain juridical ways of thought and action at the expense of an ethic of critical enquiry into the limits of and alternatives to these arrangements.[43] For Foucault, it is an important convention of the practice of freedom that we are able to call into question what is given as a boundary of reason. What holds a rule of use or boundary in place, and gives it the appearance of a transcendental standard, is engagement in, and subjectification to, the ongoing activity of questioning and arguing in accordance with it. "These foundation-walls are carried by the whole house," as Wittgenstein laconically puts it (OC § 248). We can thus learn from this investigation a crucial feature of freedom in our ongoing political language-games of critical reflection. We question and alter a subset of the rules of the games, and sometimes even make up the rules, as we go along. In our complex language-games of freedom, we provisionally follow the conventional boundaries in trying to reach understanding/agreement on some issue and we also play Foucault's game of calling into question one conventional boundary at a time (by means of a genealogy of its historical role as a boundary) and of seeking to go beyond it. As Wittgenstein puts it, a boundary of sense may be used by the conservative to keep someone in or out, but it may also be used by the radical as something to jump over (PI § 499).[44]

2.3. Questioning with the Validity Claim of Rightness

Let us consider one final example. We have seen that Habermas's validational argumentation is not unconditional. It rests on the acceptance of juridical ways of thought and action as hegemonic. Assume now that we have restored juridical practices of reflection to their proper place in our polity—as one important and reasonable type of assessment among many—and shown that the practice itself mistakenly appears to be universal as a consequence of the roles the claim of universality plays *within* the practice of trumping other forms of argument.[45] We then enter into such a practice, taking rightness as the validity claim as a matter of course and begin to validate the rightness of the claim that the workplace ought to be organized democratically. We soon find—perhaps not to our surprise—that there is widespread historical and contemporary disagreement *in* our uses of the word "rightness." Sometimes "rightness" is used in the sense of universal principles of right or justice by the modern participants in the tradition of natural law stemming from Aquinas and Kant to Leo Strauss and John Finnis. At other times "rightness" is used in the sense of "alright," or of having "a right," by modern heirs of the subjective rights traditions from William of Ockham and Hugo Grotius to Kant (again) and John Rawls. A third way of using it is in the sense of "appropriate for us," "prudent," or "right with respect to the interests of the state" by modern practitioners in the reason of state tradition, from Giovanni Botero and Justus Lipsius onward. Others, following in the well-worn footsteps of Locke and Hegel, try to show how these seemingly discordant traditions can be brought into accord. In addition, even those who are in agreement on limiting the use of "rightness" to one of these traditions disagree among themselves, as, for instance, the disagreements within the subjective rights traditions even among theorists from the same country and intellectual background, such as Robert Nozick, Ronald Dworkin, and John Rawls.[46]

For the reasons we have discussed, there is no reason to expect that our generation, or any generation, will hit on a justification of the use of "rightness" that is "unconditional" and "beyond the spatiotemporal ambit of the occasion" and, therefore, would bring agreement among these three traditions of right. Yet this consensus is necessary before the activity of reaching understanding/agreement on the rightness of Habermas's initial speech-act could begin. If the conversation turned to the question of the use of "rightness," then it would not be argumentation on the basis of the validity claim but of the use of the validity claim, and so it would not fall within the canonical form of critical reflection. This free play of democratic voices within our juridical traditions cannot be silenced except by excluding two of the three schools of thought and dissenters within the victorious school. Short of calling in the police and imposing uniformity by fiat, as Hobbes famously recommended, critically reflective political argument in an open society (and more courageously in a closed one), even when it does not involve the refusal of the terms of the argument, folds back on itself and calls into question the acceptable uses of the agreed-upon terms of the debate.[47]

Historical surveys of the ways in which members of these three schools of right have always agreed and disagreed over the criteria and application of rightness and its cognates—and so have woven, and continue to weave, a multiplicity of old and new ways of using their shared vocabulary into our juridical institutions over the centuries—bring this point home and free us from the sirens of the ideal of consensus in political argumentation.[48] Wittgenstein makes the general point with his exemplary survey of the various uses of the term "game." Rather than discovering a set of necessary and sufficient conditions for the application of such terms in every case, "we see a complicated network of similarities overlapping and crisscrossing: sometimes overall similarities, sometimes similarities of details" (PI § 66), and this complicated network is not fixed but changes over time as speakers innovate and introduce unpredictable uses *en passant*.

Of course, we often find ourselves in understanding/agreement in our uses of "rightness" in the given spatial and temporal circumstances of trying to reach understanding/agreement on other, problematized speech-acts. These are provisional agreements in what Wittgenstein calls "forms of life" in the course of reflecting on and seeking to give reasons for problematic "opinions" (PI § 241). A relatively stable use of rightness *as*, say, individual and culturally neutral rights, becomes a ground, woven into practice, in virtue of our confident abilities in using it as the unmoving "hinge" around which our reflective questioning provisionally turns, not in virtue of a transcendental property of the concept or of an explicit process of reaching agreement on it, although we are able to present all sorts of reasons for doing so when the circumstances require.[49] As a result of its hinge role it appears transcendental (PI § 104). Yet, like any hinge proposition, we can also call this particular use of "rightness" into question, extend it in new ways, propose additional validity claims and different modes of argumentation, and give reasons for and against these proposals, as we have seen over the last twenty years.

Habermas wants something more than the historical, conditional, ongoing, and changing plurality of language-games of critical reflection in which we are participants. He seeks to establish a framework of argument that is itself beyond argumentation: the "decentered understanding of the world" that will fix his three validity claims and three world relations as the independent determinants of the legitimate form of critical reflection unconditionally. For the reasons I have given, we should be skeptical of this aim. However, if it is given up, the alleged threat is that we will be left with the uncritical acceptance of the status quo and so extinguish our hard-won traditions of critical reflection. This inference, as we have seen, is equally false. Far from ending critical reflection, our new understanding of the nonfoundational and conditional role of practices of critical reflection gives a clearer view of the diverse forms they take and the boundary-challenging ways free critical reflection both rests on and questions its own conditionality.

Furthermore, if the reasonable use of words, the free exchange of reasons in agreeing and disagreeing, is, as these examples are meant to suggest, *not* "operating a calculus according to definite rules," then there is not an unconditional set of implicit rules by which we ought to proceed in the first place (PI §§ 81–82). Consequently, an idealization of a set of rules of validation cannot play the quasi-transcendental role assigned to it in this theory. The (conditional) roles of ideals and norms of judgment should be reconceived in light of what we learn about reasoning together, mutual understanding, and agreement from working through these and other examples.[50]

This is not a rejection of Habermas's immensely important clarification of the procedures for the intersubjective validation of deontological norms of cooperation among free and equal individuals by testing the norms' universality. It is to do, for his model, what he and the Frankfurt School have done for instrumental reason: to temper its comprehensive aspirations, point out its limits, and restore it to its proper place in our diverse polity, as one conditional form of critical reflection among many. This clarification should, I hope, make us less imperious in our claims for one type, which we are perhaps most often engaged in and thus accustomed to, and more open to the plurality of perspectives provided by the congeries of types available to us as participants in our complex modern political practices.

I also take this to be the *spirit* of Wittgenstein's method. He begins his *Investigations* with Augustine's "particular picture of the essence of human language" (PI § 1). By means of his many examples he shows that, while this picture describes one "system of communication" which is appropriate and useful for a number of cases, it nevertheless is not a comprehensive description: "not everything that we call language is this system" (PI §§ 1–3).

3. Interpretation as a Practice of Critical Reflection

If the clarification of the practice of validation in the previous section is correct, it would seem to lend support to the hermeneutic tradition, especially as it has been reworked and updated in our era by Charles Taylor. Taylor has always stressed our existence as practitioners in practices, the conditioning role of conventions and horizons, and our situated and dialogical intersubjectivity. In these respects and others, Taylor and the tradition of critical hermeneutics are in agreement with Wittgenstein.[51] Nevertheless, one important difference exists between Wittgenstein and some of Taylor's earlier formulations of the role of interpretation (but not in his more recent work).[52] Having successfully criticized the foundational role of representation as a form of critical reflection, Taylor occasionally transferred this elevated status to interpretation in some of his earlier writings. He writes, "human beings are self-interpreting animals."[53] He sometimes suggests by this that interpretation is not simply one method, procedure, or activity among many, but that being engaged in the activity of interpretation is our basic way of being in the world.[54]

The proposition that human beings are self-interpreting animals is often taken to advance two theses. First, the most basic ways in which humans understand themselves in the world are interpretations: "We can therefore say," Taylor writes, "that the human animal not only finds himself impelled from time to time to interpret himself and his goals, but that he is always already in some interpretation, constituted as human by this fact."[55] The second and closely related thesis is that the essential feature of personhood is participation in the reflective activity of interpretation. "We must speak of man as a self-interpreting being, because this kind of interpretation is not an optional extra, but is an essential part of our existence."[56] Philosophy is said to be a continuation of this essential activity.[57]

Just as Habermas posits that conventional speech-acts always implicitly raise validity claims, in order to give his form of critical reflection universal foundations, so the first thesis suggests that even the most conventional ways we understand ourselves and our situation are themselves interpretations. Consequently, if this were true, we would always (essentially) be involved, at least implicitly, in interpretation. This thesis is based on the widespread conflation of understanding with interpretation: that is, of treating understanding as the same as interpretation or assuming that understanding involves interpretation in some essential way. This conflation, in either of its two forms, is indispensable to the claim that interpretation is the foundational way of being in the world and, consequently, that hermeneutics is the sovereign discipline of the human sciences.[58] I wish to show that interpretation can no more play this foundational role than validation or any other practice of reflection by arguing that understanding is prior to and distinct from interpretation.

3.1. Interpretation and Understanding

To appreciate the differences between understanding and interpretation, let us return to the *Philosophical Investigations*. One of Wittgenstein's aims is to show that understanding a sign is not, in any way, interpreting it. He says that we have an "inclination" to treat understanding as some kind of interpretation, that is, to say that "every action according to the rule is an interpretation [*Deuten*]" (PI § 201).[59] However, applying his method again, if we test this thesis through examples we discover that it cannot account for the phenomenon of understanding.

The interpretation of a sign is another sign, and the activity of interpretation involves the translation or substitution of one sign or expression of a rule for another (PI § 201). If interpretation were able to account for the phenomenon of understanding, an interpretation would determine the correct use of the sign or rule it interprets, since "understanding" obviously involves being able to use the sign or rule in question. An interpretation on this account would have to be "a rule determining the application of a rule" (PI § 84). However, as Wittgenstein shows by his many examples, the giving of interpretations does not determine correct use and so does not account for understanding. The application of the interpretation always can be interpreted in various ways and, therefore, we would require another interpretation to determine the application of the first interpretation, and so on. This problem with the "understanding as interpretation" thesis is illustrated in section 85:

> A rule stands there like a sign-post.—Does the sign-post leave no doubt open about the way I have to go? Does it shew which direction I am to take when I have passed it; whether along the road or footpath or cross-country? But where is it said which way I am to follow it; whether in the direction of its finger or (e.g.) in the opposite one?—And if there were, not a single sign-post, but a chain of adjacent ones or of chalk marks on the ground—is there only *one* way of interpreting them?—So I can say, the sign-post does after all leave no room for doubt. (PI § 85)

Rather than clarify understanding, the interpretational explanation just displaces the problem of understanding one step back, to the proffered interpretation. How is it in turn to be understood, and so on? *Any* way a person follows the (endless) series of sign-posts will be in accord with the sign on some interpretation and so count as understanding. This anarchic and paradoxical consequence shows that there is some mistake in the initial inclination to assimilate understanding a rule to some kind of interpretation of it:[60] " 'But how can a rule shew me what I have to do at *this* point? Whatever I do is, on some interpretation, in accord with the rule.'—That is not what we ought to say, but rather: any interpretation still hangs in the air along with what it interprets, and cannot give it any support. Interpretations by themselves do not determine meaning" (PI § 198).

Wittgenstein then asks what can account for exactly that feature of understanding that interpretation fails to illuminate: namely, the connection between a sign or rule and its use. He answers with the explication of understanding in terms of the practice and ability, unmediated by interpretations or explanations, to use a sign and follow a rule that we saw in the section on Habermas. First, understanding a rule, and thus being guided by it, involves "training"—the acquisition through practice of a repertoire of normative linguistic abilities to use a sign and challenge conventional use in various contexts. Second, the acquisition and employment of abilities and techniques (of language use) presuppose an ongoing practice, "a regular use of sign-posts, a custom." To "obey a rule, to make a report, to give an order, to play a game of chess, are *customs* (uses, institutions)." The regular uses of signs over time sustain and are sustained by participation in practices or language-games and thus preempt the anarchy of use and meaning threatened by the interpretational account. As he sums up, to "understand a sentence means to understand a language. To understand a language means to be master of a technique" (PI §§ 198–99).

Having reminded his interlocutor of these two mundane features of understanding, Wittgenstein restates the "paradox" to which the interpretational account gives rise: "no course of action could be determined by a rule, because every course of action can be made out to accord with the rule. The answer was: if everything can be made out to accord with the rule, then it can also be made out to conflict with it. And so there would be neither accord nor conflict here" (PI § 201). The misunderstanding here can be seen simply by asking what would happen if understanding involved interpretation in an essential way, for we would give one interpretation after another and never arrive at use (i.e., understanding). The paradox is dissolved by realizing that understanding must consist in the unmediated ability to "grasp" a sign manifested in actual *praxis*:

> It can be seen that there is a misunderstanding here from the mere fact that in the course of our argument we give one interpretation [*Deutung*] after another: as if each one contented us at least for a moment, until we thought of yet another standing behind it. What this shows is that there is a way of grasping [*Auffassung*] a rule which is *not* an *interpretation* [nicht *eine* Deutung], but which is exhibited in what we call "obeying the rule" and "going against it" ["*ihr entgegenhandeln*"] in actual cases. (PI § 201)

Once understanding is seen in this correct way, there is no initial, problematic gap between understanding and use that needs to be filled in by a mediator—interpretation, representation, community agreement, or whatever. Understanding is like an immediate grasp of something. In his notebook, Wittgenstein wrote the following synoptic remark: "It is not interpretation which builds the bridge between the sign and what is signified //meant//. Only practice does that."[61]

Of course, understanding is accompanied by interpretation in some circumstances, but it cannot always be so, on pain of infinite regress and anything goes. (Interpretations come to an end somewhere.) Interpretation is a reflective activity that we engage in when we are in doubt about how to grasp or to understand a sign that is in question. But if we are in doubt about how to understand the sign then it is manifest that we do not understand it. Far from being equivalent or essential to understanding, interpretation begins when our conventional self-understandings break down and we do not know how to go on. This is why Wittgenstein concludes section 201 by cautioning against the "inclination" to say "every action according to the rule is an interpretation" and recommends that "we ought to restrict the term 'interpretation' to the substitution of one expression of the rule for another" (PI § 201).

Therefore, the first thesis that the most fundamental ways humans understand themselves are interpretations is mistaken. Moreover, interpretation is conditional on understanding. Like practices of justification, it is a practice we engage in when our understanding and use of some subset of signs is in some way rendered problematic and thrown in doubt. Here we attempt to "come to an understanding" of the sign in question by offering various interpretations, by discussing and adjudicating rival interpretations and rival accounts of the indeterminate criteria of a sign, in some cases by calling the accepted criteria of adjudication of incompatible interpretations into question in turn, and so on. However, the condition for engaging in interpretation is always that a wide range of ways of acting with words is understood, is not in doubt at all, but is followed as a matter of course in the activity of interpretation. These ways of acting, which lie at the bottom of any reflective language-game of interpretation, are not the stimulus and response of blind compulsion but the multiplicity of techniques of thoughtfully being guided—of "obeying the rule and going against it in actual cases"—short of explicit disengagement and reflective questioning. Understanding grounds interpretation. Interpretation should thus be seen as one important practice of critical reflection among many, resting comfortably in more basic ways of acting with words (self-understandings) that cannot themselves be interpretations.

It is important not to infer from this that there must be a stock of conventional uses that are permanently beyond interpretative dispute. First, the circumstances of any particular activity of interpreting a problematic sign involves the unmediated grasp of other signs, which, *eo ipso*, places them provisionally beyond interpretation. Second, it is always possible to "step back": to call into question the regular use of any of these other signs and take it up as an object of interpretation (OC § 204; Z §§ 234–35). As we have seen (in section 2), calling a background use into question and placing it in the reflective context of interpretative disputation (or validational argumentation) can and does occur in everyday conversation in the lifeworld. Wittgenstein himself celebrates this intrinsic freedom of language use: the unpredictable emergence of interpretative disagreements over the most settled uses of signs and, as a result of participation in practices of interpretation, the acquisition of the ability to see the various "aspects" (uses) of the problematic sign under different descriptions.[62]

3.2. Understanding Is Not an Implicit Interpretation

If self-understandings can be called into question and taken up in interpretive exercises, then it is tempting to defend the first thesis by replying that they are implicit or proto-interpretations that we take for granted because they have become sedimented and internalized. Nietzsche often professed this view, and it has gained a certain vogue with the slogan "Humans are interpretation all the way down."[63] While one and the same sign can function as an interpretation in one language-game (where it is the object of reflection) and as a sign understood in another (where it is the background of reflection), it does not carry over some intrinsic properties of dispositional interpretability from one role to another. The attempt to construe conventional understanding as implicit interpretation misses the revolutionary point Wittgenstein is concerned to make, namely, that the role of a sign in a language-game is the "*primary* thing," not something lying hidden behind it (PI § 656).

An interpretation is a reflection on a sign; an opinion or belief about how it should be taken. To interpret a sign is to take it *as* one expression rather than another.[64] In contrast, to understand a sign is not to possess a sedimented opinion about it or to take it *as* something, but to be able to grasp it; that is, to act with it, using it in agreement and disagreement with customary ways (PI § 241). If conventional understandings were implicit interpretations or beliefs about practice, rather than the actual abilities manifested in practice, they would not be conventional understandings, for all the reasons given above. The intersubjective speech-acts that manifest understanding ("grasp") in language-games do not raise implicit interpretation claims that need to be made explicit and adjudicated before we can go on reasonably. We have to raise the claims of reason ourselves, by performing and exchanging the wide range of illocutionary acts that bring them into question and demand reflection.

It follows that the second thesis survives in the modest and nonfoundational sense that, as Taylor puts it, interpretation is "not an optional extra."[65] Interpretation is a practice we engage in whenever we are confronted by something we do not understand and do not know how to go on, or, as initiators, when we strive to unsettle a settled understanding and show that it can be treated as one contestable interpretation among others.[66] Like "commanding, questioning, recounting, chatting," interpretation is thus as "much a part of" what Wittgenstein calls "our natural history" as are "walking, eating, drinking, playing" (PI § 25).

However, this non-optional aspect of interpretation is often overextended by an "inclination" analogous to the one Wittgenstein diagnosed above. This is the inclination to say that "every reflection on a sign is an interpretation." We can clarify the meaning and limits of interpretation by, as

Wittgenstein recommends (PI §§ 90–92), carefully surveying and discriminating—within the family of concepts we use to reflect on signs and the activities into which they are woven—between interpretation, deconstruction, evaluation, explanation, examination, interrogation, inquisition, justification, validation, verification, genealogy, problematization, and so on. Each of these concepts has a distinct grammar and complex historical genealogy as a practice of critical reflection in our natural history as language users, and none of them, as we have seen, are "closed by a frontier" (PI § 68) once and for all. Even the activity "moderns" engage in of interpreting what they call their "selves" and their "identities" is itself a recent and historically contingent way of constituting a practice of experience and reflection.[67] Our language-games of critical reflection, like our language as a whole, "can be seen as an ancient city: a maze of little streets and squares of old and new houses, and of houses with additions from various periods; and this surrounded by a multitude of new boroughs with straight regular streets and uniform houses" (PI § 18). The contemporary *and* historical study of these practices of critical reflection in Western and non-Western societies might be called "a genealogy of the critical attitude."[68]

By virtue of being participants in one practice of reflection most of time—as students or teachers, for example, in the interpretative disciplines in the humanities—we tend to take it for granted that our customary form of reflection is foundational and comprehensive. Accordingly, we equally tend to comprehend and assess other types of critical reflection in terms of the language of our customary type of critical reflection when we engage in the debate over which one is the archetype (and so arrive at the predictable answer). By disengaging from the debate and engaging in this practice of reflecting on two well-known language-games of critical reflection, we have come to understand that no type of critical reflection can play the mythical role of founding patriarch of our political life presumed of it in the debate, because any practice of critical reflection is itself already founded in the popular sovereignty of our multiplicity of humdrum ways of acting with words. This conclusion, far from leading to uncritical acceptance of the status quo, enables us to realize that submission to one regime of critical reflection, as the alleged self-certifying guarantor of our freedom, would itself mark the end of our free and critical life.

Having thus freed ourselves from this captivating misunderstanding of the use of critical reflection, we are now able to see the enlightening multiplicity of conceptions of critical reflection available to us. We can henceforth go on to use these reflective concepts as their grammar manifestly guides us in innumerable ways to do: not to provide foundations for, but to reflect critically *on*, our well-trodden ways of thought and action, rendering them less indubitably foundational, and thereby disclosing possibilities of thinking and acting differently.[69] However, since it is "our forms of language" themselves that lead us into the sorts of misunderstandings we surveyed in this chapter, it will always be necessary to bring along Wittgenstein's distinctive philosophical practice of critical reflection to test our use and abuse of these languages of critical reflection. For philosophy as Wittgenstein practiced it is just this critical attitude—"a battle against the bewitchment of our intelligence by means of language" (PI § 109).[70]

2

The Limits of Conservatism:

Wittgenstein on "Our Life" and "Our Concepts"

David R. Cerbone

> Language is, after all, not a cage.
> —Ludwig Wittgenstein, quoted in *Wittgenstein and the Vienna Circle*

> Obviously the question is meaningless—as meaningless as asking which points in Ohio are starting points.
> —W.V.O. Quine, "Two Dogmas of Empiricism"

A striking feature of the literature on Wittgenstein is the polarizing effect of questions concerning the political implications of his philosophy. Interpretive disagreement is, of course, stock in trade among scholars of any body of texts, but what I have in mind is the complete disdain with which some interpreters respond to particular ways of answering those questions. Cora Diamond, for example, in the second introduction to her *The Realistic Spirit*, sees fit to devote little more than one sentence to the charge that Wittgenstein's philosophy is inherently conservative, dismissing it with the contemptuous verdict of "nutty."[1] Though I must confess to a certain sympathy for Diamond's attitude, and even the tone she employs in expressing it, I would like, in this chapter, to give the charge of conservatism a more prolonged consideration. Doing so strikes me as called for, especially because, despite the contempt with which it is sometimes met, the charge seems to outlast any attempt to rebut it once and for all.[2] In this regard, the charge that Wittgenstein's philosophy is inherently conservative is akin to the charge that he is, the many protests to the contrary notwithstanding, an *idealist*. This is, I think, no accident.

I. A Captivating Picture

Rather than treat the attribution of conservatism as simply nutty (though the eccentricities of some particular readings tempt me considerably), what

I want to do in this chapter is demonstrate how the charge is apt to arise through a mistaken, though in many ways quite understandable, way of reading Wittgenstein at those junctures where he remarks upon the status of "our concepts" in relation to, variously, the very general facts of nature, natural history, and, most importantly, our form of life. Conservative readings of Wittgenstein, like many of those that attribute to him some form of idealism, derive from these remarks a very particular, and ultimately highly problematic, picture of our conceptual predicament, whereby "our form of life" serves as a boundary, a set of constraints, in short a *limit,* "within" which our concepts can be legitimately applied. The cogency of this picture, I want to suggest, crucially depends on the success of explaining these boundary conditions in independent terms, so that they can have the pictured relation to "our concepts." What conservative (and idealist) readings fail to realize is the extent to which the intelligibility of such an explanatory endeavor, together with its attending notion of limits, is precisely one of Wittgenstein's favored targets.

I will proceed, in section II, by developing in more detail the kind of picture I take to be at the heart of conservative readings of Wittgenstein's philosophy. Such readings, I argue, fall into roughly two varieties, depending upon just how the relation between "our life" and "our concepts" is conceived. Despite these variations, the criticisms I offer in section III are meant to be applicable to both. As will become apparent shortly, my diagnosis of the motivations for conservative readings of Wittgenstein's philosophy locates the most salient issues at a considerable remove from any explicitly political considerations, such that the relation between the issues under consideration and the political commitments that are part and parcel of conservatism might be difficult to discern. I want to note here that, first, my critique takes the particular form it does in response to the kinds of conservative readings that have been worked out by other interpreters of Wittgenstein (although I factor out those readings, or aspects of those readings, which rely heavily on biographical data),[3] and, second, that the issues under discussion *do* ultimately connect with explicitly political concerns. That is, the depiction of "our concepts" as constrained by our "form of life" can, and often is taken to, underwrite, and so legitimate, a hostile attitude toward political change; equally, the endorsement of such a depiction very often affects the attitude one takes toward the nature and possibility of social and political criticism, whether, for example, such criticism can be rationally motivated or adjudicated. In short, the pictured relations between "our life" and "our concepts" that I claim to be at the heart of conservative readings of Wittgenstein, while perhaps not necessitating a reverential attitude toward tradition, do appear to dictate a conceptual and political resistance to change. At the very least, those readings of Wittgenstein that attribute to his philosophy some form of conservatism see those commitments as emerging out of his commitment to those pictured relations, and so the question of whether Wittgenstein should be read as committed to those relations is key to assessing the charge of conservatism. I wish to argue not only that Wittgenstein is in no way committed to such a picture, and so that his philosophy is not inherently conservative, but that, by contrast, a proper reading of Wittgenstein on these issues, to which my critique in section III is meant to be a contribution, can have a liberating, transformative effect, quite the opposite of the conceptual inertia with which Wittgenstein is often saddled. In the concluding section, I lay out some of the main lines of this alternative reading.

II. Drawing the Picture: "Our Concepts" and "Our Life"

I want to begin with a remark from the relatively late *Remarks on Colour*, which, despite its brevity, can nonetheless serve to exemplify how these misinterpretations arise. The remark consists of a question followed by a single sentence offered in reply (just what kind of *answer* this reply constitutes is a delicate matter, as I'll try to show); the remark reads:

> Would it be correct to say that our concepts reflect our life?
> They stand in the middle of it. (RC III § 302)

I want to propose two readings, each of which has conservative implications, the first in a perhaps more radical (and misbegotten) manner, the second in a more subtle way. The divergence in the two readings turns on whether the sentence offered in reply to the query affirms or denies what the question asks. That is, the first reading takes the reply to be, implicitly, "Yes, by standing in the middle of it," whereas the second takes the reply to be, in effect, "No, but they stand in the middle of it." In other words, the first of the readings I want to consider affirms the idea of reflection, so that, ultimately, the *content* of our concepts is exhausted by the features of our life: our concepts record, and so are nothing other than reflections of, the patterns and processes constituting our condition. The second reading, while rejecting the idea of reflection, still locates "our concepts" with respect to those patterns and processes. It does so by understanding those patterns and processes ("our life") as providing a kind of framework *within* which our concepts can be meaningfully applied. Either version of this picture ultimately depicts our concepts as conditioned by something specifiable or characterizable independently of them.

David Bloor's sociological reading of Wittgenstein, which is both conservative and idealist, is an example of this first kind of reading.[4] (Some of Ernest Gellner's rather scattershot ruminations on Wittgenstein and what he characterizes as his "communal-cultural mysticism" seem to follow the lines of this reading as well, though on the whole, his "reading" seems to conform more to the pattern of the second variety I will consider.)[5] Central to Bloor's reading is his portrayal of Wittgenstein as stressing "the dependence of our knowledge on patterns of training" and as developing "a bold, naturalistic account of the basis of logic."[6] By "dependence," Bloor does not simply mean that Wittgenstein is pointing to the various conditions that must obtain in order for human beings to be able to recognize and articulate the propositions of logic and mathematics; rather, he takes Wittgenstein's observations to have ramifications for the *content* of the propositions of logic and mathematics. Similarly, when Bloor says that "mathematics and logic . . . both [are] equally the product of instinct, training, and convention,"[7] he means to suggest not just that our capacity to make logical inferences or formulate arithmetical propositions is the outcome of these natural and social processes, but the further idea that these inferences and propositions are in some way *about,* and in this sense reflect, these processes.

Some indirect support for reading Bloor's reading of Wittgenstein in this manner can be gleaned from Bloor's treatment of Frege in another work.[8] Frege, it will be recalled, had insisted that assertions regarding number cannot be understood as assertions about psychological events or about (the properties of) physical objects. Bloor's proposed way of accommodating this insistence is to suggest that we see "mathematics as social in nature," the social being a third category distinct from both the physical and psychological. Given the way Bloor contrasts the social with the psychological and the physical, to say that mathematics, or any set of beliefs, is social in nature is to say something about the *content* of the beliefs, not just about their status, and indeed Bloor himself does not balk at this conclusion: "If mathematics is about number and its relations and if these are social creations and conventions then, indeed, mathematics is about something social. In an indirect sense it therefore is 'about' society." Bloor further remarks that "the reality that [mathematics] appears to be about represents a transfigured understanding of the social labor that has been invested in it."[9]

Thus, to return to Wittgenstein, it appears safe to conclude that what Bloor means by "dependence," "foundation," and "product" blurs the distinction between the outcome of a process and the process itself, as can be seen in his claim that "the belief in mathematical essences is a reified perception of social processes."[10] Again, the claim is that the *content* of mathematical propositions is infused by the social structure in which the articulation of these propositions take place. We have, then, an echo of the claim Bloor advanced in his discussion of Frege: mathematics, in some indirect sense, is about society. In this way, Bloor rather unabashedly attributes to Wittgenstein a sociological variant of the kind of psychologism against which Frege had inveighed: "The idea that logic can be seen as a theory of the mind has had little support since the disciplines of logic and psychology became differentiated in the nineteenth century. Wittgenstein, however, did not swim with the tide."[11]

That Bloor's way of reading Wittgenstein has conservative implications is a conclusion that he happily draws. Logical reasoning, espoused by some as a tool of critical reflection, is, on this view, nothing more than a reflection of the social processes that found and sustain it. Since "our concepts" and "our life" stand in a relation such that the former reflect the latter, it is a mistake, to say the least, to hanker after any kind of critical perspective with respect to the particular arrangements inherent in the life we lead. All that can be said, on this view, is that we have *these* arrangements, not that they are in some way right or wrong or better or worse in comparison to some other arrangements.[12]

Such a reading can, I think, be rather quickly dismissed, primarily because of its rather glaring infidelity to what Wittgenstein actually says. At one juncture, Wittgenstein writes that "the logical 'must' is a component part of the propositions of logic, *and these are not propositions of human natural history*" (RFM VI § 49, emphasis added). Wittgenstein makes this remark as a way of defusing the worry that his talk of the facts of human natural history somehow undercuts the "hardness" of logical connections.[13] That is, his interlocutor, much like Bloor, takes him to be *combining* human natural history with the propositions of logic, such that the former infuses the content of the latter. But Wittgenstein is careful to deny this.

Wittgenstein is best read as *responding* to accusations of holding the view Bloor ascribes to him, so as to deflect a particular temptation that comes from his talk of human natural history. By means of his interlocutor, Wittgenstein persistently raises and then quells the worry that with his remarks he is blurring the distinction between being true and being taken to be true: " 'So you are saying that human agreement decides what is true and what is false?' " To which Wittgenstein responds that "it is what human beings *say* that is true and false; and they agree in the *language* they use" (PI § 241). This response indicates that he is well aware that his talk of "agreement in judgments" might seem to "abolish logic," but his repeated denial of this consequence shows that something is indeed amiss with Bloor's claim that Wittgenstein's refusal to "swim with the tide" marks a renewed advocacy of psychologism. Thus, Bloor's attribution to Wittgenstein of a view that advocates an understanding of logic and mathematics as being cleverly disguised psychological and sociological propositions runs counter to what Wittgenstein says on the matter. Indeed, Wittgenstein explicitly deflects such a view at precisely the points where his remarks appear to suggest the conclusion that logic was to be "abolished."

Perhaps, however, this first way of reading our passage from *Remarks on*

Colour is too crude in its equating the content of "our concepts" with "our life." Perhaps, that is, by declaring that our concepts "stand in the middle of" our life, Wittgenstein should not be understood as affirming the suggestion implicit in the passage's opening question to the effect that the former reflects the latter. Rather, he should be understood as in some way *correcting* this implicit suggestion, thereby offering an alternative to reflection as the best way of characterizing the relation between the two: while it would be wrong to say that our concepts reflect our life (since that would mean that, absurdly, our concepts were about our life), nonetheless they do "stand in the middle of it," in the sense that our life, its characteristic features and patterns, provides the framework within which the application of our concepts is intelligible. As such a framework, "our life" determines the limits of our concepts' applicability.

Readings of Wittgenstein along these lines are not hard to find. Thomas Nagel, who views Wittgenstein as "one of the most important sources of contemporary idealism," sees his philosophy as precisely such "an attempt to cut the universe down to size." According to Nagel, Wittgenstein's "views on the conditions of meaning . . . imply that nothing can make sense which purports to reach beyond the outer bounds of human experience and life."[14] Nagel's characterization of Wittgenstein, in its appeal to the "outer bounds of human experience and life," can readily be seen to follow the contours of the reading sketched out above. Many of Ernest Gellner's remarks likewise fit the pattern of this interpretation, since he reads Wittgenstein as offering a kind of "populist" solution to "the problem of the validation of our thought styles." According to Gellner, Wittgenstein should be read as affirming that "our conceptual customs are valid precisely because they are parts of a cultural custom. It is not merely the case that no other validation is available: no other validation is either possible *or* necessary. The very pursuit of such extra-cultural validation is *the* error of thought."[15] This "omnibus populism," as Gellner labels it, maintains "that language and thought could only be understood as part and parcel of the ongoing concrete life of such a community."[16] "Part and parcel" is not far indeed from "stand in the middle."

Gellner's depiction of Wittgenstein as promulgating a kind of "relativistic populism," such that "all cultural cocoons, all forms of life, are valid and self-sufficient," finds a more positive treatment in the work of J. C. Nyíri. On Nyíri's reading, which explicitly links Wittgenstein to conservatism, Wittgenstein's aim is "to show that the given form of life is the ultimate givenness, that the given form of life cannot be consciously transcended." Nyíri's claim that, for Wittgenstein, a "form of life, mode of thought and behaviour . . . cannot actually be criticized" because all "criticism presupposes a form of life, a language, that is, a tradition of agreements"[17] is indeed not far off from Gellner's attribution to Wittgenstein of "the doctrine that cultures were logically terminal and self-justifying, [such that] no other kind of justification [is] either possible or necessary,"[18] only it is asserted by Nyíri without a sneer. Common to Nagel's idealistic, Gellner's relativistic, and Nyíri's conservative readings is a conception of our concepts and judgments as located within, and so circumscribed by, something else: a tradition, a culture, a society, a form of life.

While the first reading of my key quote could be dismissed rather quickly, due to its glaring infidelities with respect to what Wittgenstein actually wrote, this second reading has the merit of accommodating more in the way of textual specifics. After all, Wittgenstein does write, in part II of the *Investigations*, that "what has to be accepted, the given is—so one could say—*forms of life*," and it is precisely on such an image of acceptance, or at least a particular understanding of it, that these readings focus (PI p. 226).[19] Further support may be found in the following passage, from *Remarks on the Philosophy of Psychology*, where Wittgenstein writes:

> How could human behavior be described? Surely only by showing actions of a variety of humans, as they are all mixed up together. Not what *one* man is doing *now*, but the whole hurly-burly, is the background against which we see an action, and it determines our judgment, our concepts, and our reactions. (RPPII § 629)

What Wittgenstein here calls "the whole hurly-burly," which "determines our judgment, our concepts, and our reactions," can be construed as more or less equivalent to what's picked out by "our life" in the passage from *Remarks on Colour*, and the message is in both cases the same: Our concepts stand in the middle of our life, and so our life is immune from criticism, on pain of undermining the very possibility of applying those concepts. Hence the conservatism (and idealism) that comes along with these sorts of readings.

Despite the appearance of further textual support, there are several features of this cluster of readings that make it problematic. I will postpone discussion of what I think is the most serious shortcoming until the next section, but there are others that should not go unremarked. Consider Gellner's "relativistic populism," which he sees as integral to Wittgenstein's mature views: such a view ascribes to Wittgenstein a picture wherein cultures, communities, or languages stand as hermetically sealed units, such that there can be no question of any "validation" of what such a unit does beyond the fact that it does it. What bothers Gellner is the inability of such a view to account for the overwhelming superiority of the modern, scientific account of the world, the rise of which has irrevocably changed the face of the earth and the way people live. It is not enough, for Gellner, to say that this is how we happen to do things or how we happen to view the world, there being other ways, equally legitimate in their own right. Instead, there must, it appears, be an *argument* to establish the superiority of this modern view: indeed, the very nature of the view demands it. Gellner's dissatisfaction stems from his perception of Wittgenstein as committed to the rejection of any such argument, indeed as ruling one out as entirely unintelligible.

Yet when Gellner himself, contrary to what he perceives to be Wittgenstein's philosophical convictions, begins to sketch the contours of such an argument, it quickly becomes apparent that this envisioned legitimation project cannot really go through in the manner he desires. When Gellner characterizes his own "alternative" view, which champions the unique legitimacy of "our" modern, "one-world" scientific-technological view, he includes as constitutive of that view what he himself labels a number of fundamental *assumptions:* (i) "it is assumed that like causes will have like effects, thereby making generalization and theory-building possible"; (ii) "the orderliness of the world is also assumed to be systematic: not only are there regularities to be discovered, but they also form a system, such that, if we are successful in our enquiries, the more specific regularities turn out in the end to be corollaries of more general ones." About these, Gellner says: "There is of course no non-circular way of establishing this Single World or Unique Truth." And: "In brief: the atomization of information and the orderly systematization of explanation are imperative. Neither of them is established except as a *precondition* of having real knowledge at all."[20] How then, we might ask, has Gellner himself risen above the "peasant-like shouting" he sees Wittgenstein as championing? Even at the bottom of Gellner's own "rival" worldview lie assumptions that cannot themselves be validated in terms of that view: the very intelligibility and maintenance of that view take them for granted. Even for Gellner, something "holds fast." Thus, Gellner rather unwittingly illustrates what he takes to be Wittgenstein's point.

My point in considering this aspect of Gellner's criticisms (and his own positive views) is not so much to defend Wittgenstein in the face of those charges (though some such defense can, I think, be mounted).[21] Rather, my point is to show that just what it is that critics want from Wittgenstein is often unclear. Gellner complains that Wittgenstein is omitting something important, that he is mistakenly and irresponsibly ruling out the possibility of some kind of justification for our concepts, but further scrutiny of Gellner's own position renders mysterious just what it is that he wants from Wittgenstein. That is, Gellner himself does not specify what kind of justification he has in mind, and indeed he even seems to deny the possibility of one. The question for Gellner is thus one of what kind of a justification it is, whose possibility Wittgenstein is ruling out.

III. Dissolving the Picture: Wittgenstein's Critique of Limits

Leaving aside worries about the consistency of Gellner's criticisms of Wittgenstein vis-à-vis Gellner's own philosophical agenda, I want now to consider the fidelity of both sorts of reading to Wittgenstein's philosophy. Ultimately, the complaint is not that, for example, Gellner ends up demonstrating his own confinement in one "cultural cocoon" among many, all the while bemoaning Wittgenstein's depiction of human beings as so confined: the real problem lies with this trope of confinement.[22] Both of the readings considered in the previous section deploy a version of the problematic picture mentioned at the outset, wherein some independent content can be attributed to "our life," which would then have a constraining, determining role with respect to the content or application of our concepts. According to Nyíri's Wittgenstein, for example, "it is an unalterable anthropological fact... that any human being must, in order to be a human being, be *constrained* by some form of life, by some network of tradition."[23] In doing so, both readings fail to appreciate the extent to which for Wittgenstein such notions of constraint, confinement, and limits are candidates for "philosophical treatment" of the kind recommended at section 254 of the *Investigations*. Rather than a contribution to any specific *thesis* concerning the status of our concepts, Wittgenstein's reminders concerning "our concepts" and "our life" are directed toward the urge to construct philosophically puzzling and problematic pictures of our relation to the world. A picture that depicts us as inhabiting a form of life, as something that contains and determines our applications of concepts, is one example. A careful reading of my exemplary passage, in conjunction with an examination of remarks such as those in the *Investigations*, part II, section xii, and several from *Remarks on the Philosophy of Psychology*, serves to support the more deflationary reading I want to recommend. To the extent that the articulation of a particular set of political commitments depends upon any such picture, it is mistaken, to say the least, to attribute those commitments to Wittgenstein's philosophy.

If "stand in the middle" is not to be understood as equivalent to "reflect," nor as granting to "our life" the status of a constraint for "our concepts," how exactly is Wittgenstein to be interpreted here? What sort of point is he making with respect to the "relation" between "our concepts" and "our life," if not the point articulated by conservative-minded readings? And what political implications, if any, does Wittgenstein, properly interpreted, have on these matters? I want to answer these questions eventually, but in order to do so the pictures at the heart of conservative-minded readings must be shown to be a *target* of Wittgenstein's criticism, rather than a cornerstone of it.

Consideration of the following passage (and its sequels), taken from one of the later manuscripts, provides, I think, a good beginning:

> It seems therefore, that our concepts, the use of our words, are constrained by [*bedingt durch*] a factual framework. But how *can* that be?! How could we describe the framework if we did not allow for the possibility of something else?—One is inclined to say that you are making all logic into nonsense! (RPPII § 190).

The first sentence of this passage gives voice to the picture described above: what constitutes "our life," it might be said, is the "factual framework" named here, which "constrains" our concepts, and so within which our concepts (and use of words) have their place. As with the details of Bloor's reading discussed above, Wittgenstein's opening "It seems . . . that . . ." indicates that he is well aware that his views are apt to be understood as promoting just the kind of picture conservative readings attribute to him; the subsequent questions express his exasperation over the persistence of such an attribution.

Let us consider these subsequent questions more carefully: their point, it appears, is to challenge, or in some way render problematic, the picture suggested in the first sentence. If, these questions seem to insinuate, our concepts really were constrained by a "factual framework," then that should be something we could not get any purchase on, for we would not be able so much as to imagine the possibility of facts contrary to the ones constraining us. Insofar, then, as we *are* able to pick out such a factual framework, that is, a framework of facts that strike us as important for the application of our concepts, the thesis that these facts *constrain* or *condition* our concepts loses its tenability. The sequel to the above passage helps to bring out this point:

> The problem which worries us here is the same as in the case of this observation: "Human beings couldn't learn to count if all the objects around them were rapidly coming into being and passing away." (RPPII § 191).

This "observation," trivial though it may sound, underscores Wittgenstein's point in the previous passage: although there is a connection between the relative stability of objects and our learning to count, nothing about that connection rules out as unintelligible or incoherent a situation in which such stability does not obtain.[24]

It should further be noted, in reference to the particulars of Bloor's kind of reading, that whatever this connection is between our practice of counting and such facts about the stability of objects, the latter facts are not part of the *content* of the concepts involved in the practice of counting: though our coming to say/think that 3 follows 2 may depend on, among other things, the relative stability of various groupings of objects in the world around us, that such groupings are relatively stable is not part of our saying or thinking that 3 follows 2. Thus, whatever the connection between facts and concepts, it is not that the latter are, as Bloor maintained, about the former.

A final passage from this series of remarks is worth citing here, both to reinforce the points just made, but also for the rather surprising turn Wittgenstein's discussion takes, almost without comment:

> But you can also say: "If you don't have any little sticks, stones, etc. at hand, then you can't teach a person how to calculate." Just as you can say "If you have neither a writing surface nor writing material at hand then you can't teach him differential calculus" (or: then you can't work out the division 76570 ÷ 319).
>
> We don't say of a table and chair that they think, neither do we say this of a plant, a fish, and hardly of a dog; only of human beings. And not even of all human beings.
>
> But if I say "A table does not think," then that is not similar to a statement like "A table does not grow." I shouldn't know 'what it would be like if' a table were to think. And here there is obviously a gradual transition to the case of human beings. (RPPII § 192)

I take it that the first paragraph in this passage serves to trivialize even further the notion of constraint appealed to at the outset of this sequence: whatever "constraint" the availability of writing surfaces might exercise on differential calculus, it would strain credulity, to say the least, to say that the concepts of differential calculus "reflect" that availability. The second and third paragraphs, however, appear far less trivial, though their relation to the first, and to the remarks preceding them, is far from clear. What do these new remarks about the application of the concept of *thinking* have to do with Wittgenstein's prior observations about sticks and stones? Wittgenstein's appeal to "a gradual transition" in the last sentence provides a clue: in the first range of examples—the relative stability of objects, the availability of sticks and stones, etc.—the obtaining of alternative possibilities was something upon which a fairly solid grip could be had. Even though it might be difficult to specify all the ways in which the world would be different if the possibilities envisaged obtained, the important point is that what are envisaged are *possibilities*. That this is so helps to undermine the conceit that our concepts are constrained by such possibilities in any deep sense that *prevents* us from recognizing such alternative possibilities *as* alternative possibilities.

To say "Tables might have been things which think," by contrast, does *not* appear to pick out a meaningful possibility, since we cannot, as Wittgenstein remarks, say what it would be like if tables had the power of thought. Here the concept (of thinking) *appears* to be constrained by the facts to a greater degree than in the previous examples, since here it is not at all clear how to "allow for the possibility of something else." But this appearance of constraint is misleading, since it takes for granted that the sentence "Tables might have been things which think" succeeds in picking out a possibility. Wittgenstein's point instead appears to be that it is not clear that we have cited a possibility at all; the worry instead is that we have lapsed into nonsense. But if this is so, then it's unclear what kind of "constraint" the facts exercise upon us and our concepts, since it's unclear that *something* has been ruled out that, because the facts are as they are, *we* cannot recognize (as though some other kind of being could). In this kind of case as well, the idea that the facts somehow condition or constrain our concepts and their application doesn't go through.

The distinction between this latter kind of case and the first should not be understood as hard and fast, such that some univocal relation between the facts and our concepts can be cited throughout. This is part of what I mean in saying that Wittgenstein's aim throughout his later writings is to undermine any specific thesis about the relation between our concepts and the world. *Some* departures from our usual situation are relatively unproblematic, while others produce considerably more puzzlement. The vagaries attending separation of one sort from the other, however, preclude any clean demarcation of a range of facts constituting a kind of all-encompassing framework. I will return to this issue shortly.

I want to turn to a consideration of one final remark, part of whose import is that it underscores some of Wittgenstein's deflationary aims. That, however, is only one dimension of this extremely important passage in the *Investigations*, part II, section xii:[25]

> If the formation of concepts can be explained by facts of nature, should we not be interested, not in grammar, but rather in that in nature which is the basis of grammar?—Our interest certainly includes the correspondence between concepts and very general facts of nature. (Such facts as mostly do not strike us because of their generality.) But our interest does not fall back upon these possible causes of the formation of concepts; we are not doing natural science; nor yet natural history—since we can invent fictitious natural history for our purposes.
>
> I am not saying: if such-and-such facts of nature were different people would have different concepts (in the sense of a hypothesis). But: if anyone believes that certain concepts are absolutely the correct ones, and that having different ones would mean not realizing something that we realize—then let him imagine certain very general facts of nature to be different from what

we are used to, and the formation of concepts different from the usual ones will become intelligible to him.

Compare a concept with a style of painting. For is even our style of painting arbitrary? Can we choose one at pleasure? (The Egyptian, for instance.) Is it a mere question of pleasing and ugly? (PI II § xii)

My aim in quoting this lengthy passage is to call attention to those features of it that engage the issue of conservatism. Such engagement is far from straightforward, since, in this passage, Wittgenstein can again be seen to be courting the charge of conservatism, while, I believe, ultimately avoiding it. We can begin by forging a connection between what Wittgenstein says here and what I took to be the lessons of the sequence of remarks already examined. Several thematic connections are easily drawn: the interplay between "the facts of nature" and "our concepts" (what Wittgenstein calls "a scaffolding of facts" in the other remarks), as well as Wittgenstein's denial of any interest in offering *hypotheses* about the (causal) relations between such facts and our concepts (such disinterest is signaled at the end of the first paragraph, and explicitly announced at the opening of the second).

While these connections lend support to my reading of the remarks examined previously, it would seem that this latest passage also creates difficulties for my attempts to put distance between Wittgenstein's philosophy and conservatism. The second and third paragraphs are particularly thorny on this score: although the second paragraph countenances the possibility of concepts "different from the usual ones," that possibility only becomes imaginable to the extent that changes in the "very general facts of nature" are first envisioned. Since those general facts are what they are, it would appear that the "usual" concepts are the order of the day. Indeed, despite our coming to recognize that our concepts are not "absolutely the correct ones," that doesn't make them any less entrenched: as the third paragraph makes clear, we cannot simply trade in our "usual" concepts for others at will. While perhaps not explicitly affirming any conservative doctrine, it does not appear farfetched to read this remark as articulating the beginnings of one. Wherein, then, lies the mistake of such a reading?

There are, I think, several interrelated problems that attend an attempt to wring conservative implications from this passage. The first continues a number of observations made in conjunction with the remarks examined from elsewhere in the later writings, viz., Wittgenstein's disinterest in framing hypotheses concerning the relation between "the facts" and "our concepts." One basis for this disinterest, already discussed, is a certain skepticism regarding there being any *general* relation, or set of relations, about which hypotheses could be fruitfully formed and tested: though, for example, the availability of writing surfaces is one "fact" that contributes to the continued development and transmission of differential calculus, the prospects for actually specifying that contribution appear rather dim. Moreover, Wittgenstein's adducing of a *range* of concepts, where their anchorage in various facts varies considerably (from the availability of sticks and stones to the fact that human beings are the central case of what it is to think), undermines the likelihood of there being hypotheses of general import or interest.

There is, however, a deeper motivation for Wittgenstein's disinterest, which goes to the heart of the issue of conservatism: in trying to frame such hypotheses, one cannot but *use* one's own concepts in order to delimit the facts whose causal contribution is to be determined. In other words, saying just what the facts are is not something that can be done in isolation from sorting out what our concepts are, such that the two can be seen to form two discrete realms. (It should be emphasized that Wittgenstein's talk about the formation of concepts being explained by the facts of nature never goes beyond being the antecedent to a conditional, and it's not at all clear from the sequel whether he endorses it; instead, he shifts to talking about "correspondence," which is never further explained, though we can take it to include everything from the fairly trivial observations about sticks and stones to the ones about thinking.)

What I take Wittgenstein to be challenging is the intelligibility of a standpoint where we could clearly and cleanly separate everything about human beings, everything that is a feature of our "conceptual scheme," from everything that's true about the world independently of that scheme, and then assess how these two things are related to one another. The futility of this exercise can be seen by asking how it is that the facts that constrain, determine, or condition our scheme are to be described. Either those facts cannot be described or picked out in any way, and so the exercise of wondering how our concepts fare with respect to them cannot even begin, or we avail ourselves of our language, our "conceptual scheme." On this latter option, we have not achieved the neutrality necessary to frame hypotheses, because we have made essential use of our concepts in picking out the facts. At one point in his notebooks, Wittgenstein writes: "The limit of language is shown by its being impossible to describe the fact which corresponds to (is the translation of) a sentence, without simply repeating the sentence" (CV 10). In other words, the futility of trying to specify the facts independently of language is shown by the fact that we have to use language in any such specification. Insofar as we have adopted a point of view, or occupy a perspective, we have not moved beyond, or outside of, our concepts; we continue to employ them insofar as we have a point of view at all.

While this talk of the futility of specifying the facts independently of our concepts might seem to invite the charge of idealism, as though what the facts are depended upon our concepts, further attention to what Wittgenstein says in the second paragraph of the *Investigations,* part II, section xii shows that it does not. Part of what we do in making the possibility of concepts different from our own imaginable is imagine at the same time changes in what Wittgenstein calls the "very general facts of nature." Although doing this is not meant to underwrite a hypothesis concerning the causal relations between the facts of nature and (human) beings having certain concepts, there is still the idea that one cannot pick out or describe beings as having certain concepts without at the same time saying something about what the facts of their situation are. That is, although one cannot simply read off what concepts beings have or would have given variations in the general facts of nature, the very notion of beings having concepts, even ones very different from our own, is not something that can be understood in isolation from an understanding of what the facts are, or what's true about the world. The main point is thus that it would be a mistake to think of "the facts of nature" (including facts about *human* nature) as making up a framework *within* which the formation and application of concepts happens: no clean division can be made, but instead only piecemeal observations and investigations of particular concepts in relation to particular facts. The dissolution of any kind of *general* distinction between "our concepts" and "the facts" entails the dissolution of idealism as a general thesis about *the* relation between the two: to the extent that it makes sense to talk about relations of dependence between facts and concepts, those relations must be seen to be going both ways.

If this is correct, namely that the identification of facts is inseparable from our concepts, whatever Wittgenstein means by "correspondence" cannot be taken to underwrite the kind of conservative picture(s) under consideration; the kind of constraint that is part and parcel of conservative readings cannot be made out. Nonetheless, it would be a mistake to omit Wittgenstein's talk of correspondence altogether; indeed, accommodating it will only help to undermine the picture(s) at the heart of conservative readings. The point is roughly this: that there is some anchorage of our concepts in "the facts" does not preclude conceptual change, since "what the facts are" is open to revision, alteration, and discovery. In saying this, I don't mean to be endorsing any kind of relativism; rather, my aim is to emphasize the *incompleteness* of whatever facts there are, both in terms of what facts we know, but also in the sense that, we might say, "life goes on," and so that what facts there are forms an open-ended set. The following remark from Wittgenstein's manuscripts addresses this issue:

> Do I want to say, then, that certain facts are favourable to the formation of certain concepts; or again unfavourable? And does experience teach us this? It is a fact of experience that human beings alter their concepts, exchange them for others when they learn new facts; when in this way what was for-

merly important to them becomes unimportant, and *vice versa*. (RPPII § 727)

This passage underscores the *interplay* between facts and the formation of concepts, which precludes any kind of rigid fixity of the kind that attends, for example, Gellner's "cultural cocoons."

Wittgenstein's talk of human beings altering and exchanging concepts in the above passage helps to defuse conservative interpretations but does not dispel them entirely. This is especially so when we take into consideration the third and final paragraph of this same section in the *Investigations*. There Wittgenstein emphasizes the idea that whatever the idea of conceptual change, or the possibility of concepts different from the "usual ones," comes to, such alterations cannot be considered matters of *choice*. One might contend that Wittgenstein can thus be seen to have an inherently conservative attitude toward our life with concepts, in that we are not free to decide upon our concepts or exchange them at will: even though change is possible, it is not something we can bring about, in any robust sense. While some of these points must be absorbed, they do not, I think, have the conservative implications that might be assumed. Such assumptions, I would suggest, trade on a false dichotomy: either concepts are something we freely choose (and change) *or* conservatism is correct. What I take Wittgenstein to be suggesting is that we go wrong in thinking about our concepts as *merely* matters of choice or decision: the interplay between facts and concepts discussed above helps to undermine that way of thinking. Wittgenstein is not, as I read him, ruling out (or slowing down) the possibility of conceptual change, but showing more vividly just what such a change involves, namely a reorientation in how one *lives*. Such a reorientation is by no means impossible, though it can be difficult, and it certainly requires more than an act of decision.

Consider the following remark: "The sign (the sentence) gets its significance from the system of signs, from the language to which it belongs. Roughly: understanding a sentence means understanding a language" (BB 5). Similarly, in the *Investigations* and other later writings, we find remarks such as "to imagine a language means to imagine a form of life" (PI § 19); "To understand a sentence means to understand a language" (PI § 199). "What is happening now has significance—in these surroundings. The surroundings give it its importance" (PI § 583); "I should like to say: conversation, the application and further interpretation of words flows on and only in this current does a word have its meaning" (RPPI § 240); "Only in the stream of thought and life do words have meaning" (RPPII § 504). These remarks are of a piece with Wittgenstein's talk about our concepts as standing "in the middle of our life." In making such remarks, Wittgenstein does want to establish a kind of inseparability between our concepts and our life, to show that our concepts are part of our lives and cannot be considered in isolation from them (but nor can our lives be considered in isolation from our concepts). Such inseparability does not preclude the possibility of change, but only shows what form that change must take: to change one's concepts means changing how one lives, what one takes to be important, what facts have priority. To change one's concepts is to change the "flow" of how one lives. This is not an inherently conservative point, but, one might say, a *realistic* one.[26]

What needs emphasis is Wittgenstein's rejection of the idea (or attitude) that our concepts are *arbitrary*. Such a rejection provides a way of understanding the passage from *Remarks on Colour* from which we began: to say that our concepts "stand in the middle of our life" is *not* to give "our life" some determinative power with respect to our concepts, as though the two could be prized apart. Rather, the point is that to have concepts *is* to live in particular ways. This does not mean, *pace* Bloor's kind of reading, that our concepts are *about* the particular ways we live, mere reflections of something that determines them, nor does it mean that our concepts are somehow *confined* by our life, as though what it is to lead the lives we lead could be spelled out without attending to the concepts we possess and apply. In *On Certainty*, Wittgenstein remarks that language "is there—like our life" (§ 559), which I take to mean that ultimately there is nothing outside of our lives, nothing deeper or more secure, in terms of which they can be justified. The real difficulty lies in acknowledging this without a feeling of defeat, without, that is, holding on to a picture according to which our lives, and with them our language, confine us and thereby prevent us from seeing something that lies beyond them.

IV. Liberation but Not Transcendence

In order to suggest that Wittgenstein's deflationary maneuvers do not leave us in a state of political helplessness, I want, by way of conclusion, to explore a perhaps surprising connection between Wittgenstein's critique of limits—and so of the idea that we are *confined* by our human condition—and the imagery of James Baldwin's scathing critique of *Uncle Tom's Cabin* in his essay "Everybody's Protest Novel."[27] In doing so, I want to underscore that Wittgenstein's critique of the imagery of confinement and constraint, which is, I have suggested, part and parcel of conservative readings of him, does not deny the all-too-common reality of confinement in human life: on the contrary, I want to suggest that Wittgenstein's critique can help us, by clearing away misleading pictures, to recognize such confinement or oppression for what it is, so that it might be overcome.

Baldwin's essay challenges a received conception of *Uncle Tom's Cabin* as a morally uplifting and energizing work on the horrors of slavery.[28] He argues that Stowe's work, an example of the genre he labels the "protest novel," has an almost opposite effect: the novel's excessive emotionalism serves to distance us from the horrors of slavery, while its sentimentalism, Baldwin claims, serves to mask the complexities of slavery. What Baldwin finds especially problematic is the kind of moral self-satisfaction the novel fosters, thereby providing its readers with a reassuring sense of superiority, rather than forcing them to confront their possible complicity in the concepts and categories that sustained an institution like slavery. Rather than sounding genuine protest, then, Baldwin sees *Uncle Tom's Cabin* as ultimately reinforcing a mind-set whose economy gave life to slavery in the first place.

Though it would be wrong to say that *Uncle Tom's Cabin* advocates slavery in any explicit sense, according to Baldwin, a principal source of the failure of Stowe's novel is its depiction of liberation from oppression in terms of the *transcendence* of the social conditions within which that oppression occurs. Baldwin does not deny that social conditions, the situation in which one finds oneself, can have a determinative power over one's life; indeed:

> It is the peculiar triumph of society—and its loss—that it is able to convince those people to whom it has given inferior status of the reality of this decree; it has the force and the weapons to translate its dictum into fact, so that the allegedly inferior are actually made so, insofar as societal realities are concerned.[29]

What Baldwin resents about *Uncle Tom's Cabin* is, we might say, the metaphysical status it accords to society's "triumph," so that Tom's own triumph (if it can be called that) in the novel is itself rendered in such terms: "His triumph is metaphysical, unearthly; since he is black, born without the light, it is only through humility, the incessant mortification of the flesh, that he can enter into communion with God or man."[30]

In the economy of the protest novel, social conditions are depicted as fixed, therefore, like the bars of a cage, and so only a complete escape, a complete extraction from this "cage," can effect the desired salvation. Baldwin argues that such a picture accords to the terms of oppression a kind of determinative power that ultimately has the pernicious effect of bathing the idea of liberation in the light of *fantasy*—indeed of a fantasy that effaces what Baldwin takes to be our genuine humanity:

> He [the human being] is not, after all, merely a member of a Society or a Group or a deplorable conundrum to be explained by Science. He is—and how old-fashioned the words sound!—something more than that, something resolutely indefinable, unpredictable. In overlooking, denying, evading his

complexity—which is nothing more than the disquieting complexity of ourselves—we are diminished and we perish; only within this web of ambiguity, paradox, this hunger, danger, darkness, can we find at once ourselves and the power that will free us from ourselves.[31]

Overcoming oppression is not, for Baldwin, to effect a complete escape from one's social milieu: to depict one's salvation in terms of escape is, again, to accord a kind of metaphysical status to the concepts and categories that oppress: "Now, as then, we find ourselves bound first without, then within, by the nature of our categorization. And escape is not effected through a bitter railing against this trap; it is as though this very striving were the only motion needed to spring the trap upon us."[32]

Paradoxically, perhaps, what Baldwin recommends (and it is here that he sounds his most Wittgensteinian note) as an antidote to oppression is not escape but, as his vision of humanity suggests, *acceptance*: "But our humanity is our burden, our life, we need not battle for it; we need only do what is infinitely more difficult, that is, accept it."[33] Baldwin's language of acceptance is reminiscent of Wittgenstein's ("What has to be accepted, the given, is—so one could say—*forms of life*"), and, as is the case with Wittgenstein, his language opens him up to the charge of conservatism.[34] Yet to level this charge is to ignore, first, the *difficulty* both see in coming to accept "our humanity" (like the difficulty in Wittgenstein's image of philosophy as leaving everything as it is), and, second, just how both conceive of "our humanity" as the thing to be accepted. To say, as Baldwin does, that "we need not battle for" our humanity does not imply that there are no battles to be fought, just as Wittgenstein's injunction to leave everything as it is does not imply that no effort need be expended in order to heed his words:

> Philosophy unties the knots in our thinking, which we have tangled up in an absurd way; but to do that, it must make movements which are just as complicated as the knots. Although the *result* of philosophy is simple, its methods for arriving there cannot be so. (PR § 2)

Like the "knots" in our thinking, the social configurations that oppress us serve to distort and pervert our humanity, by portraying our categories and conceptions of one another as fixed once and for all. Stowe's depiction of Tom's liberation accords to his blackness the sin slavery had ascribed to it, and inscribed upon it, and so she, as Baldwin reads her, comes no closer to accepting Tom's humanity (and, indeed, her own) than do those who would keep him in chains. Undoing these configurations is as complex as these configurations are entrenched, just as the "knots in our thinking" may be so tight and interwoven as to require a lifetime of philosophy to undo (Wittgenstein's myriad remarks, like Baldwin's decades of essays, illustrate the difficulties that attend accepting our humanity, that attend leaving everything as it is).

Accepting our humanity requires that it be freed from the illusions that haunt it, from categories that are taken to be complete, from concepts and conceptions of ourselves that serve only to confine. The aim for Wittgenstein, as for Baldwin, is to secure the possibility of liberation, not by promulgating an illusion, but by rotating "the axis of reference of our examination ... about the fixed point of our real need" (PI § 108).[35]

3

Wittgenstein, Fetishism, and Nonsense in Practice

Denis McManus

In the last hundred years, philosophy in many of its most innovative forms has declared itself, in some sense, "post-" or "anti-metaphysical." This claim, in its many different interpretations, has seemed to pose a problem for critical reflection on how we conduct our lives. The sense is that, whether through logical positivism's attack on the factual character of value or the deconstructive rejection of "grand narratives," we have lost the basis upon which we might pose any radical criticism of the forms of our social existence, moral or political. Wittgenstein has typically been seen as contributing to this same erosion. Throughout his development, Wittgenstein challenged attempts to ground our practices in accounts of the metaphysical characteristics of the world or in descriptions of the activities of the mind. Consequently, those practices possess a kind of autonomy that may seem to render them immune to the kinds of assault that we, surely rightly, have praised social critics for making. In this chapter, I sketch an alternative picture of how Wittgenstein's work might bear on our contemporary political predicament. Rather than making profound social and political critique impossible, his work suggests an illuminating and plausible view of the way in which characteristically modern critiques of our practices actually work. After describing an "anti-metaphysical" argument that figures in Wittgenstein's work early and late, an argument that challenges the possibility of evaluating practices as intelligible or nonsensical, I will set out an alternative, but still Wittgensteinian, view of how our practices may nonetheless descend into nonsense, into noise. I will outline the general character of this way of thinking before indicating how it may accommodate some of the kind of social and political critique that we feel most illuminates our modern lives. My interpretation of this kind of critique will give a sense of its power, how difficult it is to perform, and how much is at stake—it is a struggle, one might say, not merely to talk but to have something to say.

Metaphysics, Nonsense, and Critique

Metaphysical theories about the fundamental structure of reality, of the mind, and of meaning would seem to make it possible to assess which thoughts are coherent. A popular reading of Wittgenstein's early work, for example, ascribes to him a set of metaphysical theses according to which the world is constituted by the totality of facts and facts are constituted by arrangements of objects. On this basis, it has been argued, Wittgenstein maintained the further view that an isomorphism between the objects that make up facts and the elements that make up thoughts allows thoughts to describe facts.[1] On the basis of such preestablished metaphysical notions about facts, thoughts, and their structure, one might then derive a set of principles governing which thoughts are coherent and which are not.

This interpretation of Wittgenstein's work is mistaken. A fundamental strand within his thought, early and late, maintains precisely an opposed view, claiming that one cannot assess the intelligibility of a thought by reference to the reality it represents. In identifying this "reality that it represents" one must presuppose the intelligibility, the meaningfulness, of the thought. One must presuppose its meaning if one is to differentiate the parts of reality that are relevant to that thought and its coherence from the indefinitely large regions of reality that are simply irrelevant. What we are imagining ourselves assessing by reference to its conformity to reality is actually what determines how a proposition is compared with reality: "The method of portrayal must be completely determinate before we can compare reality with the proposition at all in order to see whether it is true or false. The method of comparison must be given me before I can make the comparison" (N 23). *How* we compare propositions with reality cannot itself be evaluated by comparing it with reality, and learning how to compare propositions with reality cannot itself be a process of reading something off reality:

> How is congruence or non-congruence or the like given to us?
> How can I be *told how* the proposition represents? Or can this not be *said* to me at all? And if that is so can I "*know*" it? If it was supposed to be said to me, then this would have to be done by means of a proposition; but the proposition could only shew it. (N 25)

The moral of the discussion so far is liable to chime with a well-known and widespread sentiment about the bearing of Wittgenstein's work on the work of the political theorist and the social scientist, namely, that Wittgenstein strips these observers of our practice of the means by which that practice might be evaluated. Peter Winch is perhaps the best-known example of a thinker who sought to explore the implications of Wittgensteinian insights for such social and political critique. Although his critique of positivistic social science is made up of a number of strands of thought, not all of which strike me as plausible or authentically Wittgensteinian, one strand I believe to be both and to be a variation on the above argument.

Winch challenges a particular picture of what it is to understand and assess social practices. He challenges projects that, wittingly or not, attempt such understanding and assessment by imposing "standards of rationality" (or an analogue of such) upon those practices "from without," so to speak. For example, Winch argues that Evans-Pritchard, in interpreting magical practices as inept attempts to control the natural world, retains a background commitment to a species of scientific rationality as constitutive of the rational as such.[2] Similarly, according to Winch, Pareto's explanations of phenomena such as Christian baptism and pagan sacrificial bloodletting involve the illicit imposition of conceptions of "integrity" and "purification" upon those phenomena, insinuating that these conceptions reveal something one could call the common "true character" of those practices. For Winch, such approaches fail to recognize a constitutive feature of the challenge that is the understanding of human action, a feature that distinguishes it from the forms of understanding that the natural sciences involve. Crucially, social practices are themselves constituted by particular pervading standards. Where the natural scientist imposes concepts from without, the social scientist must, at least as a first step, come to terms with the concepts used within the practices she wishes to understand. Such "social objects" are at least partly *constituted* by concepts rather than succumbing to the conceptual only when the social scientists come to town. The observer of human action who remains oblivious to the participants' own categories does not yet have the object of his study in sight.

A corollary of this argument is that any credible attempt to understand social practices must make some kind of sense of the standards they embody. This may seem to rule out as unintelligible the charge that a practice is or has become irrational or nonsensical. One can easily see how to present a Winchian case for thinking so. The events, processes, and "objects" in question are constituted by concepts. To know what they are is to know which concepts they embody. To make the connection with Wittgenstein's argument explicit, applauding or condemning a practice by reference to its "agreement" (or suchlike) with reality raises a problem: what constitutes the relevant portion of reality is something that one can only determine by coming to understand the practice. In other words, "reality is not what gives language sense." Rather "what is real and what is unreal shows itself *in* the sense that language has."[3] When we imagine ourselves judging that a practice is irrational or nonsensical, from where can we derive *relevant* standards of coherence? We would need to know what this practice is about, which is something one cannot do while nominally bracketing out its very coherence.

According to my own reading of Wittgenstein, his philosophy can be understood as an effort to show why we lose nothing when we recognize the incoherence of the confused test of meaningfulness imagined above. Wittgenstein faces a difficult task, not least because the notion of such a test supports and is supported by a powerful vision of our intellectual predicament that itself expresses a craving to found the basic terms in which we live our lives, to justify our own lives and interests. This confusion extends its influence throughout large regions of philosophy, and political philosophy is no exception. A charge that I am tempted to level against Winch is that he left his Wittgensteinian work unfinished. He demonstrated that a certain vision of the critique of our practices made no sense, but then did relatively little to show why this only swept away "houses of cards" (PI § 118). In particular, what can one make of central critical terms of social and political reflection such as "ideology" and "false consciousness" if "reality is not what gives language sense" anyway? Mustn't such a claim dislodge the point that provides us with leverage to expose these often real failures of thought and practice?

Such reasoning has led to the depiction of both Winch and Wittgenstein as perversely conservative, Winch as refusing to recognize the manifest debunking power of reflection on, among other things, our political practices. Winch insisted that his view had no such implication, and I think that he is right. My motivation here is instead something like Scott Gordon's worry that Winch gives us little concrete sense of what such debunking reflections would look like were they to take to heart Wittgenstein's insights.[4] In response, I will offer here a rather speculative sketch of a form of recognizably *political* thought that would meet Winch's strictures but retain a debunking bite. It has its origins in reflection on some of the later Wittgenstein's thoughts on rule-following, is consistent with the argument presented above against a delimitation of the "natural laws of sense," but also rehabilitates what one could call a conception of "nonsense" as a term of criticism for the political thinker. It will have the attractive feature of presenting a credible basis for the reading of some significant social and political theory of the past and will give a new twist to Winch's proposal that philosophy and the social "sciences" are more closely related than might be supposed. The form of thought I will describe takes as its target not inconsistency or contradiction but superficiality: utterances that have become empty and acts that have become token. Such "performances" do not break the rules that govern them, but this is because they have lost the content that would have made such a clash possible and significant.

Reality Shaking Off the Conceptual

In the next two sections, I will set out a possibility that Wittgenstein could recognize as real and that one might, with justification, label "reality shaking off the conceptual." One of Wittgenstein's reminders for us is that the use of concepts, as systems of description, depends upon there being a minimal degree of regularity in the results achieved when using those concepts, those systems. We use concepts in those situations where our applications are generally in agreement with each other and this reliability is multidimensional. Judgments made of a particular object may hold between different people, different times, different lighting conditions, etc. (the relevant circumstances depending on which concepts one is using). If so, judgments made by others at different times in different circumstances allow us to anticipate, for example, judgments that we will ourselves make when confronted with the objects of which these other judgments have been made.

This need for a background of agreement has a number of notable aspects. A certain degree and pattern of agreement in judgment is necessary if two people are to be talking about the same topic. Without such consistency, we see the other as, at best, talking about something else. Correspondingly, particular objects are thought of in different ways according to whether people who ordinarily agree in a certain type of judgment can consistently agree when making those judgments about those objects. Our fundamental understanding of different types of object depends upon which objects sustain such regularity with which concepts. For example, those we treat as "having a color" are those with which we find a certain regularity in our color judgments. If the fact that a flower is blue had no implications for how it appeared in other situations, what force would there be in insisting that blue is its color? In what sense does something that constantly changes color *have* a color? To what extent can we say that there is such a thing as *its color*? If the color of a chameleon really did change to match its *every* environment, what would one say "its color" was?[5] It "has" a color to the same degree as a piece of colorless glass "changes its color" as it passes in front of differently colored objects. Such a use of the idea of "an object's color," its application here to glass, seems pointless.

It seems then that it is only sensible to talk of something as having a color if this carries a suitably broad set of implications. Hence, the fact that we use a particular concept in relation to a particular object already tells us something, namely, that the kind of background identified is *already* in place. In talking about "the color of *x*'s," we are looking upon these *x*'s as things that display a certain regularity in "behavior," a regularity that makes the concept ("owned" color) and the judgments that it informs useful here (one could even say "us*able*" here—a point to which I will return). With the breakup of the generally reliable background of implications surrounding a statement such as "this object is blue," it becomes increasingly difficult for an utterance of this sentence to say anything, to be consequential. Consequently, we are faced with the need to reassess radically what we think we are judging, whether it makes sense to talk of these objects as "having a color," for example.

Now these reflections may seem to suggest a certain hermetic sealing around our life with colored objects, such that, for example, we label divergence over judgments as due to "color variation" or to the fact these objects don't "have a color." Whatever happens seems to be catered for, in that whatever happens can be assigned a description within the language of color. Nothing can happen that will rupture the covering that that language lays over reality. We may have the feeling now that our use of color terms is somehow casuistic, our commitment to their applicability unshakable by anything the world throws at us, like an item of faith or a refusal to take the world seriously. But this indicates that we are dealing with descriptions, not judgments of fact, just as the earlier Wittgensteinian argument suggests.

Also it isn't quite true to say that *anything* can happen and leave our talk of color in good repute. Let us imagine an increasing level of disagreement in color judgments. Color fluctuation becomes epidemic and even our own mastery of the colors is being called into doubt by our neighbors, whom we now see as largely color-blind. But now what are our color terms used for? In one sense, they continue to "work." But in another they don't. Orders like "Five red apples, please" are now pointless. Or one might say that such orders would be as successful as would be, in our present condition, that we should meet "at the restaurant with the nicest food" or "in the shop that sells the best records." But as a result, we cannot use these terms to do what we currently do with color terms. *Cannot* or *do not*? Let us bear this in mind, when we now ask: Has the use of color terms become nonsensical? Answering either yes or no seems wrong. Nature did not reject our color terms, so to speak. The "logic of color terms" was not violated. But we no longer behave in the same ways, are no longer bothered about the same things. The language of color has fallen silent. One might be tempted to offer an explanation here that asserts that this language has fallen silent because, in terms of our earlier purposes, the use of these terms is now pointless—they are now *unusable*. But unusable for what? The activities in which those terms played a role have also waned. We no longer argue, for example, over the color to paint a room or over the use of pigment in a picture. Concepts articulate our desires as much as our beliefs, and desires articulated in terms of color have sunk into insignificance. Their satisfaction "makes no difference," one might say. Hence, rather than being "unusable," it seems more appropriate to say that color terms simply aren't used. A whole world—populated by people with particular desires and objects of a certain sort in certain kinds of conditions—wanes. To adapt a well-known line from *On Certainty*, light *fades* gradually over the whole (OC § 141).

Mathematical Measures

Let us switch to a more complicated example, the application of arithmetic. Note, first of all, that it makes sense to talk about discovering a particular number of stones because this has a bearing on how many one can expect there to be in ten seconds time or when seen from another angle, or when counted by other people we see as competent counters. We find that when we set two stones down next to another two stones and then count the whole group we get the figure four. And so do the vast majority of other people who attempt this same exercise. This same pattern of stability is not found, however, in the case of, for example, the shadows that a group of objects throws. People may differ in how they break up the shadow and the shadows may be constantly changing. Since our "results" are so frail, so lacking in the robust implications that our enumeration of stones may boast, there is very little point in counting shadows. Similarly, imagine counting the clouds in an overcast sky or the ripples on the surface of a lake. We could, no doubt, come up with *some* figures but the results derived would be idiosyncratic and unreliable, to say the least. If our assessment of the number of stones before us varied in the same way, we could not use our findings in anything like the way we presently do. To the suggestion that one counts the stones one might reply not "Why?" but "Why bother?"

Such cases do not, of course, draw a limit to the application of arithmetic. In the face of apparent resistance to arithmetic, isn't it always possible to apply it? Isn't it simply up to us to find out how it should be done? I don't want to deny this, but let us note how it *is* done. When we pour one amount of water into a tank that already contains another amount of water, we do not get two amounts of water. But the level of the water increases. Let us suppose that each "amount" is the contents of a particular cup filled to the brim. Let us further suppose that there are gradations on the side of the tank, equally spaced all the way from the top to the bottom and that the cross-section of the tank is uniform from top to bottom. Under these circumstances, we can predict the number of gradations covered by remembering how many times we poured in full cups of water. If one cupful raises the level one gradation, pouring in another cupful will raise the level another gradation. On this basis, we can answer some interesting questions. For example, we can tell whether the cup was always full to the brim by seeing how many gradations the total amount covers.[6]

With the introduction of the "technology" of tanks with uniform cross-sections and equally spaced gradations, and the practice of using a particular container so as always to add what we call a "standard unit" volume of water, we are now treating water in a way that allows us to apply arithmetical rules to it meaningfully. We have found a way of treating this domain in a way analogous to that in which we treat other "countables," and phenomena that appeared to resist arithmetically informed description have ultimately succumbed.[7]

One might perhaps argue that, proceeding in this way, every domain will succumb to arithmetic, that such "construction" or "interpretation" may always be possible, such a "technology" always available. I do not wish to deny this. What I want to flag is the fact that such stage-setting measures are *necessary* and a sense in which such "arithmetized" phenomena may, all the same, "resist arithmetically informed description." As anticipated earlier, these phenomena may sustain enumerations and additions, but enumerations and additions that are empty, somehow *trivial*.

Consider *liberté, égalité, fraternité*. What makes this a list of three ideas? The fact that we have three separate words encourages the thought that, yes, we can count this domain too, the domain of ideas. But can we count and add ideas, or just words? Do we, after all, really have *compelling* criteria for when ideas are distinguishable? How many ideas are there in *Leviathan*, for example? Are there more or fewer in *Das Kapital*? The message of the previous section was that one could certainly *construct* or *force* opinions about such matters, sometimes very easily. For example, if asked the number of ideas in *Leviathan*, it would certainly seem wrong to say zero. But the arithmetical "interpretation" of such a domain seems simply too ad hoc for there to be any substance in the figures generated. If I say there are thirty ideas in *Leviathan* and you say thirty-one, neither of us being convicted of error, would that mean that one of us was mistaken? What, for example, would the relevant criteria of "error" *be* here?

A minimum requirement for arithmetic really getting a foothold would seem to be that we already have an established background of judgments about what makes these things separate things, about when we would say "the same one" has disappeared and reappeared or when one has been destroyed and "another" created, and so on. In our present case, such criteria seem not to exist. The problems that we face when trying to analyze a text are precisely those that will prevent us from establishing a "unit of measure," through the use of which one might start counting and adding.

Compare the utilitarian dream of adding together volumes of happiness. One very plausible interpretation of the failings of that approach proposes that, in order to apply its proposed calculus, we need to have established what "equivalent amounts" of happiness are and how much weighting such amounts should be given, and that, to have established that, we need to have solved many of just the kind of evaluative puzzles that utilitarianism promised to solve. To take a crude example, is it true that watching football generates twice as much happiness as watching opera, but that the latter is to be weighted as twice as worthwhile as the former? Obviously such questions and the issues that they provoke have generated a large literature. I wish merely to raise the possibility that the difficulty encountered here, understood within that literature as that of working out a plausible and applicable interpretation of utilitarianism, may be another case of "reality resisting a mode of description"—here, quantitative measures. Two units of happiness plus two units of happiness may give four units of happiness. But what is a unit of happiness? Two distinct ideas plus two other distinct ideas may give four distinct ideas. But what is a distinct idea?

Consider a familiar diagnosis of the perceived failures of behaviorist approaches in the human sciences. In one sense, behaviorism succeeded in describing human conduct using variables that could be handled mathematically. The sense in which it failed was that the variables it used captured aspects of conduct in which no one was interested. What we could measure quantitatively repeatedly turned out to be nothing more than weakly associated with what we wanted to measure. Quantification was achieved but only with measures of negligible "validity." Again there is a large and divided literature to be acknowledged, but my point is that the human sciences may offer us further examples of areas with a subject matter that can be described mathematically but only at the price of triviality. One generates figures, but figures that are useless, meaningless. And note here that these methods were used for a *long* time!

What do such cases tell us? I would suggest that they should prompt us to think about what we take "the applicability of a descriptive framework" to be. If arithmetic being applicable just meant "numbers can be stuck on," then, yes, arithmetic is universally applicable. But are those numbers *useful?* Can we do anything sensible with them? If that is what "applicability" requires, then just how widely applicable *is* arithmetic?

One could make the same point by suggesting that our attention needs to be focused less on whether "arithmetically compliant" results can be obtained and more on the price that we pay in order to obtain them. How much construction, technology, and triviality must we import? In an effort to understand the power of arithmetic, the simple question of "whether arithmetic can be applied" invites us to embrace a confused appreciation of "applicability" that places artificial, etiolated cases of application alongside our actual applications of arithmetic. By ignoring the "mere" circumstances, including the "mere" "practical" implications of these cases of application, we misunderstand the sense in which arithmetic "finds" application.

My perspective gives a mundane fact—that we "ordinarily" apply arithmetic only where arithmetic can be applied *significantly*—a philosophical importance beyond that of an observation about the "pragmatics" of applied arithmetic. Indeed, a proper appreciation of this fact might reveal a certain confusion in the effort to distinguish "pragmatic considerations" from something one might call the "bare applicability" of arithmetic, the "usefulness" of arithmetic from its "usableness."

Two understandings of "sensible" merge here. One could say that one *cannot* count ideas, or that one *will not* count ideas.[8] The former suggests something akin to a contradiction, the latter a mere lack of practical utility. But are we yet clear about what it means to ask whether something has a number or not, as opposed to whether or not its number is a valuable thing to know? Clouds, ideas, and so forth can indeed "be counted" but only through the construction of a highly artificial framework. The framework imposed produces a set of figures but ones in which no one really believes. Similarly, with domains such as ideas, one might say that we can *apply* arithmetic here but the figures generated have no *application*. One might say of the figures that they are not "useful" or even "usable." But, ultimately, we simply say that they aren't *used*. We don't really understand what it would be to use those figures. Arithmetic "reveals" to us certain patterns in the empirical, within which we see that adding two stones to two stones gives four stones, two liters of water added to two liters of water gives four liters of water and, in some sense perhaps, that two ideas "added" to two other ideas "gives" four ideas, and so on. But are the patterns uncovered *independently* significant? Or are these merely the patterns of a projected arithmetic, echoes of the mode of description that one is, for some reason, insisting on using? Consider this proposal of Nietzsche's:

> The invention of the laws of numbers was made on the basis of the error, dominant even from the earliest times, that there are identical things (but in fact nothing is identical with anything else); at least that there are things (but there is no "thing").... To a world which is *not* our idea the laws of numbers are wholly inapplicable.[9]

My earlier discussion suggests that Nietzsche is half right here. A certain kind of background is necessary for the application of mathematics and, in a sense, this must be *invented* (through, say, the technology of measuring tanks, etc.). But some applications of mathematics are powerful while others are merely applications of mathematics. To echo a sentiment of Nietzsche's broader philosophy, an application of mathematics might uncover a new range of truths for us, but the question remains whether these truths (and hence this application) have value.[10]

Political Critique and Pythagorean Fetishism

To see what this might have to tell us about "political critique," let us note an important source of the illusion that mathematical measures reveal the character of reality as such. That source is our tendency in some cases to treat enumerable differences as, in themselves, what matters. The tendency manifests itself in various forms of what one could call "Pythagorean fetishism." Examples might include certain brands of bureaucratic/technocratic fetishization of the mathematically measurable, our earlier example of forms of methodological fetishism in the human sciences, and, I will suggest, some of the phenomena that Marx identifies in his reflections on money and commodity fetishism. In all of these cases, a certain descriptive (here mathematical) model is introduced in order to try to track factors that are not obviously capturable in those terms—"health," "knowledge," "meaning," "value," and so on. Such approaches always have *some kind* of basis, in that there will be *some kind* of association between the factors that we do actually measure and the factor we wish to measure. For this approach to be anything other than patent nonsense, the quantifiable measure must respond in some way to the important events in the "life" of the non-quantified factor that it is meant to track. There must be some impression that the figures are rooted in non-arithmetically important events. But how successfully they track the non-arithmetical factors to be measured must be monitored and cannot itself be mathematically established, unless by other measures whose validity we are (somehow!) confident of. Failure to monitor that validity can lead to emptiness, illusion, distortion, or misunderstanding. We may come to fixate on how many orders a person issues as opposed to how authoritarian she happens to be, how many patients we get through the hospital system as opposed to how much healthier they are as a result, and how much money we have rather than what we can do with it.

And the epicycles of human thought do not stop there. If enough people come to think in the "fetishized" ways specified, then they may take on a certain kind of truth. One's status may indeed depend more on how much money one has rather than on what that money allows one to do. (Or rather, how much money one has becomes, in itself, an important determinant of what one can do, irrespective of how that money might be spent.)

Such examples indicate how certain modes of talk (and thought) can lose their import, become meaningless chatter, and that to recognize that this is so requires us to reflect on the broader context within which that talk arises. Modes of expression can become fetishized in the sense that we retain a commitment to their use despite the fact that their use no longer has the import that it is supposed to have. Exposing such situations is one of the tasks, I would suggest, that some of the most important sociological and political thinkers have undertaken. To take the most obvious example, consider Marx's reflections on money, the "universal equivalent." To rationalize this institution one might be tempted to claim that there is something called "value" that really is present in coats, boots, and linen and that is tracked by price. The implausibility of such a metaphysics would be comic but for the fact that, if Marx is to be believed, much of our life is spent in its grip. Many crucial decisions in our personal, public, and professional lives are made on the basis of questions of price. We may work longer hours for more pay on the basis of a "calculation" of how much those hours are worth to us. Or the hospital in which we work may be closed because it costs too much money to run, a decision made on the basis of "value for money." There clearly are situations in which the tool of money helps us. But equally well, the tool can take on a life of its own, use-value being marginalized and a means by which it can be represented taking center stage.

We do, as a matter of fact, have to make decisions that require us to compare the "worth" of "commodities," the *forms* of worth of which are not at all obviously commensurable. But do we *articulate* this question of competing worths when we reformulate the issue in terms of price? Or do we simply *replace* one question with another? It may be undeniable that a choice has to be made and a desire to make the decision sensibly or rationally may drive us to seek a "method" for making that decision. But is the "method" we choose in deciding to compare prices a sensible or rational one to use. After all, tossing a coin is a decision procedure! That a method such as pricing allows us to make a decision does not demonstrate its worth unless all we care about is having *some* decision. In this way, pricing may not resolve but instead simply replace important evaluative questions, moral and political questions about how we wish our society to be. Then, like Wilde's "cynic," we will "know the price of everything and the value of nothing."

This is, of course, only one interpretation of the practice of pricing, and by no means the most obvious. Money contributes to the expression of a range of other normative commitments, some of which endow it with the significance that our Marx-inspired story claims is illusory. But also the invocation of pricing when faced with substantive moral and political issues can be presented precisely as a positive step as a means of removing such decisions from the purview of governmental or religious elites. Notionally at least, a commodity's price expresses "the people's evaluation" of its worth, the condensation into a single figure of fifty million or more judgments of how much of something else an individual would sacrifice to obtain this item. Such a story, along perhaps (as Weber and Merton have argued) with notions of entrepreneurship, ambition, frugality and honest hard work, can free the pursuit of money from an idolatrous miserliness and pricing from an arbitrariness or a fear of hard decisions.

Floating at this point where these many different tides meet is the mode of representation that is money and our judgments of an item's price. How is one to determine which of these many forces is driving our choice of price as a basis for action? The problem appears as difficult as, perhaps even the same as, that of determining who we are and what we want and value. From the perspective I have offered, the fetishism of commodities can be seen as an instance of the fetishizing of modes of expression. Such modes have life, and we can say and do something with them only under certain conditions. But those modes of expression may nonetheless be brought into play or may remain in play when those conditions do not hold. Then we are liable to misunderstand the life that our words have and what it is that we are doing and saying when we use them. As an intentional agent, this is to misunderstand myself.

Consider another example, one close to home, which indicates how we might place the work of Weber on rationalization and bureaucratization within the framework I have sketched. Consider the effort to guarantee the delivery of good education to university students through the construction and formal review of formal structures of "quality assurance." Such an effort seeks to generate a self-conscious pursuit of educational excellence. But does it? A constellation of forces loom not dissimilar to those associated above with money. The appropriateness (necessity?) of such an approach rests upon concerns with accountability and equity. Its target is incompetence, laziness, and prejudice. It hopes to develop an environment within which such vices become visible and hence can be eradicated. It hopes to make this vision concrete through the formulation and application of measures of educational success and the formulation and application of rules of "due process" in the "delivery" of education.

But such an approach presents other aspects. In particular, we might wonder whether the procedures in question offer us real traction on the phenomenon of education or merely the impression that we have such traction. To echo the familiar refrain about tests of IQ, such measures of quality of education may, in fact, measure the rigor with which an institution approaches its paperwork and the capacity to make its students feel content. One suspects that at some point in the development of the measures in question, it was decided that, verily, education *shall* be so accounted and hence shall be so account*able*. To adapt words attributed to Galileo: "Formalize what is formalizable, and make formalizable what is not so."[11]

Nevertheless, there clearly are whole areas of research devoted to the development and refinement of such measures and many of those who think seriously about such measures will no doubt insist on their status as "indicators" rather than "criteria" of success. But taking such measures *as* indicative rather than as criterial is a matter not of how such measures are labeled but of how they are used, and such measures are used not only by those who think seriously about them. If they provide the basis for decisions on the financial support of an institution (or its withdrawal), then knowledge of that fact, combined with an understanding of the measures, may put pressure on staff not to focus first and foremost on the rigor and fairness with which the institution promotes education but on the scale and organization of its paperwork, and not on the students' fulfilling their potential but on their being content. Incompetent and lazy staff may be forced to change their ways but perhaps only in that they now, like the able and once well-motivated staff, may come to worry about paperwork and discontented students.

Perhaps such measures can be refined so as not to cause such destructive conflicts. Or perhaps the success that they wish to capture formally cannot be so formalized. Perhaps there remains the need for a species of judgment that cannot be replaced by "going by the book" (however extensively refined that book might be). Abilities may exist that are passed on by exposure to their practice and unstructured discussion of that practice (discussions without agendas or "aims and objectives"). There may be species of professionalism that one can grasp and assess as well or poorly practiced only by becoming oneself a good professional of that sort. This vision will be intolerable for adherents to a certain ideal of "accountability": whatever is being assessed must be "transparent" to the "man on the street" (perhaps a juror or a taxpayer, for example!). And, no doubt, some practitioners of these now "dark arts" have hidden their incompetence, and rested complacently, behind claims to "know better." But perhaps such turpitude is best spotted by diligent and able practitioners of these professions. The validity of formalized measures will rest upon how they are applied, and, for that, diligent and able practitioners of the "dark arts" would be necessary anyway.[12] Such voices may need to be heard in order to detect when particular formalized measures have simply become irrelevant or silly, by virtue of dissociation from educational objectives that have not been, and perhaps may never be, articulated in the formal terms that would render unnecessary such a species of "dark" professionalism.

The most worrying twist that the commitment to "accountability as formal measurability" could take (is taking?) would be to allow this demand to alter our conception of educational quality. Terrified by the perceived indeterminacy of what students are being taught and teachers are being paid to teach, we may instead demand that something *else* be taught. Courses would then be designed with different aims—aims that are (or can be made to look more) measurable. Then indeed the formalizing approach may "succeed," in the sense that it may be possible to enhance the teaching of these measurable skills. Are these skills the ones we wished to have taught? Quite possibly. But are they *all* we wished to have taught? I have no proof to offer here but merely wish to flag how the use of certain descriptive tools may become an end in itself, and in the process render invisible or even come to destroy the valuable "commodities" that we sought to produce with their help. That this is indeed happening is something that the final section of this chapter will argue may be beyond demonstration—because the issue in question is one regarding what constitutes an adequate description of what is happening.

In the preceding paragraph, I spoke of the "perceived indeterminacy" of some traditional measures—"perceived" because the charge of indeterminacy may itself merely express a commitment to certain measures,[13] and may reflect a refusal to accept as a real assessment the view of competent professionals, on the grounds that whether someone is such a professional is itself an issue "bedeviled" by the very same "indeterminacy." Indeed I suspect that the mere fact that quantitative and other formal methods of description yield descriptions with a certain kind of determinacy sometimes gives these descriptions an added and possibly unwarranted weight. (The kind of determinacy in question is no doubt that of the natural sciences.) "Compared with other descriptions," we may think, "at least we know here what we are talking about." But this, of course, forgets, first, that once the decision has been made to apply such methods of description, all one possibly *can* get are "determinate" results and, second, that maybe one gets those results because these methods just don't track the distinctions that matter! Instead they may draw distinctions that don't matter and simply fail to respond to distinctions that do. There is art, guile, and craft to the application of descriptions, and consequently it should be no surprise that many such descriptions are applied superficially, ineptly or confusedly. The results will, nonetheless, remain "determinate," even if meaningless.[14]

From my perspective, the above cases may illustrate a species of fetishism, a fetishizing of a certain mode of expression, of a certain mode of thought. Unfortunately, we are capable of transplanting an idiom and its associated values and habits of thought out of contexts in which they "work." And there is no obvious reason why the new subject matter should indeed not be better understood by importing this new way of life. After all, "reality is not what gives language sense." My point rather is that the business of detecting nonsense is more difficult than metaphysicians and, perhaps, positivistically minded political theorists have wanted to believe. My examples have hopefully shown how something that one might call a "political imagination" might be necessary, an effort to imagine what difference these utterances make in the lives of the people who utter them.

The model of criticism set out here strikes me as capturing the slow, almost invisible leaching away of sense from our practices that some of the most radical species of distinctively modern social and political critique target. The form remains, but the lives that would animate these practices slip away. These practices may then become ceremonial, but not *merely* so. Instead they may express commitments on our part, such as a refusal to countenance a morality in politics beyond a "balancing of the books," or a professionalism or art in education beyond that which could be outlined or defended in a court of law or to a taxpayer who happens to know nothing about the subject being taught. But perhaps more characteristic of these questionable practices of judgment is ambiguity. For example, in the work of Weber on "rationalism," Foucault on psychiatry, and Freud and Elias on "civilization,"[15] we see an Enlightenment ordering and something like a Romantic expressivism, neither of which we wish to renounce. To take one last very brief example, in the cynicism enveloping contemporary talk of "rights," one has the sense of nonsense encroaching upon us, not by the violation of moral or political rules but through the withering away of the life within which the invocation of rights has content. The range of phenomena over which people may claim to have rights has extended from the likes of their life, property, and freedom of speech to include their body parts, their image, and their freedom to drive to work. Is debate over such issues enhanced or clarified by talk of "rights"? Or is it rendered hysterical? May such talk serve only to maintain the impression that the claims in question or the participants in the debate are being taken seriously? May such talk constitute another way of avoiding serious moral and political debate rather than a way of articulating it?[16] No doubt different judgments are appropriate in different cases, and we must battle to prevent a mere language[17]— and the *impression* of a mode of thought that accompanies it—from disguising those differences. Our responses to political problems may retain a form we value, but it takes more than that to retain its content. Vigilance over whether that significance, that life, has indeed slipped away (leaving the words, like ghosts, behind) will be "a battle against the bewitchment of our intelligence by means of language" (PI § 109).

What Kind of Thinking Is This?

A final, natural question to ask now is: What is the epistemology of this kind of critique? Is the emergence of mere talk something that one might *note*? In one sense, yes. Such breakthroughs are expressed through observations about our situation, about the lives in which we find ourselves mired. But in another sense, no. There is no set of criteria that one might apply to determine whether we had entered such a situation. Paralleling Winch's critique of positivism, it is confused to think of such a predicament as one to be scientifically observed, because the predicament is one in which our powers of observation themselves have become exhausted. We do not observe contradictions in our beliefs, such as might provide opportunities for the falsification of sociological claims about our situation. For example, in our chaotic color world, the language of color neither runs out of things to say nor finds itself contradicting itself. If, for some reason, one insists on continuing to describe that world in color terms, it can still be described as one of objects changing color in front of color-blind people. Similarly, the language of capitalism can, in one sense, describe everything that can happen in our world, and a bureaucracy has a description for every element of this heterogeneous life of ours that passes before it. Our web of judgments becomes threadbare, purely decorative, but does not tear.

Similarly, the signs of "anti-mathematical revolt" to which I have pointed are, without doubt, ambiguous. It is not at all obvious that one cannot measure happiness or describe human conduct quantitatively and informatively. Inasmuch as there are some individuals who "believe in" such assessment, it also isn't obvious that formal assessments of education do not determine which universities will teach well. But I suspect that it is characteristic of such situations to present themselves in this ambiguous manner. We are dealing with cases where a favored descriptive tool—mathematics, say—is struggling to find application. This, of course, is another way of saying that we are unsure how to describe such cases. There seem to be several different ways of reacting to them:

- Is it that we do have real or genuine measures of what we wish to measure but ones that for some reason aren't very useful?
- Have we, in trying to measure one thing, ended up measuring something else?
- Perhaps our measures simply have not yet achieved the necessary level of refinement, and more work is needed.
- Or might we even say that what we are trying to measure is unreal and that we should instead be focusing our attention directly on what we can measure, which we had previously thought of as merely associated with, or as symptomatic of, the real underlying issue?

Compare the uncertainty that we might have over whether to say the chameleon has a color:

- One could say that it does but that it keeps changing.
- Or that it doesn't.
- Or that it does, but one can't do much with that fact.
- Or that it does, but we need a special technology to measure it, reaching for our slow motion camera. But does our camera show unambiguously that the chameleon does have a color? Or are we measuring something else here? After all, our procedure and our results are more akin to those involved in, say, mapping the reflected light on the surface of a pool. Just what kind of "property," then, are we tracking here?[18]

When we imagine the collapse of the color world, we experience similar uncertainties. In our journey there from our present condition, we pass through situations in which we would not know what to say. Are these fluctuations in color due to the objects, to the conditions, or to us? Where one lays the blame becomes increasingly arbitrary with the disintegration of the conditions under which blame can be laid. We are envisaging circumstances in which our descriptions become not false but empty, in which our descriptive vocabulary loses import. Our predicament is that we are using that vocabulary to describe its decline. The objectives that we may feel we are no longer achieving are articulated by the very concepts whose use we may fear has become pointless, ceremonial, as it were, expressive of one's commitment to a mode of thinking rather than an instance of that thinking. The observation of facts will not help one determine whether one's observations are fruitful or these facts salient. Yet our descent into barren action and mere chatter is what the "social situations" to be identified represent. In none of these situations can the measures involved be seen to somehow recoil from the reality to which they are applied, to expose themselves as incoherent or contradictory. The problem rather is that they only measure what they measure.

Before closing, I want to indicate a continuity with a certain line of thought to be found in philosophy, a line of thought whose success or failure exhibits the kind of indeterminacy described (or perhaps a form of determinacy qualitatively different from that which characterizes well-executed natural science). Kierkegaard, Nietzsche, and, I have suggested, Wittgenstein himself have, in their different ways, expressed doubts about a certain fetishization of truth, at the expense of whether the truths sought are those that matter. Philosophy itself has been targeted by these thinkers as a major culprit, attempting to convert problems with our lives into problems with our beliefs, and responsibilities for our actions into care about our worldview.[19] From the perspective offered here, this is a reflection of the futility of trying to master the danger of nonsense with a body of the kind of doctrine that metaphysics provides. Given the account of the emergence of nonsense sketched here—nonsense as noise or emptiness—it is also unsurprising that such a critique has also brought in its trail a certain kind of cultural critique, a certain kind of political, sociological or psychological reflection (least obviously in the case of Wittgenstein, but there are signs of it nonetheless). Such criticisms of metaphysics yield critiques of "the present age" as populated by the merely "aesthetic" or by "last men" or as having progress as its "form," "rather than making progress being one of its features" (CV 7). Note also the kind of difficulty that we face in deciding whether these critiques are correct. Just as the utilitarianism of the English gentlemen that Nietzsche despised is itself perfectly *coherent* in its own terms, the steps from Kierkegaard's aesthetic to the ethical to the religious are *leaps*.

This sense of our predicament dovetails with a certain reading of the remarks in the *Tractatus* on ethics and the meaning of life. The world we face sustains a multitude of different, noncompeting descriptions yielding a multitude of different, noncompeting facts. In this sense, when one comes to wonder which description to act on and live by, the facts leave one in the lurch. As one might put the point, "ethics is transcendental." Alternatively, one might say, that there is no problem of the meaning of life if that is understood as the problem of *discovering* which descriptions one ought to take seriously.[20] One is left, one might say, with a matter of *conscience*.[21] This no doubt sounds a rather backward-looking or "irrationalist" proposal.[22] But ultimately, such conscientiousness may have a rigor of its own, precisely not that of living by the book or following methodological guidelines. Indeed a craving for a methodology may itself express precisely the delusion described in this chapter, a belief in a form of words that cannot succumb to emptiness, a belief in a system of description or explanation that somehow cannot be used superficially or stupidly.[23]

To conclude, I have argued that we can make sense of a species of reflection on our situation which reveals a species of nonsense in our lives and provides a Wittgensteinian model for radical political critique. The model hopefully captures the difficulty and seriousness of such thought, the rare kind of insight required, and just how much is at stake. The vice we seek to expose is not that of speaking falsely or of acting contrary to principle. Rather it is the descent of our talk into meaningless chatter and our action into token gesture.[24]

4

Genealogy as Perspicuous Representation

David Owen

> Only the art itself can discover its possibilities, and the discovery of a new possibility is the discovery of a new medium. A medium is something through which or by means of which something specific gets done or said in particular ways. It provides, one might say, particular ways to get through to someone, to make sense; in art, they are forms, like forms of speech. To discover ways of making sense is always a matter of the relation of an artist to his art, each discovering the other.
>
> —Stanley Cavell, *The World Viewed*

Wittgenstein's significance for reflection on political philosophy is not, I think, to offer any substantive theses concerning political philosophy or its traditional topics of enquiry. Rather if his work has salience for the engagements of political philosophy, it lies in his understanding of philosophy as a form of therapy and, more particularly, in a conception of philosophy as an activity oriented to dissolving a certain class of nonphysical constraints on our capacity for self-government, which I'll refer to as "aspectival captivity." Consequently, in the opening section of this chapter, I'll advance and defend the claim that Wittgenstein's way of conducting the activity of philosophy is best understood, in its ethical and political aspect, as oriented to a particular aspect of self-government (where "self-government" should be understood simply as the capacity to make and act on one's own judgments). On the basis of this argument, I will advance the further claim that genealogy, in the sense in which this mode of critical reflection is conceptualized and practiced by Nietzsche and Foucault, is *one* way in which political philosophy can acknowledge and address our exposure to this form of nonphysical captivity.

I

In one of the most widely cited remarks from *Philosophical Investigations*, Wittgenstein remarks: "A *picture* held us captive. [*Ein Bild hielt uns gefan-*

gen.] And we could not get outside it, for it lay in our language and language seemed to repeat it to us inexorably" (PI § 115). This remark sets the scene for Wittgenstein's sketch of the practice of philosophy as seeking to release us from the grip of such captivity in which a picture functions *either* as the implicit background or horizon of our practices of thought and action *or* as an explicitly acknowledged limit that cannot be otherwise because it is held to be "universal, necessary, obligatory" (in Michel Foucault's perspicuous phrase).[1] Three issues are raised by this remark. First, what does Wittgenstein mean when he talks about "a picture"? Second, in what sense can a picture hold us captive? Third, what are the sources of our vulnerability to such captivity? This section sketches responses to each of these questions.

First, in *Philosophical Investigations* Wittgenstein provides a variety of examples of pictures; most famously, for instance, he considers a picture of language (articulated by St. Augustine) as a system of propositions that are (ultimately) composed of names and logical connectives, where naming "appears as a *queer* connexion of a word with an object" (PI § 38). As Wittgenstein notes: "This queer conception springs from a tendency to sublime the logic of our language—as one might put it. . . . And you really get such a queer connexion when the philosopher tries to bring out *the* relationship between name and thing by staring at an object in front of him and repeating a name or even the word 'this' innumerable times" (PI § 38). Wittgenstein goes on in *Philosophical Investigations* to show how this picture of language is connected to a specific picture of the inner as a private realm (accessible only by introspection) composed of private objects, names, and relations.[2] However, Wittgenstein does not restrict himself to examples of philosophical pictures. For example, in "Remarks on Frazer's *Golden Bough*," Wittgenstein shows how Frazer's analysis involves a scientistic picture of knowledge as well-supported hypotheses and, relatedly, a picture of human societies as occupying discrete positions on an evolutionary scale of development—the so-called "stages view of history."[3] Yet further examples are given in *On Certainty;* for instance, Wittgenstein writes: "We form *the picture* of the earth as a ball floating free in space and not altering essentially in a hundred years. . . . The picture of the earth as a ball is a *good* picture, it proves itself everywhere, it is also a simple picture—in short, we work with it without ever doubting it" (OC §§ 146–47).

I introduce this last example for two reasons: first, to remove the risk of giving the erroneous impression that Wittgenstein regarded pictures per se as bad (on the contrary, the value of a given picture is given by its capacity to orient our practical judgments such that we can go on in the world, that is, experience ourselves as agents); second, to draw out the centrality of pictures to our lives as necessary conditions of thought and action. The picture of the world as a ball is, Wittgenstein points out, not simply an arresting image but a system of judgments. In this respect, pictures are the element in which mind has its life: "All testing, all confirmation and disconfirmation of a hypothesis takes place already within a system. And this system is not a more or less arbitrary and doubtful point of departure for all our arguments: no, it belongs to the essence of what we call an argument. The system is not so much the point of departure, as the element in which arguments have their life" (OC § 105).

Wittgenstein's concern with pictures is, it seems, a concern with the mindedness of our lives, with our lives as minded. It is also, in addition, a reflection on how we stand to ourselves as minded: "But I did not get my picture of the world by satisfying myself of its correctness; nor do I have it because I am satisfied of its correctness. No: it is the inherited background against which I distinguish between true and false" (OC § 94). Acquiring a language (i.e., becoming minded), we inherit that agreement in judgments that composes a form of life. Seen under the aspect of judgments, Wittgenstein puts it thus:

> We do not learn the practice of making empirical judgments by learning rules: we are taught *judgments* and their connexion with other judgments. A *totality* of judgments is made plausible to us.
>
> When we first begin to *believe* anything, what we believe is not a single proposition, it is a whole system of propositions. (Light dawns gradually over the whole.)
>
> It is not single axioms that strike me as obvious, it is a system in which consequences and premises give one another *mutual* support. (OC §§ 140–42)

And again:

> The child learns to believe a host of things. I.e., it learns to act according to these beliefs. Bit by bit there forms a system of what is believed and in that system some things stand unshakeably fast and some are more or less liable to shift. What stands fast does so, not because it is intrinsically obvious or convincing; it is rather held fast by what lies around it. (OC § 144)[4]

Thus, in becoming minded, we inherit a system of judgments—and this inheritance guides our practical judging and, thus, activity within the world; it enables us to make sense of (and hence to experience) ourselves as agents in the ways that matter to us. But, given changes in the conditions of worldly activity, we may come to experience our world-picture or some aspect of it as problematic in that we are increasingly unable to make sense of ourselves as agents in this way. In other words, a disjuncture may emerge between our ways of making sense of ourselves, on the one hand, and our cares and commitments, on the other. It is in precisely this respect that it is vital that we can call a given picture into question in order to assess its *value,* that is, its capacity to guide our judgments and activity such that we can make sense of ourselves as agents, such that we are intelligible to ourselves as agents, in the ways that matter to us. This is just where the issue of being held captive by a picture becomes pressing, since it suggests that in conditions where our picture is increasingly unable to guide our judgments such that we can make sense of ourselves as agents, we may find ourselves held captive by this picture and thus unable to revise or replace it in the ways required for us to make sense of ourselves as agents in ways that matter to us.

Let us turn, then, to the thought that we may be held captive by a picture. What is the sense of this claim? To begin with, note the way in which the opening sentence of section 115 of *Philosophical Investigations* invites us to consider two different images of being bound. The first is given by reading the sentence thus: "A picture—held us captive." Here the sense of the sentence is of being bound by force, of being held in captivity (as if in chains). The second is given by the stressing the sentence thus: "A picture held us—captive." The sense of the sentence here is of being spellbound, of being captivated (as if hypnotized). Both ways of understanding this remark point to us as being enthralled by a picture and, thus, to a condition that obstructs self-government; indeed, the two ways of taking Wittgenstein's remark illustrate the two uses of the concept "enthrall" (i.e., enslave and entrance). The former highlights the obstruction of that aspect of self-government that concerns our capacity for agency, our capacity to act on the basis of our own judgments; the latter foregrounds the obstruction of that aspect of self-government that concerns our capacity for judging, our capacity to make our own judgments. Acknowledging these senses of Wittgenstein's remark guides us to the recognition that in this passage he is drawing to our attention the way in which the exercise of our capacity for self-government *qua* agency is blocked by our captivity to a picture because the exercise of our capacity for self-government *qua* judging is obstructed by our captivation by this picture: we are enslaved because we are entranced. I'll refer to this condition as "aspectival captivity."

An example that illustrates this point is given in *Culture and Value:* "Someone is *imprisoned* in a room if the door is unlocked, opens inwards; but it doesn't occur to him to *pull,* rather than push against it" (RCV 48). Imagine: entranced by a picture of doors as opening outward, Wittgenstein's man pushes and pushes with increasing frustration, with an increasing sense of powerlessness—and so experiences himself as imprisoned, as subject to external constraints on his capacity for agency, precisely because the idea that doors only open outward is taken as prior to judgment, as a principle of judgment rather than as subject to judgment. The problem here is not simply that this man has a particular picture of doors that guides his judgments and actions in infelicitous ways, it is that he is captivated by this picture and, thus, is incapable of calling it into question. Hence Wittgenstein's point is that being able to evaluate the value of the pictures that compose our ways of going on in the world, our practical identities, is integral to self-government—and this requires that we can free ourselves from this captivity (i.e., change the aspect from which we consider our situation) such that we can make sense of ourselves in ways that connect up to, and enable the expression of, our cares and commitments.

It is this condition of aspectival captivity that Quentin Skinner refers to when he remarks that "it is remarkably difficult to avoid falling under the spell of our own intellectual heritage." "As we analyse and reflect on our normative concepts, it is easy to become bewitched into believing that the ways of thinking about them bequeathed to us by the mainstream of our intellectual traditions must be *the* ways of thinking about them."[5]

The danger here is that one "thinks that one is tracing the outline of the thing's nature over and over again, and one is merely tracing round the frame through which we look at it" (PI § 114). What matters in this context is our capacity to free ourselves from our captivation to the ways of thinking in question—to recognize and loosen the grip that the picture expressed by these ways of thinking has on us that means, in part, grasping the workings of our language "*in despite of* an urge to misunderstand them" (PI § 109). The role of philosophy is to counteract this urge: "The work of a philosopher consists in assembling reminders for a particular purpose" (PI § 127). Thus Wittgenstein's purpose, expressed through his advocacy of "perspicuous representation" (PI § 122), is that of philosophy as directed to enabling us to free ourselves from our captivation to pictures that, as Gordon Baker puts it, "generate insoluble problems by exercising an imperceptible tyranny over our thinking":

> The cure is to encourage surrender of the dogmatic claims "Things *must/cannot* be thus and so" by exhibiting other intelligible ways of seeing things (other *possibilities*), that is, by showing that we can take off the pair of spectacles through which we now see whatever we look at. . . . To the extent that philosophical problems take the form of the conflict between "But this isn't how it is!" and "Yet this is how it *must* be!" . . . they will obviously be dissolved away once the inclination to say "must" has been neutralised by seeing another possibility.[6]

This is one aspect of the sense in which philosophy is "a battle against the bewitchment of our intelligence by means of language" (PI § 109), and we should note that what is involved in this account is *not* a matter of acquiring new knowledge: "These problems are solved, not by giving new information, but arranging what we have always known" (PI § 109). One type of such perspicuous representation is intellectual history. As Skinner comments:

> The history of philosophy, and perhaps especially of moral, social and political philosophy, is there to prevent us from becoming too readily bewitched. The intellectual historian can help us to appreciate how far the values embodied in our present way of life, and our present ways of thinking about those values, reflect a series of choices made at different times between different possible worlds. This awareness can help to liberate us from the grip of any one hegemonal account of those values and how they should be interpreted and understood. Equipped with a broader sense of possibility, we can stand back from the intellectual commitments that we have inherited and ask ourselves in a new spirit of enquiry what we should think of them.[7]

By reorienting our relationship to our current ways of thinking, the intellectual historian can elicit another way of seeing this heritage that enables us to free ourselves from our all-too-human forgetting, our tendency to fall under the spell of our inherited ways of thinking. This characterization of intellectual history may appear to run contrary to the claim that freeing ourselves is a matter of rearranging what we know and not of new knowledge, but it does not. Although the intellectual historian may impart new knowledge, what counts is the reorientation of our relationship to our current ways of thinking, and this is a product not of new knowledge but of the arrangement of knowledge. Important examples of this type of perspicuous representation in political philosophy are provided by Skinner's own recent work on liberty and James Tully's work on constitutionalism.[8]

How, though, do we come to be captivated by some picture or other? What leads us into this state of captivity? Here we need to distinguish between two modes of vulnerability to captivation. The first mode is that forgetting that is an immanent dimension of our habitual activity as language users and attends the form of aspectival captivity that operates when a picture functions as the uncontested implicit background or horizon of our practices. Thus, for example, a simile or an analogy or a method of projection is absorbed into the forms of our language; it becomes part of the *grain* of our language and thus seems ineluctable. The second mode is what one may call a form of philosophical repression and attends the form of aspectival captivity that operates when a picture is subject to reflection and taken to be universal, necessary, or obligatory. It is this mode of vulnerability to which Wittgenstein refers when he talks of the danger that attends our "craving for generality," a danger that he associated particularly (but not exclusively) with the philosopher's tendency to succumb to the attractions of scientific method (not least as a form of self-legitimation). Thus: "Philosophers constantly see the method of science before their eyes, and are irresistibly tempted to ask and answer questions in the way science does. This tendency is the real source of metaphysics, and leads the philosopher into complete darkness" (BB 18).

It seems that while Wittgenstein holds that both of these modes of vulnerability are immanent to the human condition, he is particularly concerned with the way in which philosophy—or at least certain forms of philosophy—can generate the condition of aspectival captivity through the repression of other possible ways of reflecting on a given topic that attends the quest for generality. Here the importance of Wittgenstein's approach is to loosen the grip of this mode of philosophical reflection by exemplifying a different mode of philosophical investigation oriented, on a case-by-case basis, to the problems to which the craving for generality gives rise. It is this method of philosophy as expressed through the idea of perspicuous representation that accounts in large part for the structure of *Philosophical Investigations* as a text.

In respect to these arguments, we can say that the significance of Wittgenstein's approach for political philosophy is threefold. First, it specifies a particular kind of problem: a nonphysical constraint on our capacity for self-government (to which we are vulnerable through natural forgetting or philosophical repression). Second, it offers a medium for dissolving instances of this type of problem, which Wittgenstein calls "perspicuous representation": showing us how we can see things differently and thus enabling us to free ourselves from the despotic demand of the "must" characteristic of our captivation by a given picture. Third, it exemplifies a case-oriented mode of philosophy that aims to let us free ourselves from (or weaken our susceptibility to) the craving for generality expressed in modes of philosophy modeled on the natural sciences, modes of philosophy that heighten our vulnerability to being enthralled by, and in thrall to, a picture. In the remainder of this chapter I will try to illustrate this threefold significance by considering, first, the place of this type of problem in political philosophy; second, the practice of genealogy as a form of perspicuous representation; and, third, the role of perspicuous representation with respect to the orientation of political philosophy.

II

The condition of aspectival captivity contrasts with another form of self-imposed, nonphysical constraint on our capacity for self-government, namely, captivation by false beliefs or ideological captivity. This contrast is significant because a powerful tradition in political philosophy, running from Plato's parable of the cave to Marx's analysis of ideology to Habermas's theory of communicative action, treats *all* forms of nonphysical captivity as captivation by false beliefs.

The main feature of ideological captivity can be elucidated by reference to the concept of "false consciousness." This concept refers to the condition of holding beliefs that are both false and compose a worldview that legitimizes certain oppressive social institutions, where this condition is a noncontingent product of inhabiting a society characterized by these social institutions. As Raymond Geuss has pointed out in his classic study of critical theory, it is not difficult "to see in what sense the 'unfree existence' from which the agents [characterized by false consciousness] suffer is a form of *self-imposed* coercion": "Social institutions are not natural phenomena; they don't just exist of and by themselves. The agents in a society impose coercive institutions on themselves by participating in them, accepting them without protest, etc. Simply by acting in an apparently 'free' way according to the dictates of their [worldview], the agents reproduce relations of coercion."[9] Thus, ideological captivity is characterized by self-imposed coercion because the agents concerned are subject to "a kind of *self-delusion*," where the power of this coercion "derives *only* from the fact that that the agents do not realize that it is self-imposed."[10]

The main contrasting feature of aspectival captivity is that whereas the condition of ideological captivity is necessarily tied to the falsity of the beliefs held by the agent, the condition of aspectival captivity is independent of the truth or falsity of such beliefs. This becomes clear when we note four points that follow from the discussion in the preceding section. First, the concept of a picture refers to a system of judgments in terms of which our being-in-the-world takes on its intelligible character. Second, there are two necessary features of such systems of judgment. On the one hand, such systems govern what is intelligibly up for grabs as true or false. They do not determine what *is* true or false, but rather what statements or beliefs *can be* true or false. As Wittgenstein puts it, a picture "is the inherited background against which I distinguish between true and false" (OC § 94). On the other hand, such systems are "partial" in the sense that they involve pre-judgments (i.e., judgments that act as principles of judgment) that are themselves not grounded in more basic judgments but rather in (nothing more *or less* than) our ways of acting in the world. Third, the value of a picture or perspective is dependent on its capacity to guide our reflection such that we can make sense of ourselves in the ways that matter to us. Fourth, to be held captive by a picture or perspective is to be captivated such that one cannot reorient one's reflection. This is a state of unfreedom. Thus, what matters in this context is *(a)* our capacity to free ourselves from our captivation to the ways of thinking in question—to recognize and loosen the grip that the picture or perspective expressed by these ways of thinking has on us—in order *(b)* to evaluate the value of this picture or perspective relative to other possible pictures or perspectives. Hence, as Foucault remarks, the point of this kind of philosophical work consists in "the endeavour to know how and to what extent it might be possible to think differently."[11]

At this stage, it should not be difficult to see that the "unfree existence" to which those held captive by a picture or perspective are subject is a form of self-imposed constraint on their capacity for self-government. It is a constraint on their capacity for self-government because it prevents those subject to it from exercising their powers of judgment concerning the value of such and such a picture or perspective by presenting this picture or perspective as the *only* way of reflecting of the topic in question. This constraint is self-imposed because it is grounded in our contingent practices. To adapt Geuss's remark concerning false consciousness, we might say that the agents reproduce their condition of subjection simply by acting in an apparently "free" way according to the dictates of their world-picture, and that the power of the subjection to which agents are subject derives solely from the fact that they do not realize that it is self-imposed. Now we might be tempted to say that in a certain respect this kind of self-imposed captivity does, like ideological captivity, involve a false belief but that it does not involve a false first-order belief; rather it involves a false belief about one's beliefs (i.e., a false second-order belief). This way of reflecting on aspectival captivity would lead us the following claim: aspectival captivity involves the agents' holding the false belief that the range of possible beliefs (whether true or false) open to them is the only possible range of beliefs open to them. But to accept this conceptualization of aspectival captivity would be misleading and mistaken for the following reason: an agent held captive by a picture cannot have second-order beliefs about the range of first-order beliefs available to him or her; there is, as it were, no logical space for such beliefs to arise. The point can be put this way: it is a necessary condition of the agent's having such a false second-order belief that the agent recognizes the possibility of such a second-order belief being true or false, but to be held captive by a picture or perspective is just to fail to recognize this possibility as a possibility.

Consequently, while both of these cases call for the use of practices of critical reflection that enable us to free ourselves from our self-imposed condition of captivity, the case of ideological captivity calls for a form of self-reflection appropriate to guiding us from error to truth, whereas the case of aspectival captivity calls for a form of self-reflection capable of guiding us to see ourselves differently in a way that enables us to assess the value of the picture in question. An example of the former is the tradition of ideology-critique *(Ideologiekritik)* developed by the Frankfurt School, and an example of the latter is genealogy as conceptualized and practiced by Nietzsche and Foucault.

The point of this contrast has been, first, to indicate the place of being held captive by a picture within political philosophy (i.e., as a form of self-imposed, nonphysical constraint on our capacity for self-government) and, second, to provide a contrasting representation of types of self-imposed, nonphysical captivity, thus loosening the grip of the thought that holds that all cases of self-imposed, nonphysical captivity are cases of ideological captivity. It is not part of my claim that there are no cases of ideological captivity; on the contrary, I think that subjection to this form of captivity is a common and significant feature of human beings, which political philosophy does well to address. Rather I aim simply to make the point that reflection on ideological captivity addresses that aspect of self-government that concerns the fact that our judgments are guided by beliefs that can be true or false, while reflection on being held captive by a picture attends to that aspect of self-government that concerns the fact that our judgments are situated in systems of judgment that can be of greater or lesser value in terms of their capacity for enabling us to make sense of ourselves as agents in ways that matter to us. At this stage, I want to turn to redeem the claim made here that genealogy is best characterized as a practice of critical reflection directed at captivation by a picture and oriented to eliciting aspect change. For the sake of clarity, in performing this task, I'll continue the contrast between aspectual captivity and ideological captivity.

III

Insofar as ideological captivity is characterized by holding false beliefs that legitimize oppressive social institutions, and by being blocked in some way from recognizing the falsity of these beliefs, the aim of the practice of ideology-critique is to enable the recognition of this fact. As Wittgenstein put it:

> One must start out with error and convert it into truth. That is, one must reveal the source of error, otherwise hearing the truth won't do any good. The truth cannot force its way in when something else is occupying its place.
>
> To convince someone of the truth, it is not enough to state it, but rather one must find the *path* from error to truth.[12]

Hence, the key feature of ideology-critique is to produce a form of self-reflection whereby agents subject to ideological captivity can recognize the falsity of the beliefs that they hold. The nature of the self-reflection involved in this process—and hence the form of the critical theory—will hang on the account of the mechanism through which agents are currently blocked from achieving such recognition; what is certainly the case is that this process of self-reflection will involve not only liberation from the false beliefs in question but also, and immanent to this process, a recognition of how they came to be held captive by these false beliefs. Hence, as Geuss puts it, "a critical theory has as its inherent aim to be the self-consciousness of a successful process of enlightenment and emancipation."[13] The form of this process of self-reflection within the tradition of the Frankfurt School has been specified by Geuss as follows:

> A critical theory criticizes a set of beliefs or world-picture as ideological by showing:
> (a) that the agents in the society have a set of epistemic principles which contain a provision to the effect that beliefs which are to be sources of legitimation in the society are acceptable *only if* they could have been acquired by the agents under free and uncoerced discussion;
> (b) that the *only* reason the agents accept a particular repressive social institution is that they think that this institution is legitimized by a set of beliefs embedded in their world-picture;
> (c) that those beliefs could have been acquired by these agents *only* under conditions of coercion.
> From this it follows immediately that the beliefs in question are reflectively unacceptable to the agents and that the repressive social institution these beliefs legitimize is not legitimate.[14]

In other words, through a process of self-reflection, agents come to recognize the falsity of their false beliefs. An integral part of this process is that these agents are brought to see that their failure to recognize this fact prior to this process of self-reflection is part and parcel of the oppression to which they were subject and which—at the level of social institutions—they are still subject. Hence, ideology-critique is successful if and only if the agents subject to ideological captivity are enabled to free themselves from this captivity and, through this process of enlightenment, become motivated to engage in a process of emancipation, that is, to fight against the oppressive social institution in question.

The state of unfreedom described by the concept of aspectival captivity is, as we have seen, logically distinct from that described by the notion of ideological captivity, most notably in that aspectival captivity is independent of the truth or falsity of the beliefs held by the agent. Hence, too, the kind of practice of criticism required to address this condition of unfreedom—namely, genealogy—is also logically distinct in kind from ideology-critique. Genealogy, as will become clear, also has as "its inherent aim to be the self-consciousness of a successful process of enlightenment and emancipation," albeit one of a somewhat different kind.

In so far as aspectival captivity is characterized by agents' reflecting and acting on themselves as subjects in terms of a given picture as the *only* possible picture open to them, the initial aim of genealogy is to enable them to free themselves from aspectival captivity by exhibiting the possibility of other pictures. Hence, as James Tully notes, Foucault's genealogical exercises consist of "historical studies undertaken to bring to light the two kinds of limit: to show that what is taken for granted in the form of the subject in question has a history and has been otherwise"; and to show "in what has been given to us as universal, necessary and obligatory, what place is occupied by whatever is singular, contingent and the product of arbitrary constraints." These studies enable us "to free ourselves from ourselves," from this form of subjectivity, by coming to see that "that-which-is has not always been," that it could be otherwise, by showing how in Western cultures people have recognized themselves differently, and so to "alter one's way of looking at things."[15]

However, as we have noted, what motivates genealogy is not simply the condition of being held captive by a picture, but the recognition that this captivity prevents us from making sense of ourselves as subjects in the ways that matter to us. In other words, whereas ideology-critique seeks to disclose a contradiction between our beliefs and our epistemic principles, genealogy aims to elucidate a disjuncture between our intelligibility to ourselves as agents, our form of subjectivity, and our cares and commitments. Two examples may clarify this point.

The first is given by Nietzsche's *On the Genealogy of Morality*. Nietzsche's concern is that European peoples are held captive by a picture of morality that has been fundamentally shaped by Christianity and that, after the death of God, renders us increasingly unable to make sense of ourselves as moral agents. An instance of this captivity is provided by Kant's famous argument in the "Critique of Teleological Judgment" that morality (in Nietzsche's narrow sense) requires certain matters of faith and that without the *res fidei* there is only nihilism, where nihilism can be glossed as the condition of being unable to make sense of ourselves as moral agents.[16] Nietzsche agrees that this picture of morality does require such matters of faith—but the point of his efforts to enable us to free ourselves from this picture of morality is to free us from the entailment of Kant's view that, once we acknowledge the death of God, nihilism is all that remains. Hence, Nietzsche's task is to free us from captivity to this picture—a task that he takes up by providing a genealogical account of how we have become subject to it. There are three stages in this genealogical process of self-reflection. First, by providing an account in which two types of morality stand in relation to one another, Nietzsche unsettles the view that what he refers to as "slave morality" is the only type of morality. Second, by giving an account of the emergence and development of the ascetic ideal, Nietzsche shows us how we have become captivated by this picture of morality and how this captivation leaves us open to the threat of nihilism. Third, in devaluing this picture of morality by showing that it entails our becoming obscure to ourselves *qua* moral agents, Nietzsche's account motivates us (through our own commitment to making sense of ourselves as moral agents) to engage in the practical task of revaluing our moral values. In other words, Nietzsche's genealogical account attempts to articulate a way in which we can make sense of ourselves as moral agents—and, in particular, make sense of our current failure to make sense of ourselves as moral agents—that guides us to engage in the revaluation of our moral values.

The second example is provided by Foucault's work in *Discipline and Punish* and *The History of Sexuality*, volume 1. Here, Foucault's concern is based on the thought that we are held captive by a picture of political relations (and of the relationship between the growth of capabilities and the growth of autonomy) fundamentally shaped by discourses and practices of sovereignty—a picture that leads us to assume that sovereignty is the preeminent locus of political reflection:

> At bottom, despite the differences in epochs and objectives, the representation of power has remained under the spell of monarchy. In political thought and analysis we *still have not cut off the head of the king*. Hence the importance that the theory of power gives to the problem of right and violence, law and illegality, freedom and will, and especially the state and sovereignty.... To conceive of power on the basis of these problems is to conceive it in terms of a historical form that is characteristic of our societies: *the juridical monarchy*.[17]

The substance of Foucault's concern is that our captivation by this sovereignty-based picture of political relations facilitates forms of domination based on forms of power not disclosed by this picture (such that the growth of capabilities is connected to the intensification of power relations) and, hence, undermines our capacity to make sense of ourselves as political agents in ways that foster our capacity for self-government. His task is, thus, to enable us to free ourselves from this picture, such that we may consider how the growth of our capabilities can be disconnected from the intensification of power relations—or, in other words, how we may begin to make sense of ourselves as political agents in ways that support, rather than undermine, our capacity for self-government. Again, there are three stages to the process of genealogical self-reflection. First, Foucault provides an account of two types of political relations, those organized around sovereignty and those organized around bio-power, and their relation to each other, in order to unsettle the grip of the sovereignty picture on our political imaginations. Second, by giving an account of the emergence and development of the sovereignty picture, Foucault shows us how we have become captivated by it and how this captivation leads us to fail to make sense of ourselves as political agents insofar as we fail to make sense of our own unfreedom as political agents. Third, by enabling us to make sense of ourselves as "unfree" political agents and, in particular, to reach an understanding of our current failure to make sense of our own political unfreedom, Foucault's account motivates us, in terms of our own commitment to self-government, to engage in the practical task of overcoming this condition of unfreedom. It does this through redirecting our political subjectivity toward experiments with altering our games of government to minimize the degree of domination within them.[18]

Self-reflection of the kind that genealogy aims to produce, then—starting from an inchoate sense that some feature of our subjectivity, of our ways of reflecting on our experience, is a conflict between "But this isn't how it is!" and "Yet this is how it *must* be!"—has the following form in both Nietzsche and Foucault:

a. It identifies a picture that holds us captive, whereby this captivity obstructs our capacity to make sense of ourselves as agents in ways that matter to us;
b. this account involves a redescription of this picture that contrasts it with another way of seeing the issue in order to free us from captivity to this picture;
c. it provides an account of how we have become held captive by this picture, which enables us to make sense of ourselves as agents and, more particularly, to make sense of how we have failed to make sense of ourselves as agents in ways that matter to us;
d. insofar as this account engages with our cares and commitments, it motivates us to engage in the practical working out of this reorientation of ourselves as agents.

It is in this way that genealogy performs its inherent aim to be the self-consciousness of a process of enlightenment and emancipation. As Foucault puts it, genealogy "will separate out, from the contingency that has made us what we are, the possibility of no longer being, doing, or thinking what we are, do, or think . . . seeking to give new impetus, as far and wide as possible, to the undefined work of freedom."[19] It is in this way that genealogy functions as a form of perspicuous representation.

In this chapter, I have argued that Wittgenstein's significance for political philosophy is to alert us to a specific type of nonphysical constraint on our capacity for self-government and to provide a way of addressing and dissolving such constraints, which he refers to as "perspicuous representation." I have also contrasted this type of nonempirical constraint with that of ideological captivity and argued that genealogy is one example of the forms that perspicuous representation may take in the context of moral and political philosophy, not least insofar as it immunizes itself against the craving for generality that renders us most vulnerable to being held captive by a picture. It is no part of my argument to claim that genealogy is the *only* practice of political philosophy that exhibits the features of perspicuous representation; my claim is simply that it is an important example of this approach. Despite its limited scope, this argument has considerable significance for the practices of political philosophy. If we begin by recalling the two sources of our vulnerability to being held captive by a picture, we can draw two morals for our practices of political philosophy. First, our practices make us vulnerable to being held captive by a picture, via natural processes of forgetting, to the extent that these practices do not cultivate a historical or comparative sensibility.[20] Second, our practices make us vulnerable to being held captive by a picture via processes of philosophical repression to the extent that these practices are characterized by the craving for generality. Hence, insofar as the condition of aspectival captivity is a significant issue for political philosophy—and the work of Foucault, Skinner, and Tully suggests that it is—the clear implication is that we would be well advised to cultivate practices of political philosophy that are oriented to particular cases and are characterized by a historical or comparative sensibility.

Part II

A Wittgensteinian Politics

5

Notes on the Natural History of Politics

Allan Janik

> Is it wrong that I direct my actions on the basis of the propositions of physics? Should I say, I have no good reason for that? Isn't it just that, which we call a "good reason"?
>
> Suppose we met a people who did not regard that as a telling reason. Now, how do we imagine this? Instead of the physicist they consult an oracle. (And for that we consider them primitive.) Is it wrong for them to consult an oracle and be guided by it?—If we call this "wrong" aren't we using our language game as a base from which to *combat* theirs?
>
> —Ludwig Wittgenstein, *On Certainty*

I take the fact that language-games can "combat" one another as proof positive that Wittgenstein recognized the political dimension of language. How might he have developed his insights? Can we learn something about politics from the later Wittgenstein? In answering these questions we should begin by reminding ourselves of certain basic features of philosophical problems as he conceived them.

In the *Philosophical Investigations* Wittgenstein begins his discussion of the nature of philosophical problems by referring to St. Augustine's conundrums about time in the *Confessions*. There Augustine remarks with perplexity that he knows what time is until somebody asks him, then he is at a loss to explain what he knows. Thus knowing something that one cannot put into words upon request, Wittgenstein insists, is typical of what philosophical problems are all about. So, a Wittgensteinian philosophy of politics begins by observing that the question about the nature of the beast, the ultimate philosophical question in Aristotle's eyes—What is it that we are talking about?—catches us off guard, leaves us uncomfortable, puzzled, and perplexed. The question, What is politics? almost always provokes a mixture of disquiet and curiosity.

If we are to reach an answer from the way in which Wittgenstein approaches epistemological problems, we will have to ask questions and study examples of what is taken to be political. Since Wittgenstein believed that philosophical problems originate when we let language trap us into asking about only one thing, when in fact we should be investigating many different phenomena, we should probably begin by asking how many different things do we include under the rubric of politics. The following brief list of questions should illustrate a wide-ranging set of political questions, from the familiar to the controversial:

> Should education have a higher budgetary priority than military spending?
> Who should pay for social services?
> Should there be unrestricted access to abortion?
> Should gays be allowed to marry or adopt children?
> What is the relationship between the political traditions that we parade on holidays and our actual traditions of political practice?
> In what respects is the relationship between parent and child political? That between husband and wife?
> Are Marcel Duchamp's "ready-mades" art?
> Should I have any compunction about enjoying a luxurious lifestyle?

The issues at the top of the list are clearly part of our common understanding of politics; they might be generally accepted as central to an education in political science. Those in the middle would be identified by mainstream political scientists as boundary issues between politics/law and ethics; they are questionably political. Yet there are grounds to insist that all the questions have a political dimension. Wittgenstein invites us to consider how the term "politics" is used, and we find ourselves in deep conflict about which uses are more or less appropriate. The conflicts, paradoxically, are themselves political. Thus a Wittgensteinian political philosophy will need to start from the essentially contested nature of its own object of inquiry.

A second Wittgensteinian move in philosophical investigation of politics would be to ask how it is that our very involvement in politics (whatever that might happen to mean) obscures the answer to the original question and systematically conceals the plurality of political phenomena that our set of questions points to.

I want to suggest that a Wittgensteinian philosophy of politics would be neither merely an analysis of what is normally understood as political behavior (party politics, office seeking, determining public order, setting social priorities, and so on) nor a "political theory" (conceived either as philosophy or social science) in the sense of a normative account of any political arrangements that could count as rationally justified. Rather, a Wittgensteinian political philosophy would have to deal with the multiplicity of ways that politics enters into the life of an animal that uses language; for to the extent that there could be a Wittgensteinian philosophical investigation into politics, that investigation would have to bear upon the role of politics in concept formation and the ways that our actual concept use all but systematically obscures its own political dimension. Moreover, to be true to the spirit of Wittgenstein's philosophizing, that investigation would have to reject social criticism for a form of redescription of political phenomena that would cease to make them problematic to us. To achieve a philosophical perspective on politics the philosopher would have to remain outside the sphere of the political: a citizen belonging to no community. This requirement would tend to disqualify nearly everybody writing on the subject of political philosophy today, including many people who draw liberally from the Wittgenstein philosophical arsenal in their efforts to do, say, political theory, political philosophy, or the philosophy of social science. It is, nevertheless, strictly in accord with Wittgenstein's own perspective on the matter. That is, of course not to say that the way such scholars make use of Wittgenstein's thought is illegitimate, but simply to observe that they seldom practice the philosophy of politics in what is sometimes referred to as the "quietistic" spirit that Wittgenstein did—nor do they tend to employ his peculiar style. I suggest that there is a certain kind of discipline bound to Wittgenstein's alleged quietism and that his style is not as irrelevant as one might think at first glance.

In this chapter I propose to answer the question, What is political? by assembling some Wittgensteinian reminders of the role of the political in human experience that enable us to grasp how politics fits into human natural history. I do so, of course, without endeavoring either to justify or to condemn existing political arrangements. It should be clear from the start that I am not aspiring to produce a theory of politics any more than Wittgenstein himself was interested in producing a theory of knowledge. Rather, I want to get straight about the way politics attaches to everyday concepts and conflicts.

Perhaps our endorsement of Wittgenstein's so-called quietism will seem offensive or absurd to politically engaged philosophers and intellectuals generally. So I would do well to assert my conviction at the beginning that the solution to political problems as I understand them comes in the way we live, not in the theories we hold. Politics is about real conflicts, and conflict solving in the real world is a matter of will, of living differently. The opposite of political insight and sound judgment in ticklish situations is not ignorance but tragedy, as Aristotle knew well.[1]

I depart from conventional political science and political philosophy in assuming that the question of what is political extends far beyond the "politics of the politicians" to every sphere in which human beings compete to influence one another's behavior. The main clue in our search for the political is implicit in the question, What constitutes a political problem? Our concerns as philosophers will be with the ways in which our everyday concepts are politically laden. This approach takes its cue from those social critics, typically outsiders, who see the normal agenda of party politics as sweeping important political matters (say, within the family) under the carpet, and those political theorists, be they philosophers or social scientists, who insist that politics too has a conceptual dimension that students of politics neglect at their peril. Some of the latter have already found their way to Wittgenstein. I would like to deepen and extend the insights for politics that they have drawn from his work and show how we might obtain a certain clarity about the political by leaving things as they are.

On the face of it there seems to be something very odd about approaching a subject that played virtually no role in Wittgenstein's life or thought from a perspective drawn from his later philosophy.[2] This deserves comment. In the *Tractatus* he sharply demarcated what could be put into words precisely (unambiguously) from what could not. Indeed, he confused a whole generation of philosophers and scholars by identifying the precise as the meaningful and the ambiguous as the meaningless (forgetting that there is a meaningful form of ambiguity: metaphor, a generally neglected topic in his philosophizing). The sphere of the meaningful was the subject of science; the sphere of ambiguity he designated ethics. Later, in his "Lecture on Ethics," he cast a little light upon the obscurities of this effort to consign ethics to silence by distinguishing matters of absolute value from matters of relative value. The former referred to questions about God, the sense of the world, and the meaning of life, whereas the latter seemed to refer to concerns such as utility or distributive justice. It is necessary to emphasize that Wittgenstein was so little interested in questions of relative moral value that he never specified what he meant by the term "moral," except to say that these questions were all the questions in ethics that were not concerns of absolute value. It is obvious from his text and everything else he wrote, as well as the testimony of his lifelong friends, that questions of relative value (including questions about politics—but not, say, questions of aesthetics) interested him not in the least. So, it is indeed strange to discuss the implications of his later philosophy for our understanding of politics. However, we should not forget that Wittgenstein's own mode of describing what he was doing is by no means infallible. For example, what he termed ethics in the *Tractatus*—questions about God, the meaning of life, and the limits of language—have been treated by other philosophers (such as Karl Jaspers) as metaphysics or the meeting point of ethics and metaphysics. Moreover, the conception of language as limited from within and thus crystalline, which facilitated gesturing at the ethical in the *Tractatus*, is precisely what is no longer available in his later philosophy, despite the fact that Wittgenstein never revised his views on the matter. Yet, there is much to suggest that perhaps he should have. Perhaps we ought to look upon his later philosophy as he did himself upon his earlier philosophy as somehow including what he had *not* said as well. Here it is important to stress that I am not suggesting that this ought to have been a part of Wittgenstein's philosophical agenda; but there is noting about his later philosophy that excludes looking at the sorts of philosophical questions that arise in connection with politics. Be that as it may, "What is political?" is just the sort of conceptual question that fascinated him. Its very simplicity and familiarity obscures the difficulties it presents. Moreover, as William Connolly has suggested, Wittgenstein's family-resemblance character of concepts replaces the neat world of precise description and introduces an implicit political dimension to his account of concept formation.

To say that it is strange to discuss Wittgenstein in relation to politics is by no means to assert that it is pointless, as an increasing number of scholars have emphasized. Consider these examples (which I have discussed at length elsewhere):[3] Hanna Pitkin insists that there are important implications for our understanding of political theory in the late Wittgenstein's concept of language as constituted through cues rather than labels as well as in his view of philosophy as leading to self-awareness. J. C. Nyíri has argued that Wittgenstein was in fact a conservative thinker, who devoted himself to developing the philosophical underpinnings of conservatism in asserting, for example, that we follow rules blindly. Ferrucio Rossi-Landi, on the other hand, has linked him to Marx in describing him as the analyst of linguistic alienation. For David Rubinstein, Wittgenstein can be construed as closely complementing Marx's account of practice and providing a sounder foundation for social theory than any of the other currently available philosophical alternatives. More recently the research of David Bloor and the Edinburgh School, Charles Taylor, and, above all, Theodore Schatzki have made an increasingly strong case for the general relevance of Wittgenstein's philosophy for the philosophy of social science.[4]

As provocatively stimulating as all of these efforts to associate Wittgenstein and politics are, they for the most part ignore the *spirit* in which Wittgenstein wrote, to the extent that he explicitly stressed how little his work belonged to the main current of European and American civilization in the age of fascism *and* socialism (CV 6). He was less interested in erecting structures than he was in examining the foundations of existing ones. To accomplish this he thought that the philosopher had to renounce citizenship in any human community (contra Otto Neurath and the left wing of the Vienna Circle) (Z § 455).[5] If these sentiments are not mere willfulness—and what follows endeavors to articulate how they are not—they not only are central to his concept of philosophy as necessarily leaving things as they are but also have wide-ranging implications. His perspective on the world was one that eschewed looking forward or backward to see where we are but planted itself firmly in the present (the comparison with Nietzsche's notion of Eternal Recurrence suggests itself here).[6] As in the case of Nietzsche, Wittgenstein seems to suggest that there is a certain disciplining of the philosophical mind required of philosophers if they are to see what is always before their eyes. In short, Wittgenstein was profoundly apolitical both as a person and as a philosopher, and it is paradoxically precisely this apolitical stance and what it enabled him to observe that constitutes his importance for political philosophy (here a curious comparison with Orwell at the moment of his disillusionment with socialism—not earlier or later—suggests itself). In his efforts to avoid being blinkered by the ubiquitous ideologies in his world, cultural ones (e.g., the Vienna Circle, Bloomsbury, and the Brenner Circle) as well as political, he developed an eminently anti-ideological mode of philosophizing, with at least implicit resources for our understanding of politics.

Here is perhaps a good place to counter a standard objection, namely, that in philosophy one should not bring historical or biographical considerations to bear upon philosophical positions: the views of the philosophers must stand or fall on their own merits. This is to ignore the obvious importance of the historical/biographical for determining the meaning of texts. Take the case of Karl Marx's *Communist Manifesto*: the fact that is was written in aid of educating a group of conspiratorial Belgian tailors with respect to the dynamics of history is anything but irrelevant to any discussion of Marx's goals both as a philosopher and as a politician. So there can be no good reasons for ignoring what we know, and we have all sorts of good reasons for considering the historical context within which philosophizing takes place in our efforts to assess its significance.

Be that as it may, for the sake of those skeptics who find Wittgenstein's dictum that philosophy leaves everything as it is a hopelessly unacceptable endorsement of the status quo, it should be emphasized that his approach entails only that philosophy inevitably fails in its task of understanding the world when it also directs itself to changing it. The history of Marxism after Marx, and above all after Lenin, well illustrates how wishful thinking has a way of impeding the vision of politically engaged philosophers. How the world really gets changed for the better is a matter concerning which, Wittgenstein believed, nobody has an answer. Wittgenstein dismissed activism, as he dismissed theory in epistemology, in order to attain a more radical philosophical perspective on the nature of human action, one that would allow him to go to the root of the problems that have tormented philosophers for so long, such that they "dissolve" of themselves.[7] The main lines of his critique of traditional epistemology from Descartes to Russell are well known (even if the centrality of Wittgenstein's open-textured notion of rule-following with its radical implications concerning the ultimate indescribability of human action has tended to be neglected).[8] The issue then is, How does the radical character of his critique of classical epistemology illuminate the question of what is political? For on the surface they are worlds apart.

For all the merits of subsequent work in the field, William Connolly's effort to do political theory in Wittgenstein's name, however tentatively, is particularly challenging and largely neglected. His brilliant *The Terms of Political Discourse* deserves special attention as a Wittgensteinian critique of conventional political "science."[9] To act, Connolly argues, is to employ concepts. In the course of acting we sometimes discover that the concepts we employ (his examples include responsibility, power, interest, and freedom) are not wholly shared by other members of the community but are the objects of bitter conflicts. His merit is to have demonstrated that these conceptual conflicts are the very stuff of political life. He has trenchantly lain bare the role of essential contestability in political struggle and thereby exposed the politics of "politics." On Connolly's view the very concept of politics turns out to be itself political.[10] Because many of the concepts we employ are complex, rooted in traditions with a branching development and open to yet further modification, they are capable of being construed *legitimately* in different ways by bitter opponents, who are nevertheless acting in good faith. His analysis of the ways in which "freedom," "power," and "interest" are essentially contested, while by no means drawn from Wittgenstein, is explicitly in aid of the Wittgensteinian goal of establishing a "grammar of politics," which in turn is continuous with Wittgenstein's efforts to analyze philosophical problems on the basis of the "depth grammar" of our language. Thus, while Connolly does not explicitly emphasize the connection between essential contestability and the family resemblance character of concepts, it is at this point that his analysis complements Wittgenstein's later philosophy. The point is that our ability to "follow the rule" in new and unexpected ways leads to a situation where the referents of terms form families, only loosely and indirectly related to one another. Such referents are not the compact classes that set theory describes, with the result that the various senses of a word like "fair" can clash with one another. For example, "fair" can imply "gained on the basis of fair exchange in the market" or fair in the sense of "equally distributed among all citizens" (Marx's example in the *Critique of the Gotha Program*).[11] No small part of Connolly's argument for the crucial character of essentially contested concepts depends upon the notion that the very act of classifying a situation entails judging both its moral and its political significance in a way that is wholly unavoidable (think of the difference it makes whether you call an act "euthanasia" or "assisted suicide"). This implies that "political science" cannot be done from a perspective *au dessus de la mêlée*. Our very descriptions of the world are charged with evaluations that are fundamentally political in nature. The political scientist who ignores the biases in everyday classifications ends up practicing politics surreptitiously and unconsciously—and, therefore, confusedly—rather than analyzing it. Thus Connolly will insist that no small part of Wittgenstein's significance for political analysis is to help us to grasp why such analysis is (1) unprivileged with respect to its ability to describe political phenomena, (2) written from within political contests, and (3) addressed to fellow citizens. In short, "political *science*" turns out to be a contradiction in terms.

What follows is an exploration of some prominent features of that terrain, beginning with this question: On the basis of Wittgenstein's later philosophy, how is politics at all possible? The question may ring Kantian but the effort in fact bears upon a Wittgensteinian rehabilitation of the Aristotelian concept of *praxis*; our investigation is Wittgensteinian in the sense that it aims to "show" how politics too is rooted in certain general facts about the destiny of a language-using animal and, therefore, how it forms a part of the natural history of human beings.

William Connolly's work is crucial to that task because he proceeds from the problem of establishing the conceptual dimension involved in adequately describing political life and draws its implications for both political conduct and analysis. One of his merits is to have demonstrated with help from Wittgenstein that there is an important link between Aristotle's two definitions of what it is to be human, the *zoon politikon* (roughly: a social and a fortiori political animal) and the *zoon logon echon* (roughly: a rule-following animal). In Wittgensteinian terms, speaking a language involves following rules where there are no explicit rules but only examples to go on. The lack of explicit rules and the fundamentally ambiguous, metaphorical character of their employment insures that there is always a plurality of ways of following a rule: we invent new ways of doing so continually. Thus following a rule can lead to conflict where there is more than one way to do so and the various senses to terms clash with one another. Classical examples of the resulting "essentially contested" concepts are art, democracy, and Christianity. Their historical development has been so complex and ramified that it is possible to argue about their meaning endlessly but by no means irrationally. How does Wittgenstein help us to see how such conflict is "natural"?

If one knows anything at all about Wittgenstein's later philosophy, it is that Wittgenstein insists that a private language—that is, one that comes into being as I create names for my sensory experiences—is a conceptual impossibility. Since sensory experience is serial, it would never be possible for me to confirm that I use the name that I had previously assigned to a past sense datum correctly in assigning it to the present one. Using names thus involves appealing to criteria in a situation where we are potentially mistaken. The use of criteria presupposes regular procedures for correction, and this cannot be something that one person does once. Regularity is involved, and that regularity is a public matter. "Private languages" such as codes are thus parasitic upon public, meaning-constituting practices. The idea of a private language can be entertained precisely because we have illicitly smuggled in the notion of language through the side door. Positing the idea of a private language in fact involves transgressing the limits of language and saying something just as nonsensical as suggesting that one commit adultery with one's own wife (an example of a pragmatic contradiction that Aristotle uses somewhere). The difference is that in the case of private language the nonsensical character of the assertion is covert.

Speaking a language involves mastering a technique or following rules that the individual who is learning did not and could not create, for the simple reason that the said individual does not know the point of mastering the technique. The why and the wherefore of doing what we must in learning only becomes clear to us ex post facto—so clear that we "never give the matter another thought" once we have, say, learned how to swim or ride a bike. The substance of the rules does not matter in establishing the routine. To learn, then, is to follow rules or master a technique that you did not create and, in the course of mastering it, gradually to come to grasp the point of doing so. To use language, then, is, in a certain sense, to be *ruled* in the sense of being disciplined. The whole question of why we do what we do and not something else just does not arise, except much later in a very different context.

What does it mean to be "ruled" in this sense? For a start, it means to be subject to behavioral regularities that we have neither created nor necessarily approve of (think, for example, of learning "manners") and that, as we later learn, might be other than they in fact are and thus do not in any strict sense demand our acquiescence. It does not take profound reflection to discover that the rules that any given individual has learned do not have to be what they are. Rousseau seems to have got it backward; for it seems that human beings are born helpless only to become constrained by rules not of their making, which are at once contingent and nevertheless necessary if they are to act at all. Further, this has to be the case; for we cannot learn to learn without learning specific survival skills that have to be communicated as infallible commands to begin with (*hot!* has to produce the sort of hasty retreat on the part of the toddler that excludes thinking). Moreover, it is precisely this mastery of technique that enables us to navigate safely through our environment and at the same makes us the persons we are. Practical rules, then, are a priori in that they make action possible. It is precisely the quasi-synthetic and a priori character of rules that makes them invariably political—a curious kind of synthetic a priori indeed!

Neither Wittgenstein nor anyone else ever suggested that the rules mastered in childhood were anything but contingent as to their substance. The rules we internalize as we are enculturated could be different (as Foucault never tired of reminding us). Each of us, for example, could have had a different mother tongue from the one we in fact have and with it a wholly different "culture." The rub, however, is that, being the kind of creature that we are—namely, a speaking animal—we have to learn to follow rules blindly if we want to learn anything (as all army sergeants, novice masters, and athletic coaches well know). To become your own person, it seems, you have to first become what your guardians (tutors, superiors etc.) want you to be, not in the sense that your personality is necessarily established or fixed for all time by the rules you master and how you master them, but in the sense that their rules establish the range of possibilities open to you and thereby condition your future development. To realize any human potential whatsoever we have to learn language and, therefore, to master a plethora of techniques that, from the point of view of their stipulations, are arbitrary and coercive, and we soon realize that they could be different. What we realize only later, if at all, is that our capacity for action is bound to the discipline that simultaneously constrains and facilitates that action. Belonging to another social class, living in a different place, having different parents, and so on would make a great difference in what we learned but—and this is often overlooked—little difference in how we learned. To follow rules at all is to be always potentially in a situation where we are bound in ways that are at once necessary but could, nevertheless, paradoxically, be different. In this sense rule-following is a sort of "synthetic a priori" behavioral foundation for knowledge (even if, unlike Kant's synthetic a priori, it does not involve propositions).

To take this view, however, is to see only one side of the implications of Wittgenstein's concept of rule-following; for he emphasizes that the very repetition that makes concept formation possible makes it no less difficult to throw off a concept at will than to acquire one that way. On this view to realize that there is an alternative to the existing order says nothing whatsoever about the "availability" of that alternative. Frequently, in our media-dominated society with its constant flow of new images, we are tempted to confuse the fact that we can conceive of an alternative to existing social relations and political states of affairs with that alternative being a real (workable) possibility. While the substance of the rules we have mastered determines what constrains us politically (i.e., what makes politics in the ordinary sense possible), it is the activity of rule-following that determines our capacity to change our behavior patterns. As the two become detached from one another the scenario gets more complex: new possibilities for "entanglement in the rules" arise.

Connolly has rightly identified the political character of essential contestability; what he has not undertaken to do is to argue that politics inheres in the family resemblance character of concepts. He has written, "When groups range themselves around essentially contested concepts, politics is the mode in which the clash is normally expressed."[12] What is obscured in this sentence is the fact that for a concept to be essentially contested, groups must have already in some sense ranged themselves around it, since a concept has no existence outside of human actions. Wittgenstein's notion of rule-following emphasizes how this happens in the normal course of events. Concepts, he insists, do not permit of neat delimitation or definition by genus and specific difference, in Aristotle's terms. Rather, they are looser groupings with significant overlap but lacking in a set of shared "universal" characteristics, like members of a family who share subsets of characteristics without sharing any "essential" set of common characteristics. Wittgenstein's well-known example is that of games. He is anxious to defend the view that games do not share any single finite set of properties by virtue of which they are called games—nor should they be expected to. Implicitly he is claiming that on Aristotelian criteria we are never able to define what we commonly group under the heading "game." (This is, in itself, something that Aristotle would agree with; his concept of definition is intended only to apply to natural kinds and not to artifacts. The differences between Aristotle and Wittgenstein here run deep indeed.) In fact, common usage decides what a game is, such that, when the philosopher produces a definition of "game" that, say, precludes games played alone from being termed games properly so-called, the objection "You have omitted solitaire and a variety of things that language users normally term games" must be taken seriously. Wittgenstein insists that it is well-established social practice, rather than philosophical fiat, that decides what is real.

We call things "games" or "representatives" or "works of art" because they fit into practices such that the analogies between them suggest that they are members of the same family. Thus there are closely related cousins such as soccer and ice hockey and more distantly related ones like chess and charades or football and guessing riddles. In many instances (for example, basketball), we know exactly what analogies (with football) were drawn upon to constitute the game. Admission to the family rests upon the role that the activity plays in our practices as opposed to any of the specific characteristics of the game itself. (The actions involved in playing chess might well belong to a religious ritual rather than a game, and there is nothing about the rules that tells us that chess is a game—that is something we know, in the end, because we know the English language.) However, because a given individual must learn specific usage to learn language and because we can invent games (something that never would have occurred to Aristotle as relevant to our understanding of concepts, as it might have to Protagoras or Isocrates), it is possible to find ourselves in a position of arguing about, say, whether or not taking cabbages from other people's gardens on Halloween is a game. In this case the line between games, pranks, and vandalism (i.e., the point of the practice, which determines its political significance) is mighty thin. However, to have made this suggestion is to initiate a political discussion about who belongs to the family, for although our concepts are flexible, this by no means implies that they are arbitrarily used. Just how flexible is our usage as regards the term "game"? What kind of games can we invent? What can count as "game behavior"? How much do the surrounding practices with regard to, for example, property permit us to consider something that would frequently be termed "stealing" a game? Here we are confronted with a classical political issue. At stake is not only the usage of the term "game" but the redefinition of a whole series of practices. It is also noteworthy that the considerations that would lead us to accept the putative innovation—for example, the gamelike character of helping ourselves to other people's cabbages in a way that is neither altogether malicious nor entirely innocent—are largely incommensurable with the kinds of objections that might be raised to such a suggestion. Therefore, the elements that come into play in resolving the question will also be subject to dispute.

The family resemblance character of concepts, in turn, is rooted in Wittgenstein's central insight that to have a concept is to have learned to follow a rule. This rule disciplines us in a particular way. It is of the essence of a rule, however, that it also be supple—that is, that there be more than one way of following the rule. This is not to assert that rule-following is arbitrary, but that the context in which rules are applied can determine variations in how the rule is interpreted. Throughout Europe, for example, one raises one or more fingers when ordering glasses of champagne at the opera. However, in England or Norway one counts from the index finger, whereas in France and Austria one begins with the thumb. To learn to count on one's fingers, then, will be different depending upon where one has learned a practice. Now it is the conventional element in the practice (as opposed to its intrinsic order) that is potentially political. This potential is actualized when for whatever reasons such customs come into conflict (rather like the way the word *filioque* in the Creed could precipitate the Great Schism within Christianity). For this reason "political" debates are sometimes skirmishes over the borders of concepts—that is, over just what falls under a certain term. Connolly has provided an admirable account of how political contests in the normal sense are inter alia constituted by conceptual disputes about the nature of notions like "interest," "freedom," and "power." My aim here has been to bring out just how this is part and parcel of language use and, a fortiori, of human nature.

The changing character of the context and the point of employing a technique can also have consequences for our understanding of politics. In the last hundred years the point of, say, horseback riding, has changed radically, whereas the technique has hardly changed. In 1900 it was an essential mode of transportation; today it is an expensive sport. The concomitant change has not had much to do with politics. However, when we consider the parallel case of hunting (where we must admit weapons have changed the techniques somewhat) we see that what was once a respectable mode of obtaining food has become in the eyes of many (especially in contemporary France) completely unacceptable as a sport.

This is perhaps a good point for a reminder: the aim here is not to provide a comprehensive account of the political role of concepts but to illustrate how "politics" in the conventional sense depends upon the family resemblance nature of political terms and the necessity of rule-following. This it what is means to speak of the philosopher's task as one of determining how politics fits into our natural history. The political analyst (e.g., William Connolly) wants to explain how it is that concepts constitute political debate. The political philosopher, on the other hand, wants to show why the politicization of concepts has to be the case given the kind of creature that we are. In effect, to draw this distinction is to distinguish between the dimension of grammar (in Wittgenstein's sense of logical grammar) and the place of politics in our natural history—the two are distinguishable even if they are not separable from one another. The matter might be summed up this way: political analysts want to understand how political concepts work, whereas political philosophy aims at answering the metaphysical question of how politics is at all possible.

To sum up: the essentially contested character of concepts is a constitutive element in political contests, but, more than that, it is the very defining characteristic of political conflict. Essential contestability is rooted in the family resemblance character of concepts. Concepts have this character because (1) to possess a concept is to be able to apply a rule and (2) rules can be applied in a variety of ways. This is because they have to be learned in the context of specific practices, which themselves take their character from neighboring concepts (we do not learn isolated judgments but nests of judgments: we do not learn to ride but we acquire the skill to use a horse, say, as a means of transportation or as a source of power or as a sporting activity).

All of this in turn implies that the life of a speaking animal is shot through with politics in the sense that the very first skills we acquire are imbued with a contingent and therefore political character. It is our fate to be political, curiously the more so when we become masters of ourselves in a mundane sense. Following a rule to the point that we are capable of varying the practice in question is a highly political activity, even if we are not inclined to think so. Politics, then, does not refer merely to those aspects of public life surrounding lawmaking; it is an ineliminable element in concept acquisition and use. If this is correct, radical revision of the nature of social science is required, in that to understand "politics" we shall have to grasp how it grows out of the political dimension of our practices (language-games). Moreover, it follows that we shall have to make important adjustments as regards our understanding of the ways that politics enters into our lives, for now it becomes tied to our very first—and all subsequent—learning experiences. Thus interpersonal relations, scientific debates, and artistic creation, for example, will have to be understood as having a political dimension. Politics, as Connolly rightly emphasizes, pervades our very descriptions of the world.

It might be objected here that Wittgenstein is not necessary to obtain such a perspective on the political dimension of human activity. This is partly true and partly beside the point. It is true in the sense that such a perspective might just as easily be derived from, say, a certain reading of Hegel and Marx. However, the point here has been in part to break new ground by identifying the implications of Wittgenstein's later philosophy for issues with which he has only recently been associated (it also complements Charles Taylor's efforts to link Wittgenstein to Hegel in comparing the relationship between Wittgenstein's objections to the idea of private language and Hegel's critique of the notion of immediate knowledge).[13] But there is still something specifically Wittgensteinian that has not yet been explored, which has very important implications for what is normally termed "political science."

It would seem that political science would have to take on a universal character if all parts of the social world are potentially political. Political knowledge seems to encompass everything. However, there are strong reasons for thinking that Wittgenstein's view of rule-following entails the view that we cannot get into a position from which we can know (in the scientific sense) the social world. To see why this is so will be to articulate, however imperfectly, something implicit but unarticulated in Wittgenstein's later philosophy—the relationship between rule-following and his injunctions about what it is to do philosophy (the form of his philosophizing). Wittgenstein's remarks that philosophy can only describe practices, that it should not aspire to alter them, have been construed as politically conservative as well as capriciously perverse. This is because they have been read in isolation from his central notion that to acquire a concept is to follow a rule. It must be added that Wittgenstein himself is not especially illuminating about this connection, so it is not altogether strange that such difficulties with interpretation should arise. Even if what has been alleged concerning the political stipulations of rules and the conceptual link between family resemblances and essential contestability is wrongheaded, there is one point where Wittgenstein and the political analyst must converge. They must both describe practices, although they do so differently because they have different ends. Two points need to be emphasized: first, although Wittgenstein insists that description must replace explanation, one finds in his works precious few descriptions of practices in the sense that, say, phenomenologists understand the term, and almost all of these few descriptions are merely a sort of gesturing at practices; and second, this is probably not accidental given the difficulties inherent in describing our rule-following behavior. These difficulties with respect to describing action are slowly being recognized by some social scientists. To see why this should be so we will do well to recall what is required of a description of action—something philosophers from Aristotle onward have unquestioningly assumed we could do.

The first difficulty in describing action arises from the fact that our subjective accounts of action do not have to be correct for them to be orderly and "useful" to us in the sense that they facilitate self-understanding. It is quite possible, for example, for people to believe that an all-grapefruit diet is healthy and therefore decide to eat only grapefruit. Such a diet is hardly healthy. We can think that we are behaving healthily when we in fact are not. So, the first rule as regards descriptions of behavior is that first-person accounts of what someone is doing need not be correct. Paradoxically, they are indispensable, for it is not possible to decide what people in fact are doing unless we know what they think they are doing. A second problem in interpreting action is presented by the fact that there are any number of actions that cannot be understood unless the interpreter has mastered the practice in question. This is because they will not be in a position to recognize what counts as a mistake unless they already know how to do what they are observing. Moves in chess, calculations, blessings, toasts, and the like are examples of actions that are opaque to individuals who could not in principle be performing them. The interpreters' skill is thus bound to their own experience as much as it is to the intelligibility of what they observe. There are, then, beyond doubt serious difficulties surrounding the interpretation of action, only two of which have been touched upon here. But this is surely no secret except to the most naïve positivist. Wittgenstein's position here is interesting precisely because it is so radical.

For Wittgenstein the task of philosophy is to describe, but Wittgenstein does not himself describe much by way of actual behavior. His other account of what it is to do philosophy—the idea that the task of the philosopher is to assemble reminders—is at once more illuminating of his own work and more consistent with his insistence upon the primacy of rule-following in understanding meaning and action. There are, he insists, things about which it is difficult to remind ourselves. It is precisely this difficulty that obscures the roots of thought in action. One suggestion is that our difficulty here arises because it is possible to follow a rule without being aware that we are doing so in any explicit sense (it is probably not accidental that Wittgenstein gives no examples of the kinds of rules we actually follow but only evokes what it is to follow rules in discussing games like chess). This can happen because we are taught rules as techniques to be applied (as judgments). Along with those techniques we are given examples—or better, we learn those techniques through grasping examples as regularities—

which we can fall back upon when there arises some difficulty about how the rule should be applied. Wittgenstein sometimes likens this to using a color sample to check whether a given color is in fact, say, puce. As long as we can rely upon these examples, we know our way around. Our problems arise when we, for whatever reasons, no longer can rely upon them. The result is confusion. The point is that to apply these rules—to use our color sample—we do not have to be able to explain what we are doing. Thus we can have problems explaining ourselves when we are asked, even though we know what we are doing. From a Wittgensteinian-Aristotelian perspective, Socrates missed the point when he found it a failing in the artisans that they could not give an account of what they did.

At this point Wittgenstein becomes frustrating, for he only tells us that there are things concerning which it is difficult to remind ourselves, and he admonishes us that we should not try to explain this away but instead simply describe our practices. Yet there is clearly something that requires explanation here. Why are we in this position? Is this a matter of fact or of logical grammar? Wittgenstein is silent beyond a few scattered hints. These hints point again to what is involved in following a rule. To follow a rule we do not have to be able to report upon the technique we have mastered. The point is that it is conceptually impossible to do this in any rigorous way. To do so would be a matter of being able to say clearly what it is like not to have mastered that technique, which is impossible before mastering it, because we do not know what it is that we do not know (we do not know our way around). After we have mastered the technique (say, simple arithmetic) phenomena are available to us ("the numerable") that were not before. Learning rules has opened up a range of possibilities that were literally unimaginable to us before we mastered the technique. But, having mastered the technique, we have only the foggiest idea of what it was like not to have mastered it. In this respect my knowledge of myself before I could speak or calculate is not essentially different from my knowledge of another person's color-blind state. To understand myself in this situation I must turn to others (as Augustine points out in the passage from the *Confessions* with which the *Philosophical Investigations* opens). Because this is the case, philosophy cannot be carried on in the manner of a theory, since we cannot be in a position to describe in detail what it is to follow a rule. We can only do this indirectly, by reminding ourselves of what we had to learn to be able to do what we do. We can form no exact comprehensive picture. So, it is not that we can say nothing whatsoever but that there is a conceptual (grammatical) limit to what we can say. All we can do is to evoke our grasp of what it is to follow the rule; the experience upon which that activity is based is not our own and only indirectly available to us. Nor will anyone else be in a position to do this for me. The bases of our action, the training upon which concept use rests, does not lend itself to scientific analysis. It is not simply that the rules do not form a system, but that we are not in a position to formulate them in any precise sense. This is why Wittgenstein must explain language through gestures such as the unanswered question, the (counter)example, the analogy. It further illuminates why all understanding must be historical and also why history must be open-ended. It is from the situation or the context that we know the point of applying the technique or the meaning of the practice, and only when we know this can we be said to be following the rule. However, since there can always be new and unexpected ways of following the rule, we can never give the sort of final specification of what it is to follow a rule that, say, a definition would demand. For this reason Wittgenstein would ask himself whether he was not getting closer to the view that the logic of language cannot be described. To understand a practice in the concrete is to understand it as a historical phenomenon.

The point of all this is by no means radical skepticism but, rather, a genuinely modest skepticism. We can clearly formulate pictures in the form of ideal types or paradigmatic examples of many of our practices. We do have more than a vague grasp of that form of life that was, say, the Italian Renaissance. So it is not impossible to obtain a perspective on rule-following. What we cannot do is to provide a comprehensive systematic analysis of "the social system" we are enmeshed in. If this is right, the very concept of a science of action (a social science) is part of an inverted world picture: we cannot ask what the necessary and sufficient conditions for action are because there is no action as such, only rule-following within the context of specific practices in which words and actions are woven together. This can be grasped in two ways: first, contextually ("from without," as it were) either by assembling reminders in the form of series of examples or on the basis of a synoptic view of the peculiar "nesting" of practices that constitutes a certain form of life, such as the Italian Renaissance. Second, rule-following can be grasped by experienced individuals, but in a mode tied to their experience in such a way as to be inarticulable apart from it (what Thomas Aquinas called knowledge by co-naturality).

How does the politics of rule-following relate to "politics" in the mundane sense? Some suggestions have already been made. Perhaps the most important one is that rule-following produces a kind of regularity in our behavior that limits the ways we can expect to alter our practices. Just as certain sports such as tennis and swimming cannot be pursued seriously together on account of the contradictory ways that they develop the body, the ways we would change society do not have to be compatible with one another. To change society has to entail not simply changing the ruling ideas (the substance of the rules we abide by) but changing our mode of rule-following itself. If we need an example of the difficulty referred to here, we need merely consider what the introduction of democracy into the undemocratic societies of Central Europe after World War I accomplished: it turned out to be a necessary condition for the development of the new forms of absolutism (now populist, not elite) that are associated with fascism (the depressing fact is that only Czechoslovakia of the newly founded republics in the interwar period remained democratic). So, even if we can change our political organization, the ways in which we adjust to the political innovation pretty clearly cannot be decreed from above, since we are not in a position to articulate precisely what we are doing when we are under the sway of sets of rules. For this reason the Wittgensteinian political analyst ought to be very interested in the flexibility of rule-following behavior in the society he or she studies, not simply in what rules are followed but how they are followed. This will clearly have not a little to do with how the practices that constitute that society "nest." It will be of the utmost importance to discern how meaning-constituting practices intersect and determine one another.

We may conclude that a Wittgensteinian political philosophy provisionally promises the following: first, it establishes how constraints are built into those rules through which our very ability to act is constituted; second, the family resemblance character of concepts illuminates how it is at all possible for there to be a conceptual—and potentially tragic—dimension to politics, that is, how political conflicts are rooted in rule-following; third, the specificity involved in mastering a technique explains why there cannot be acontextual criteria for rationality, as, say, Kant would suggest; fourth, the Wittgensteinian assault upon private language, often derided for its abstruseness, in fact casts light upon the Aristotelian notion that politics is implicitly present throughout human activity and not merely in one sphere of action; finally, the difficulty in representing our own mastery of techniques to ourselves (not simply the difficulty in answering the myriad questions Wittgenstein puts to us in his later work) indicates that grasping, let alone altering, the rules we follow is radically limited by our very rule-following activity.

It would be folly to think that the Wittgensteinian perspective on the political developed here is anything other than crude. But crude is not the same as unilluminating—nor is it incompatible with the promise of further accounting for the ways our conundrums about the political are rooted in language itself, and ultimately in entanglements in the rules we follow.

6

Wittgenstein and the Conversation of Justice

Richard Eldridge

Political thinking has appeared in many different circumstances, displayed many different styles, and argued for many different substantive commitments. Despite these differences, however, it is possible to isolate three broad traditions of style and substance within this thinking.

Political Theory, Political Science, and Political Judgment

Classical political theory, as in Plato's effort to describe the ideal state, seeks to sketch the form of social life to which we rationally ought aspire, as offering us the necessary and perhaps even sufficient condition for the full realization of our rational humanity. The city of words that Socrates and his interlocutors found is "a model laid up in heaven, for him who wishes to look upon, and as he looks, set up the government of his soul. It makes no difference whether it exists anywhere or will exist."[1] One who gazes on this model of political life and who then sets up the government of his soul accordingly will "follow the wisdom-loving part" of the soul, with the result that "there is no internal dissension . . . and each part [of the soul] will be able to fulfill its own task and be just in other respects, and also each will reap its own pleasures, the best and the truest as far as possible."[2] This picture of political theory and its relation to ethical life has significant appeal and plausibility in broad outline. It seems hard to believe that we altogether lack the capacities to imagine and to assess alternative futures and courses of life for ourselves, and if we possess these capacities even in part, then why not exercise them as best we can? The details of political theory and ethical theory then arise out of the exercise of these capacities, as we seek in reflection to take responsibility for who we are and what we do, both socially and individually.

Political science would have it otherwise. It is hopeless to try to determine the conditions of the acquisition of the best and truest pleasures, because we are not creatures who are made to be content in doing whatever reflective reasoning most fully recommends. Rather, we move on from desire to desire and from action to action, seeking security and the effective power to fulfill our ever-arising desires within a framework of competition. As Hobbes puts it,

> the Felicity of this life, consisteth not in the repose of a mind satisfied. For there is no such *Finis ultimis* (ultimate ayme,) nor *Summum Bonum*, (greatest Good,) as is spoken of in the Books of the old Morall Philosophers. Nor can a man any more live, whose Desires are at an end, than he, whose Senses and Imagination are at a stand. Felicity is a continuall progresse of the desire, from one object to another; the attaining of the former, being still but the way to the later. The cause whereof is, That the object of mans desire, is not to enjoy once onely, and for one instant of time; but to assure for ever, the way of his future desire.[3]

Since there is no ultimate aim and hence no perfect felicity in fulfilling it, the best anyone can do is to secure the effective power to satisfy ever-changing desires. We are dominated by "a perpetuall and restlesse desire of Power after power, that ceaseth only in Death." Given the further "diversity of passions, in divers men," given the need for "Riches, Honour, Command or other power" in order to satisfy these passions, and given the scarcity of these powers, it follows that human beings "enclineth to Contention, Enmity, and War: Because the way of one Competitor, to the attaining of his desire, is to kill, subdue, supplant, or repell the other." If this is the way things are, then there is little point to imagining reflectively the conditions of ideal felicity, for there are none. The best we can do is, first, to trace the patterns and sources of persistent conflict and, second, to describe the merely comparative advantages of obeying "a common Power" that might afford human beings "protection from some other Power than their own."[4] What the sources and patterns of conflict are, and how and why human beings as they stand might best manage their conflicts, independently of empty reflections on any ultimate aim, are matters for empirical investigation. Generalizations about what people are likely or liable to do in certain circumstances are ready enough to hand to support a descriptive science of political life, that is, of the shape of the competition to satisfy desires under given social conditions. It seems hard to believe that such generalizations are either altogether unavailable or irrelevant. A descriptive science of what people naturally tend to do seems to erase the possibility and importance of deep normative reflection and to substitute pragmatic assessments of what happens when certain natural tendencies are acted on under various conditions. Political science leaves no room for classical political theory.

Interpretivism: Yet it also seems that not all political reasoning either is or should be so immediately consequential. Sometimes, it seems, judges do and ought to reason more imaginatively and less consequentially. Even if they do not appeal deductively to comprehensive political or ethical norms, they must sometimes issue verdicts about how the present conditions of political compromise *ought* to be understood or might best be understood. There is, as Ronald Dworkin notes, sometimes "theoretical disagreement in law." That is, even where there is agreement "about what the statute books and past judicial decisions have to say" about a certain class of problems,[5] there can nonetheless be disagreement about whether or how a new case falls within the relevant class. There may have been unambiguous good reasons provided by statute and precedent for deciding a set of past cases in a certain way, but in the face of this new case the situation is unclear. Do the past reasons for decision apply here, in a situation not explicitly addressed by statute or precedent? In such cases, Dworkin argues, a judge will have to determine what the law is, doing so interpretively and judgmentally. Judges should neither merely "enforce special legal conventions" nor act "as independent architects of the best future, free from the inhibiting demand that they must act consistently in principle with one another." Rather their determinations of law should flow from "more refined and concrete interpretations of the same legal practice [the law] has already begun to interpret."[6] On Dworkin's model of the interpretive determination of the law, "propositions of law are true if they figure in or follow from the principles of justice, fairness, and procedural due process that provide the best constructive interpretation of the community's legal practice." In arriving at the best constructive interpretation of legal practice, the judge is to be neither a passive, deferential historicist, insensitive to what the law implies but does not explicitly state, nor a buccaneer activist substituting personal judgment on questions of policy for that of the legislature. Judgment—flowing from the interpretation of legal practice, and expressing how we are in that practice "united in community though divided in project, interest, and conviction"—is crucial.[7] Here the exercise of judgment involves something like Aristotelian *phronesis* updated in Hegelian fashion by including a commitment to democratic community. Neither ideal models of the political good nor consequential assessments of the effects of various regimes, but rather interpretive judgment, expressive of and on behalf of the ways of a democratic political community, is to determine what the law is.

Dworkin's model of the interpretive determination of the law is subtle, and it seems to offer a way between the sometimes heavy-handed and potentially tyrannical appeals to ideal models of social and personal life that are distinctive of the classical tradition in political theory and the consequential assessments that express no aspiration to common rational citizenship and social reciprocity that are distinctive of the post-Hobbesian tradition of political science. But is this model coherent and tenable? Just what do Dworkin's judges do, and how do they do it? For all his talk of the ideal judge as an interpreter "sensitive to the great complexity of political virtues" and embracing "popular conviction and national tradition whenever these are pertinent,"[8] it remains at least unclear what room there is between appeal to ideal models and consequential assessment of effects. Suppose judges try to express the value commitments of their community to justice, fairness, and procedural due process in a genuinely new case that is not unambiguously settled by statute or precedent. What do they do? Do they say what these values in fact require in a present case, that is, what people really ought to believe about how best to fulfill these values? Or do they consult the actual preferences that people have about how to go on? Either, it seems, the judge must act from claims about values themselves, where these claims may to an outsider appear as the whims of tyranny, or the judge must act from the verdicts of empirical research into the felt consequences of political and legal arrangements. The judge must be either an active thinker, guided by political theory or whim (depending on one's own view of the judge's values), or a passive respecter of the empirical results (of, say, market behavior theory) about how conflict might be minimized and decent chances at satisfaction maintained. How is it possible at the same time to be both an active thinker, drawing on ideals, and a passive deferrer to strict precedents and empirical results? Is the interpretivist picture of an ideal judge coherent?

There is quite likely no straightforward answer to these questions independently of close critical readings of what judges and other political actors have done and might do in furthering the ways of a democratic political community. Dworkin himself discusses in detail both the complex values that have informed democratic political practice and how judges either have addressed or might address in hard cases the question of how best to further those values in a particular present. The chief point of Dworkin's emphases on interpretation and judgment is that there is no "algorithm for the courtroom" or for the legislative assembly:[9] to see what might best be done in any particular case will require a reflective survey of what has been done in past cases coupled with intimate normative assessments of how best to go on now. Still, how does one know how to go on?

Wittgenstein on Judgment

"A philosophical problem," Wittgenstein writes in *Philosophical Investigations,* "has the form: 'I don't know my way about' " (PI § 123). Throughout *Philosophical Investigations,* the condition of the human subject in attempting to come to judgment, both as a self-responsible agent and in relation to ongoing linguistic practice, is continually reenacted.[10] The protagonist of

Philosophical Investigations carries on an internal dialogue with himself, in which he seeks to make judgments in accordance with *both* rationally well-founded standards for correctness *and* the more flexible ways of common practice. This internal dialogue is broken off, rather than concluded in a final discovery of how we are to judge, so that, insofar as we identify with the voices of this internal dialogue, we are cast as subjects for whom judgment is always a problem, involving the claiming of responsibility, and never something properly determined by a method. Hence this internal dialogue in *Philosophical Investigations* offers us—to the extent that we might identify with its voices—a chance to recognize in a new way what we do and might do in judging, in politics as in other domains.

One prominent thought in this internal dialogue is that in attempting to apply our words, we should attend patiently to ordinary uses of language, rather than trying to discover philosophical superfacts (for example, about forms or essences) that are properly legislative for ordinary practice. For example, "What does it mean to know what a game is? . . . Isn't my knowledge, my concept of a game, completely expressed in the explanations that I could give? That is, in my describing examples of various kinds of game; shewing how all sorts of other games can be constructed on the analogy of these; saying that I should scarcely include this or this among games; and so on" (PI § 75).

Here knowing what a game is does not imply knowing an explicitly formulated definition, vouchsafed by philosophical investigation into essences, but rather simply being able to apply the word "game" to various sorts of ordinary cases. "One gives examples and intends them to be taken in a particular way.—I do not, however, mean by this that he is supposed to see in those examples that common thing which I—for some reason—was unable to express; but that he is now to *employ* those examples in a particular way. Here giving examples is not an *indirect* means of explaining—in default of a better" (PI § 71).

One's knowledge of a concept or of the application of a word is *expressed in* ordinary practice, in doing *what is done:* "there is a way of grasping a rule which is *not* an *interpretation,* but which is exhibited in what we call 'obeying the rule' and 'going against it' in actual cases" (PI § 201). If this is so, then the best we can do is to stop hunting about for justifications of linguistic and conceptual practice, ordinary or otherwise, and instead clear up "misunderstandings concerning the use of words, caused, among other things, by certain analogies between the forms of expression in different regions of language" (PI § 90). It is in ongoing ordinary practice alone that criteria of correctness are laid down; there is no point or possibility of assessing, explaining, or justifying that practice. "Philosophy may in no way interfere with the actual use of language; it can in the end only describe it" (PI § 124).

This line of thinking may well appear to be of little help when we are actually faced with hard cases of judgment. In politics, it looks like an endorsement of conservatism or traditionalism, and the impression that Wittgenstein is somehow conservative or traditionalist, especially in politics, is not uncommon. But this line of thinking about judgment in *Philosophical Investigations* is *not* the end of the story. There is a second line of thinking according to which it is not so easy always to rest in doing what is ordinarily done. "You will find it difficult," we are reminded, or Wittgenstein reminds himself, "to hit upon . . . a convention [for the exact use of a word]; at least any that satisfies you" (PI § 88). While this remark reminds us to attend to varieties of actual use rather than to seek any explicit definition of at least some concept words, it also suggests that the convention to *do whatever is done in using a word* is not satisfying either. One can "adduce only exterior facts about language" (PI § 120), rather than explaining or justifying ordinary usages. This in turn means that those usages seem to hover in the air. They come from us, or from our engagements with the world. Surely there are questions to be asked about how they arise and about how they might best be continued, especially in relation to hard cases. If these questions turn out to be unanswerable, then that leaves us disappointed with ordinary usage as it stands, leaves us wanting either a normative theory of what we ought to say or an empirical account of how many people are naturally caused to say what they say. This want or wish goes unappeased by the simple recommendation to attend to what we say. This difficulty is insisted on in *Philosophical Investigations* itself. "We are therefore as it were entangled in our own rules. This entanglement in our rules is what we want to understand (i.e. get a clear view of)" (PI § 125). Our wanting to understand does not lapse in the face of the varieties of ordinary practice that we encounter, but is rather nourished by them. Hence, despite the fact that it is fruitless, we *do* "predicate of the thing what lies in the method of representing it" (PI § 104). We seek to find *in* the thing some *essence* that *requires* us to judge it to be what it is, rather than resting content with the thought that criteria for judgment are only laid down in ongoing practices. We seek either a normative theory of what we ought to do or a causal explanation of what we in fact do in using language. It is not so easy—as the continuing self-interrogations, the continuing swerves by the protagonist into and back out of philosophy show—to stop doing philosophy. There is nothing, these swerves suggest, deeper than ordinary practice that is available to guide it, and yet that practice does not run smoothly for us on its own: we want more.

No one has been more continuously and closely attentive to these opposed lines of thinking about ordinary practice in the text of *Philosophical Investigations* than Stanley Cavell. One way of characterizing Wittgenstein's efforts that Cavell has offered is that Wittgenstein "undertook to trace . . . the ways in which, in investigating ourselves, we *are led* to speak 'outside language games,' consider expressions apart from, and in opposition to, the natural forms of life which give those expressions the force they have."[11] What Cavell has in mind here—in speaking of how, according to Wittgenstein, we *are led* to speak outside the ordinary—is the philosophical search, in thinking about our prospects (political and otherwise), for standing terms or principles that are decisively authoritative in setting norms for our practice. People ordinarily do all sorts of different things. In philosophy one is tempted to try to discern what they all rationally ought to do, no matter what. Perhaps one's succumbing to this temptation is motivated by a fear of the unruliness and unintelligibility of the muddle of ordinary practice as it stands; perhaps it is motivated by a wish that one should oneself possess perfect authority; perhaps it is motivated by a sense of the pains and difficulties of bearing responsibility within ordinary practice, where the normative principles of correctness are unarticulated or unclear and hence where challenges to what one does are always possible. In any case, succumbing to this temptation and thinking philosophically about what all rational creatures ought to do is natural enough, even human, all too human. We *are led* to speak "outside language games."

What then in turn mostly happens, however, is that this effort misfires. Seeking to think, judge, and speak with perfect authority, somehow in touch with absolute norms, "we lose . . . a full realization of what we are saying; we no longer know what *we* mean."[12] That is, rather than speaking within the terms of ordinary practice—conversationally or dialectically, one might say—where challenges are always possible, we instead seek to speak as more than a finite and situated subject. Hence we come to speak inhumanly, as we refuse the role of an ordinary speaker in relation to an ordinary interlocutor. Nothing, again, is more natural than to be tempted to do this. But when we do it, we lose a sense of ourselves as finite subjects in conversational and other practical relations to other finite subjects. The only cure for this loss is to return to ways of ordinary thought and interlocution, with all their unclarities, imperfections, and pains. But to do this is to return to the very scene in which the temptations and wishes to speak otherwise, to speak absolutely, arose.

Hence there is in us, in Cavell's reading, something that is expressed and exemplified within the continuing drama of *Philosophical Investigations:* "[an] irreconcilability . . . between our dissatisfaction with the ordinary and our satisfaction in it, between speaking outside and inside language games, which is to say, the irreconcilability of the two voices (at least two) in the *Investigations,* the writer with his other, the interlocutor, the fact that poses a great task, the continuous task of Wittgenstein's prose, oscillating between vanity and humility."[13]

Read in the light of this sense of the irreconcilability for us of our dissatisfaction with the ordinary and our satisfaction in it, both intellectualist idealism and empiricist naturalism appear as misbegotten efforts—albeit inevitable ones—to close or foreclose this irreconcilability. Intellectualist idealism, of which classical political theory is an instance, offers us the form of the good, the essence of the just state, *the* aim of human life, intellectually grasped and thence to be realized in practice guided by that grasp; all that remains is administration. "The Form of the Good . . . must be reckoned to be for all the cause of all that is right and beautiful, . . . and he who is to act intelligently in public or in private must see it."[14] The trouble with this proposal is that it removes us from our role as finite human speakers always working out with others critically the terms of going on with our lives, and in doing so it makes us (all too humanly) inhuman. Empiricist naturalism, maintaining contact with what is ordinarily done, offers us results about how most effectively to satisfy preferences as they stand—about how to manage conflict or distribute scarce resources efficiently, blocking no trades. The trouble with this proposal is that it scants our powers for reflecting and for desiring otherwise, more deeply and humanly than one once did, say, as a child.

The advice of *Philosophical Investigations,* as Cavell reads it, is then to "see how philosophical explanations [intellectualist and empiricist alike] will seek to distract you from your interests (ordinary, scientific, aesthetic); how they counterfeit necessity. That this advice is all but impossible to take is Wittgenstein's subject."[15] In an odd way, the truth of this situation—that we remain caught up in that irreconcilability, both able to reflect and act beyond the ordinary or departing from it, but never to do so perfectly and alone—is expressed better by the skeptic than by either the intellectualist idealist or the empiricist naturalist. The skeptic at least sees that there is something wrong, that we live in a condition in which we continue to wish for something that continually does not come true. "The threat or truth of skepticism [is] that it names our wish (and the possibility of our wishing) to strip ourselves of the responsibility we have in meaning (or in failing to mean) one thing, or one way, rather than another."[16]

How are we then, humanly, to live with this wish, no longer entranced by counterfeit necessities? Cavell's suggestion is that we do live with it, both as individuals and as communities of interrelated subjects, by swerving back and forth between moments of acceptance of the ordinary and moments of criticism of it. Cavell's own name for this ongoing process of swerving is *the argument of the ordinary:* the argument of the ordinary with itself over its possible perfection, carried on in and through us. "The human capacity—and the drive—both to affirm and to deny our criteria constitute the argument of the ordinary."[17]

Living out this capacity and drive involves a double movement. Sometimes there are times "to be the one who goes first."[18] The present conditions—that is, present practices and the criteria in use there—have grown repressive, stultifying, or conformist. It is time to mark out a new path, to think and thence to propose new criteria. The risks of such a path are isolation and madness, failing to speak as a genuinely human subject at all. Hence there are also times to wait, to find one's voice only in its engagement with what is ordinarily said and thought and done. To go on in thought alone and against the sways of the ordinary is to risk unintelligibility; to remain within those sways is to risk human nonexistence by falling into thoughtless conformity.

To move between and within these risks is to participate in the argument of the ordinary. This participation involves seeking further intelligibility both of oneself to oneself and of the community to itself. Cultivation or perfection is the ongoing aim of this participation, as one seeks both *actively and independently* to think and judge and also to think and judge cooperatively, in reciprocity and acknowledgment with others who actively think and judge likewise. To do all this is further to take part in *the conversation of justice:*

> Perfectionism's emphasis on culture or cultivation . . . is to be understood in connection with this search for intelligibility [to oneself], or say this search for direction in what seems a scene of moral chaos, the scene of the dark place in which one has lost one's way. Here also the importance to perfectionism of the friend, the figure, let us say, whose conviction in one's moral intelligibility draws one to discover it, to find words and deeds in which to express it, in which to enter the conversation of justice.[19]

Where, at last, does this picture of our plight as subjects leave political theory, political science, and political judgment? In one way, interpretivist political judgment seems to be the best form of thinking about politics, the form most faithful to our ongoing engagements in the argument of the ordinary and the conversation of justice. The best we can do, it seems, is to demonstrate interpretively and narratively how our practices have expressed our most important political commitments in the past and how they might be continued or recast so as best to further their expression at present, just as Dworkin suggests.

Yet this result faces two related difficulties. It has, first of all, too much the air of a triumphant metaperspective. "At last," it proclaims, "we know what we're doing when we're thinking well politically; we're thinking narratively and interpretively." As perhaps with most metaperspectives, this one seems not to offer us much help in coping with any particular present problem of political practice. Instead of engaging *in* the conversation of justice (as he does elsewhere), Dworkin as a theorist offers us more an illusion of method (and its securities) than anything that actually generates a result.

Here the interpretivist metaperspective seems to encourage distance from both the practices to be attended to and from full engagement in any practice of close interpretation. It's all just another interpretation, another story, whatever one does. This thought forecloses the *agon* of seeking intelligibility to oneself in and through one's conversations with others about how one's culture might best be perfected toward becoming a fit home for human agency. It is not so easy to escape this *agon* into the thought that anything one says will be an interpretation, and if one does so escape then one is no longer quite in the conversation. In contrast to any stance of detachment, Wittgenstein in *Philosophical Investigations* presents himself not as a master of either interpretations or interpretive strategies, but rather as caught up in the contending claims that are made *on him* by various accounts of judgment. Likewise, Cavell engages densely with specific literary and philosophical texts, in doing so bearing a sense that he is letting himself be read by them. Not only must we generate interpretations and claim to have reasons, we must also be open to the claims made on us by texts and *their* reasons.

What is "consideration" in the theory of contract in this hard case, or what is "the best interest of the child" in contemporary family law? These are substantive, arguable questions. Disagreements about answers to them arise out of, and are woven into, disagreements in ways of life. To say, in response to these questions, "Construct the best interpretation you can of the meanings of these phrases that are latent in our practice," is to step aside from the substantive debate, not to enter it. Entering the debate is inseparable from living argumentatively within its terms, in one contending way rather than another. As Pierre Bourdieu notes, "the art of applying knowledge, and applying it aptly in practice . . . is inseparable from an overall manner of acting, or living, inseparable from a habitus."[20] Dworkin's methodology seeks to rise above the entanglements that come with living within contending habituses, and it fails.

Second, the interpretivist metaperspective and the injunction always to tell the best story one can about past and prospective practice misses the fact that both theoretical idealizations and empirical results will figure within any good story. This is the obverse of the first difficulty: urged alone, interpretivism is too empty and abstractly distancing; actually done closely—it now appears—it is continuous with both ideal theory and empirical inquiry. In attempting interpretively to develop and exercise political judgment it will sometimes be important to articulate intellectually a new ideal (or a new version of an ideal) of how we might best arrange our common life; it will sometimes be important to be the one who goes first to denounce present injustice and to point the way forward. Religiously motivated abolitionists, say, in the grip of an ideal of comprehensive human reciprocity, are examples of figures who, by forcing imaginative confrontation with the facts of slavery, went first. Sometimes it will be important to change past practice radically.

But it will also sometimes be important to carry out and take seriously straightforward empirical investigations into what human beings actually do care about most deeply; it will sometimes be important to take seriously the ways of the ordinary. Empirical inquirers who have reminded us that most people care to have a modicum of private life to pursue happiness as they see fit, or that people typically seek advantages for their children about whom they care deeply, are good examples of those who have rightly chastened utopian would-be engineers of human souls who have supposed we might follow an ideal of universal comradeship, say. Sometimes it will be important to remind ourselves of what we mostly just do prefer in our social arrangements.

Judging in accordance with the reminder that we are always to construct the best interpretation we can of what we have been and might be seems to miss the force of the more committed political insights that stem from both ideal political theory and empirical political science. Each of the three styles of political thinking—political theory, political science, and political judgment—depends on the others for appropriate correction of its own partialities of insight. Each of them figures rightly in certain moments of the argument of the ordinary and of the conversation of justice. Cavell remarks that he thinks of "philosophy as the achievement of the unpolemical, of the refusal to take sides in metaphysical positions."[21] That this is an achievement—the refusing of counterfeit necessities in favor of the acceptance of thinking and listening as a human subject in relation to human subjects—albeit one that it is almost impossible for us to manage, is something we might learn from Wittgenstein's voices.

What follows, then, from the condition of the human person that is enacted in *Philosophical Investigations* is, I think, a kind of substantive or weak perfectionist liberalism in the style of Joseph Raz,[22] as opposed to the neutralist, proceduralist, rights-oriented liberalism of Dworkin. Political proceduralism in general faces the following dilemma. Either the procedures urged for resolving disputes and establishing sociopolitical arrangements are sharply specified: in that case they will reasonably appear to some to be tyrannical in forwarding an uncongenial way of life; or the procedures urged will be fully neutral among contending ways of life, but empty, both incapable of yielding resolutions and incapable of commanding allegiance from within a way of life.[23] Here the fate of putatively necessary political procedures parallels the fates of the necessary explanations of thought and language that are traced in *Philosophical Investigations;* such necessary explanations haunt and tempt us but never quite coherently engage wholly with the ordinary.

The way out of proceduralism and toward substantive liberalism is then to see different ways of life as reasonably contending ways of embodying the good. These ways of life are in genuine contention with one another. It is not easy for the Amish fully to see the value of the life of those living within consumer society and vice versa. Affirmative tolerance and talking will often be in order,[24] including feeling in oneself measures of both resistance and attraction to what is other. So will waiting: sometimes there will be nothing to say, though nonetheless the hope of reciprocity and social perfection does not lapse. So will a political framework of mutual respect: hence the liberalism. But this framework will express a commitment to a substantive good—personal autonomy;[25] it will not of itself neutrally settle conflicts about the scope and value of this good. No political decision procedure will. But then human life is complicated and interesting, in its entanglement in the conversation of justice.[26]

7

Doing without Knowing

Feminism's Politics of the Ordinary

Linda M. G. Zerilli

> A *picture* held us captive. And we could not get outside it, for it lay in our language and language seemed to repeat it to us inexorably.
> —Ludwig Wittgenstein, *Philosophical Investigations*

A good friend of mine tells me that she visited a website that was recommended to her by a female-to-male transsexual whom she had met on a female body-building discussion list. The site included a summary of the argument from a book called *The Apartheid of Sex* by Martine Rothblatt.[1] There was an elaborate sort of questionnaire followed by a grid that showed there was no valid form of argument or proof that could answer the question, What is a woman? with any kind of rational consistency. There was also a new way to think of people, regardless of sex/gender, and this was as individuals, each with a different combination of three aspects that were called something like nurturing, aggressivity, and eroticism. Everybody has these in different proportions, and may couple with others with complementary assortments. "How's that for an alternative to the heteronormative myth of woman?" comments my friend, while adding: "And I think it totally works." Convinced by the argument, will she surrender her belief in woman?

I assign an article by Anne Fausto-Sterling, "The Five Sexes: Why Male and Female Are Not Enough," to my undergraduate class in feminist theory.[2] The feminist biologist shows that at least 4 percent of the population are born intersexed, that is, with some mixture of male and female characteristics. Depending on how one classifies them, there are five sexes, maybe more. Our culture's surgical enforcement of the idea of either male or female on the intersexed infant is symptomatic of its deep investment in sexual dimorphism. Proponents of that idea say it reflects the facts of biology, but Fausto-Sterling says it is a social norm posing as a fact of nature, a norm for which the documented existence of intersexed bodies is a scientific scandal. And that these intersexed bodies really exist is a scientific fact, one that can be proven with a correspondence theory of (sexual) truth. Will my students now relinquish their belief in a world that is naturally and exclusively divided into male and female?

I propose these vignettes of "gender trouble" as a place from which to begin thinking about the state of contemporary feminist theory. I deeply appreciate the efforts of thinkers like Anne Fausto-Sterling and Martine Rothblatt, but increasingly I have come to see the limits of that sort of theory for feminism. I mean the sort of theory that presents tightly structured arguments carefully documenting the logical and empirical exceptions to the rule of sex and gender in an attempt to prove that sexual dimorphism—like every effort to define woman—is a fraud. I want to say: You can't get to what is truly fascinating in both Fausto-Sterling's and Rothblatt's accounts—an imaginative space in which intersexed bodies would not be immediate candidates for surgery, and in which "individual" is not just another term for man—(simply) by traveling the route of logical argument, epistemic justification, or scientific verification. Why? Because the powerful hold that "the straight mind" (as Monique Wittig calls it) has on our subjectivity and our practices—our thinking, acting, and desiring—is not dependent, finally, on a network of knowledge claims. These claims exist (in the millions, in fact), and one can make counterclaims (as feminists have done and should continue to do).

But what if it turned out that these knowledge claims and counterclaims themselves amounted to little more than window-dressing over prior agreements in judgment about what counts as a woman and what counts as a man? What if all those claims and counterclaims turned out to share a lot more than might at first seem apparent, and more than those who make them appear to think? What if our ability to judge these claims and counterclaims were somehow parasitic on a whole series of assumptions that do not enter our frame of reference as objects that can be contemplated, debated, verified, or refuted? What if that frame were the invisible "scaffolding of our thoughts," to cite Wittgenstein, the ungrounded ground that doesn't get questioned, and that keeps the various language-games of sex and gender going? (OC § 211).

Suppose I say: "There are men and women in the world." It is quite likely that you will wonder: what other interesting information does she have for us? Or, what on earth does she mean to claim by telling us that? Is it supposed to be an empirical proposition?[3] Then again, because you are a sophisticated audience, because this is a scholarly book, and because you may know that I go under the sign of a feminist theorist, you might be willing to grant that statement as (potentially) meaningful, as introducing a meaningful statement, or simply as one academic's idea of an opening joke. But if I were to announce to the stranger who sits next to me on the subway: "There are men and women in this car," that stranger would quickly change seats. I would most likely be taken for a lunatic. It is just so obvious (that there are men and women here, in this car)! What could an appropriate reply be? "I know, but thank you for reminding me." No one is going to say "I know" to a statement like that unless she or he thought that there was some way in which I could think that she or he might not know. But what would it mean not to know something like that? What does it mean to *know* it? How does one know that one knows?

You will recognize in these questions the skeptic's objections. Second-wave feminism is deeply indebted to the modern skeptical tradition, which raises the problem of our knowledge of the external world (and of other minds), and concludes that we know nothing. I will address various aspects of skepticism in the course of my discussion. I should say at the start, however, that my essay concerns not philosophical skepticism as such but the extent to which contemporary feminist debates about gender are shaped by—and trapped within—the frame of the traditional epistemological project that generates the skeptical problematic.[4] I am generally concerned with the way in which philosophical categories, especially those relating to foundationalism, have come to define and to limit feminist understandings of politics. More specifically, I want to explore how certain epistemic commitments have come to define discussions about the category of women.

What I would like to emphasize at this point, then, is that important strands of contemporary feminism employ the skeptic's deceptively simple question, How do you know? to unsettle the sedimented certainties of everyday life, one of which is that "there are men and women in the world." If this claim sounds strange from a feminist perspective, it is not because what is claimed is just so obvious but because it is not, where "obvious" means taken for granted. That's what I call the feminist practice of defamiliarization, the early master of which was Simone de Beauvoir. That's also one reason why savvy feminists will often wrap the word "women" in scarequotes, as if those diacritical marks defended against predicating of the object what lies in the mode of representing it, as if one could thereby divest oneself of the predicative moment of all judgment and speaking. I put "women" in quotation marks to indicate that I know—smart feminist theorist that I am—that "women" as a certain kind of (universal) being does not exist (to say nothing of "Woman"). I want to mark the distance between me and this word that I speak but that invariably ends up speaking me, that is, on my behalf.

In contemporary feminist theory, quite a lot is at stake in the word "women." Once herald as the successor to "Woman" (the masculinist monolith) and as the mark of a political constituency bound by a shared identity and common experience, "women" has lost its appeal as a category of feminist theory and as the subject of feminist praxis. The debates over "the category of women" have taken on the tone of a war of differences in which each attempt to theorize is subjected to accusations, which more or less cluster around the problem of exclusion: every theoretical and political claim to the category brings with it a normative conception of women which excludes those who do not conform. What has been rejected by a wide array of feminists is the notion that there is a woman part of me which connects me to other women and which is somehow distinct from the race part of me or, for that matter, from any other aspect of my social identity and experience. What has been likewise rejected is the idea that the woman part of me (gender) is a cultural interpretation of a biological constant (sex).[5] The result of these critiques has been the collapse of the category of women as the ground of political action—that is, as far as certain feminist theorists are concerned—and tremendous skepticism toward the sex/gender distinction as a conceptual tool of feminist analysis.

In the view of some feminists, however, the price for abandoning the coherence of the category of women has been the loss of a coherent feminist politics. Who is the subject of feminism if not women? How can feminism organize in the name of no one and without a sense of collective interests? The debates go back and forth, circling around the question of whether one does need to posit a subject (women) in advance of political action; whether one could posit such a unitary subject without excluding some individuals (typically those that do not conform to the white, heterosexual, middle-class standard); whether one does have to lay down foundations before acting politically, to know who "we" are and what "we" want, as it were. The essentialist scare of the 1980s gave way to the poststructuralist scare of the 1990s, in which feminist critics of foundationalism were accused of having taken things too far. The idea of using the category of women for strategic purposes (sometimes called strategic essentialism) took on appeal as feminists looked for a way out of the dilemma that the collapse of women as the subject of feminism presented for collective action.

Considering "women" as a strategic category of feminist politics, I am struck by the implicit assumption that one could think like a skeptic but act like a foundationalist. The logic of this position runs as follows: As a feminist theorist I would doubt the category of women, but as a feminist activist I would take it as the ground of political action. Hence the category is strategic. What is significant about this position is not only that it assumes that one could control the meanings that flow from the pragmatic use of the category of women,[6] but also that it reflects a characteristically Humean attitude toward knowledge: namely, that there is an irreconcilable conflict between our everyday attitudes toward the world around us, on the one hand, and the critical attitude we adopt as soon as we stop to reflect on them, on the other. For Hume, skepticism is philosophically irrefutable but "practically barren." There are two ways of looking at the world, and the gap cannot be breached between what we simply take for granted in the course of ordinary life and what we know to be the case when we reflect philosophically, namely, that all is in doubt. For example, I might question the existence of the table in front of me and still take it for granted as the writing surface on which I pen the essay that puts it into doubt.

Hume thought that the doubts we raise in the act of reflection were as natural as the certainty with which we act on our beliefs in everyday life. In his view, then, skepticism is part of the human condition.[7] Questions can be raised, however, about the conditions under which Western philosophy has raised doubts about the external world: more often than not these have taken the form of extreme abstraction, decontextualization, and radical subjectivism. In this reflective stance, all that is real is our experience, and, according to the skeptic, we cannot move from our experience to the objective existence of physical objects. (How do I know that I am really sitting at my desk writing this essay? It could be a dream or a hallucination. I could be a "brain in a vat," receiving external stimuli. And so on.) At the center of philosophical discussions is what Stanley Cavell calls a "generic object," an object that is chosen precisely because of its familiarity (say a table or a chair).[8] In these discussions the generic object, ripped from its context in the ordinary, becomes paradigmatic. Generalizing from the generic object considered in utter abstraction to the object as it is given to us in a multiplicity of everyday contexts, we forget the context and have only our subjective experience of the object before us—and from there it is not a long step to raising questions about its existence and essence.

Working both with and against this philosophical tradition, feminist theory has not been exactly immune to this theoretical practice of decontextualization and abstraction from the ordinary. Now what happens when the generic object under consideration is not a table or a chair but "women" or "woman"? Consider the founding text of second-wave feminism, Simone de Beauvoir's *The Second Sex*, which opens by wondering whether "women still exist" and by posing the metaphysical question "What is a woman?" Taking up the generic object that has occupied the minds of (male) philosophers, Beauvoir repeats a wide range of statements on Woman in the hope of exposing them as nonsensical. In the introduction to part II of the text, "L'expérience vécue" (Lived experience), Beauvoir cautions her readers that, in contrast to the philosophers (and the scientists and all the other masculine authorities on what a woman is), "when I use the words *woman* or *feminine* I evidently refer to no archetype, no changeless essence whatever; the reader must understand the phrase 'in the present state of education and custom' after most of my statements. It is not our concern here to proclaim eternal verities, but rather to describe the common basis that underlies every individual feminine existence."[9] And that attempt to articulate contingent commonalities in the place of eternal verities is where all the power and all the problems of second-wave feminist theory began.

The Second Sex is a powerful work because it confronts (the masculinist myth of) "Woman" with (the feminist category of) "woman"; and the latter, unlike the former, is not assimilable to a natural kind. The text is powerful because it confronts the generic object of the philosophers (Woman) with the critical object of feminist theory (woman), and the latter, unlike the former, is rooted in what Beauvoir called lived experience.[10] Notwithstanding these strengths as well as Beauvoir's advice about proper reading protocols, feminists have come increasingly to doubt that there is in fact a difference between her use of words such as *woman* and that of the masculine authorities. In those controversial accounts of femininity (e.g., motherhood as a narcissistic flight from freedom or the female body as abject immanence), just *who* is speaking? we might well ask. Despite Beauvoir's claim to distinguish "eternal verities" from contingent commonalities, it is not at all clear where the myth called Woman ends and the empirical beings called women begin.

Whether vilified or admired (or both), Beauvoir's text framed the terms of the second-wave feminist debate. The difficulty she faced trying to distinguish between the social realities of women's lives and the masculinist myth of femininity speaks to what Teresa de Lauretis calls "the complex and contradictory relation of women to Woman."[11] It is this relation that Beauvoir navigates in the opening pages to *The Second Sex* when, refusing both essentialism (the idea of "fixed entities that determine given characteristics, such as those ascribed to woman") and nominalism ("women are merely the human beings arbitrarily designated by the word *woman*"), she finds—to her own surprise—that to "face the question: what is a woman?" she has to declare: " 'I am a woman'; on this truth must be based all further discussion."[12]

Declaring "I am a woman," Beauvoir implicitly recognizes something important about the conditions of doubt, of feminist critical practice: namely, that something must stand fast if something else is to be questioned. What she wants to question (Woman) is not an empirical proposition or set of propositions; it is not a knowledge claim that can be refuted or a scientific thesis that can be falsified; it is not something Beauvoir can locate, isolate, and undo with her amazing powers of philosophical rigor and rhetorical brilliance. For Woman is everywhere and nowhere, part of a world-picture, the taken-for-granted background that forms the context of Beauvoir's own practices of thinking, speaking, and acting. What would it mean to raise doubts about something like that? Skepticism is no answer: "To decline to accept such notions as the eternal feminine . . . is not to deny that . . . women exist today—this denial does not represent a liberation for those concerned, but rather a flight from reality."[13] More to the point: for Simone de Beauvoir, a woman, to deny that women exist would be like effacing the conditions of her speech, like ceasing to exist.

Declaring "I am a woman," Beauvoir recognized the paradox of speaking for women, which is to say, the (background) conditions of the language-game of gender that she was trying to disrupt. Beauvoir had to make the claim "I am a woman" in order not to be Woman. By saying, "I [Simone de Beauvoir] am a woman," by saying the obvious, the author of *The Second Sex* called attention to the certainty with which her readers assume it. She anticipated that they would identify her as a woman author anyway, all the better to discredit her, as in "You think thus and so because you are a woman."[14] Inhabiting the discredited place of woman, Beauvoir also achieved some distance from it, not by denying that women exist or putting the word "woman" in quotation marks, but by making claims from that (impossible) enunciative position: "I am a woman and I say . . ." In other words, she spoke and she made judgments. Beauvoir questioned the language-game of gender, but she did not do so in words—or from a place—that pretends to float free of some sort of context.

When Luce Irigaray, writing thirty years after Beauvoir, is asked, "Are you a woman?" her reply is: "A typical question. A man's question?" It is, in any case, a question that she can only refer back to him and say: "It's your question." When asked, "What is a woman?" Irigaray responds: "I believe I've already answered that there is no way I would 'answer' that question. The question 'what is . . . ?' is the question—the metaphysical question—to which the feminine does not allow itself to submit."[15] Irigaray refuses the question because, in her view, its grammar structures what could so much as count as an answer. Still, when asked what has prompted and sustained her work, Irigaray replies:

> I am a woman. I am a being sexualized as feminine. I am sexualized female. The motivation of my work lies in the impossibility of articulating such a statement; in the fact that its utterance is in some way senseless, inappropriate, indecent. Either because woman is never the attribute of the verb *to be* nor *sexualized female* a quality of *being,* or because *am a woman* is not predicated of *I,* or because *I am sexualized* excludes the feminine gender. In other words, the articulation of the reality of my sex is impossible in discourse, and for a structural, eidetic reason. My sex is removed, at least as the property of a subject, from the predicative mechanism that assures discursive coherence.[16]

And yet there is no other place from which Luce Irigaray, a woman, might speak.

Part of what concerns Irigaray here is what Wittgenstein calls grammar. "Grammar tells what kind of object something is" inasmuch as it defines what can be meaningfully said about it (PI § 373). Arbitrary and autonomous, neither reasonable nor unreasonable, "grammar constitutes our form of representation, it lays down what counts as an intelligible description of reality, and is hence not subject to empirical refutation."[17] What is at issue in grammar is not a metaphysical given but our form of representation, which sets limits to what it makes sense to say, and which is held in place—I do not say justified—not through grand theories but small acts: daily, habitual practices of speaking, acting, and judging. Irigaray recognizes the restraints that grammar places on the use of the word "woman" and the nonsensical nature of making claims that grammar prohibits. Saying "*I* am a woman" is, for Irigaray, as nonsensical as saying "bachelors are married men" is for Wittgenstein. The feminist project is not to find a place in the existing grammar where "am a woman" would be predicated of "I," but to put the conditions of predication themselves in question, to "jam the machinery," and to refuse the metaphysical lure of the verb, "to be."

Irigaray's passionate call for "another 'syntax,' another 'grammar' of culture"[18] entails no redefinition of woman—which follows from the metaphysical "what is . . . ?"—but the creation of a "space, previously non-existent and still 'unreal,' in which radically different speculation can take place," to borrow Lucy Sargisson's account of utopian thought.[19] But that space is unreal only to the extent that it is not yet realized through our actual practices of speaking. There is nothing in the grammar of woman—in the rule for the use of the word—that determines how we (must) speak, which means that there is nothing in the word "woman" (or "women") that determines what it can mean when spoken in various contexts. A rule, as Wittgenstein argues, is not an essence that governs our practices of speaking from above; it is a standard of correctness that is sustained by countless practical instances of individual acts of speaking (PI §§ 200–201).[20] A rule, like the general form of representation of which it is a part, is subject to change, but that change is extraordinarily difficult, precisely because it is not achieved through the force of arguments: grammar antecedes all such practices of justification. Changing the grammar or rule for the use of the word "woman" will entail not its falsification but the introduction of a new concept—actually, a new way of seeing what has been there all along.

Although every act of meaningful speech will entail following a rule—If I say, "Woman is a color," I will not speak meaningfully, though one could imagine contexts in which that utterance might be meaningful—what makes possible Irigaray's call for another syntax from within the interstices of the given syntax is the indeterminacy of the rule itself. Not only is a rule not (metaphysically or conventionally) fixed, according to Wittgenstein, it is not even intrinsically better than (what within our form of representation counts as) deviant practice. Use cannot justify a rule, let alone some essence of language. Alternative rules or forms of representation are not irrational in any absolute sense. To call for another grammar of sexual difference is to make "a passionate commitment to [another] system of reference" (CV 64) and to open oneself to a new way of seeing, but not because it more accurately symbolizes woman (or the essence of reality). Luce Irigaray is calling for change at the level not of theory and knowledge but of imagination and action. The "feminine" is groundless: from its "locus" one does not contest Truth with new truths, Reason with better reasons, or the myth of Woman with the empirical reality of women. If you want to elaborate another society, a new form of life, another syntax, you don't need another argument, you need a sense of humor. *"Isn't the phallic tantamount to the seriousness of meaning?* . . . Besides, women among themselves begin by laughing. To escape from a pure and simple reversal of the masculine position ["a utopia of historical reversal"] means in any case not to forget to laugh. Not to forget that the dimension of desire, of pleasure, is untranslatable, unrepresentable, irrecuperable in the 'seriousness'—the adequacy, the univocity, the truth . . . —of a discourse that claims to state its meaning."[21]

At the risk of turning Irigaray's call for laughter into a serious matter, I want to emphasize its affirmative character for feminism. The laughter is not nihilistic; it is an expression of creative potential that enables us to distance ourselves from words, to be at odds with any given utterance, and to assume own unique attitude toward it, but without assuming the detached position of the skeptic. This distance is crucial when the topic is Woman. As both Beauvoir and Irigaray in their different ways recognize, Woman is a mythology. A mythology cannot be defeated in the sense that one wins over one's opponent through the rigor of logic or the force of the evidence; a mythology cannot be defeated through arguments that would *reveal* it as groundless belief (e.g., the postmetaphysical feminist project). A mythology *is* utterly groundless, hence stable. What characterizes a mythology is not so much its crude or naive character—mythologies can be extremely complex and sophisticated—but, rather, its capacity to elude our practices of verification and refutation. A mythology, as Jacques Bouveresse observes, is the force of an idea, a form of representation, a manner of speaking that provides a universally valid explanation of my world, convincing me "a priori because of the desire, and not the thought, that it should be able to account for every case."[22] Strange as it sounds, it is a lot easier to adopt a new mythology (with equally universal explanations) than it is to fine-tune an old one (make it more sensitive to the particular case). To understand why this is so, I turn now to Wittgenstein's account of the difference between knowledge and belief, and come back to the question: Do I know that there are men and there are women in the world?

The issue Wittgenstein puts before us is this: Is it possible that a great deal of our world, as it is now, is made up of propositions that can be neither justified nor doubted, and that are neither reasonable nor unreasonable, since their certainty is presupposed in all judging and at the origin of all our language-games? "I am a human being," "I have two hands," "The earth has existed for a long time"—these are some examples of the class of propositions that Wittgenstein called "hinge propositions" and that he examined in his response to G. E. Moore's refutation of skepticism and defense of common sense. Wittgenstein agreed with Moore that one could be *certain* of these sorts of propositions, but he contested the idea that one could *know* them. Among other requirements, the claim to know something entails being able to give reasons for how one knows: to know means being able to give grounds, evidence (see OC §§ 15–18, 21, 550). But what sorts of reasons or grounds or evidence could I possibly give for claiming, as Moore did: "Here is one hand. Here is another. Therefore two hands exist"? Wittgenstein showed that Moore's "proof" does not guarantee anything. It merely invites the skeptical objection: How do you know? As Wittgenstein wryly puts it: "If you do know that *here is one hand,* we'll grant you all the rest" (OC § 1).

Exploring the space between skepticism and foundationalism, Wittgenstein examines propositions for which no proof can be given, but which can be asserted with no small measure of unshakable conviction. "What would it be like to doubt now whether I have two hands? Why can't I imagine it at all? What would I believe if I didn't believe that? So far I have no system at all within which this doubt might exist" (OC § 247). "My having two hands is . . . as certain as anything I could produce in evidence for it." Moreover, it "isn't just that *I* believe in this way that I have two hands, but that every reasonable person does" (OC §§ 250, 252).[23] If someone were to doubt that he had two hands, if he were to keep looking at them to make sure they were still there, "we should not be sure whether we ought to call that doubting"; we would more than likely call it a "mental disturbance." Likewise, if someone said "he doubted whether he had a body, I should take him to be a half-wit. But I shouldn't know what it would mean to try to convince him that he had one" (OC §§ 255, 73, 257). How could you *convince* someone who wasn't sure he had two hands, or a body, or, for that matter, who wasn't certain that the world has existed for a long time? What evidence could you possibly bring to convince him otherwise? According to Wittgenstein, you might be able to *persuade* him otherwise, but that will look more like a (religious) conversion to an alternative "system of reference" than like an intellectual agreement about the "facts" of reality.[24] It will be more like a change of attitude than of rational outlook. Far from being a position one rigorously holds and is prepared to defend, "certainty is *as it were* a tone of voice" (OC § 30).

More to the point of my essay is this example from *On Certainty:* "That I am a man and not a woman can be verified, but if I were to say I was a woman, and then tried to explain the error by saying I hadn't checked the statement, the explanation would not be accepted" (§ 79). Why not? I think

Wittgenstein is saying that the subjective certainty that he or any other "reasonable" person has—with "reasonable" being defined in very specific ways through specific cultural practices—about his sex is: (1) not a matter of "agreement with reality"; (2) not something that can be known by checking the statement to see if it corresponds with the "facts" of that reality (e.g., the genitalia or the chromosome test); and (3) not something he can be "mistaken" about. In other words, if L. W. were to claim, "I am a woman," and then try to correct the claim by saying, "Oops! Sorry, I forgot to check," that explanation would not be accepted because the relation that one has to one's sex—like that which one has to one's hands—is not a matter of knowledge (and least of all of a correspondence theory of truth) but of (subjective) certainty.

Wittgenstein does not argue that no questions can (ever) be raised about something that now stands fast for us; the taken-for-granted background of our language-games is not frozen or fixed but indeterminate. Contrary to the foundationalist claim that what supports our language-games is certain to the extent that it is noninferential and noncontingent knowledge, Wittgenstein holds that what is certain is not something we "know" and that it is contingent (i.e., nonnecessary).[25] Still, what stands fast for us at any moment will be experienced as simply given. Certainty is a doing, not a knowing: "Why do I not satisfy myself that I have two feet when I want to get up from a chair? There is no why. I simply don't. This is how I act" (OC § 148). A day may come when I formulate my having two feet as an empirical proposition in need of verification, but within my present frame of reference I just get up and walk. And every step is a further enactment—I do not say confirmation—of that certainty.

Wittgenstein elaborates the complex relationship between what is subject to doubt and what is not with this river metaphor:

> It might be imagined that some propositions, of the form of empirical propositions, were hardened and functioned as channels for such empirical propositions as were not hardened but fluid; and that this relation altered with time, in that fluid propositions hardened, and hard ones became fluid.
>
> The mythology may change back into a state of flux, the river-bed of thoughts may shift. But I distinguish between the movement of the waters on the river-bed and the shift of the bed itself; though there is not a sharp division of the one from the other. . . .
>
> And the bank of that river consists partly of hard rock, subject to no alteration or only to an imperceptible one, partly of sand, which now in one place now in another gets washed away, or deposited. (OC §§ 96–97, 99)

What this means is that the Heraclitean dictum ("all is in flux") is not quite right. We both do and do not step twice in the same river: some things must be—or more exactly, simply are—held constant (the hard rock) for other things to change, be that change quick (the flow of the waters) or slow (the sand bank).[26]

What stands fast, then, is neither forever beyond doubt nor metaphysically guaranteed. To return to Wittgenstein's example of the subjective certainty about his sex, we could say that what stands fast does not take the form of empirical propositions that concern the relation between him and a fact in the world (which is how science raises the question of sex, and which is at issue in the verification of the statement "I am a man"). Thus Wittgenstein is saying something like this: My sex is not something I know (where to know means to give grounds), but it is something I am certain of. That I, L.W., am a man is a hinge proposition that grounds my language-games but itself is ungrounded. If I, L.W., say "I am a woman," there is no fact that anyone could bring in evidence to convince me that I am really a man. What is at issue here is something we would call not a "mistake" but a "mental disturbance." "Not every false belief of this sort is a mistake" (OC §§ 73, 72).[27] That it counts as a mental disturbance turns not on some absolute standard of correctness—a transcendent rule—but, rather, on our standards of correctness, the ones we have inherited, the ones we practice, and the ones we sublime into absolute standards. We would not say to a man who just claimed he was a woman: "I think you are mistaken. Why don't you check?" But how do *we* know that he is disturbed? Because, after all, it is obvious that he is not a woman? In the same way that it is obvious that there are men and women in the world? In the same way that it is obvious to you, my reader, that I, L.Z., am a woman?

"When you meet a human being, the first distinction you make is 'male or female?' and you are accustomed to make the distinction with unhesitating certainty. Anatomical science shares your certainty at one point and not much further," writes Freud. Indeed, science tells you things that "run counter to your expectations and "confuse your feelings" about the "natural distinction" between the sexes. Science might lead me to "conclude that what constitutes masculinity and femininity is an unknown characteristic which anatomy cannot lay hold of."[28] But can it lead me to doubt the certainty with which I determine whether an individual is male or female? Freud calls on science to put into question that certainty, but he also suggests that science traffics in truths that do not touch it. Because science raises the question of sexual difference at the level of anatomy and tries to settle it through a correspondence theory of truth—and in the last instance by pointing—science can never persuade me to abandon the certainty with which I answer (without so much as even posing) the question—male or female?—for myself, daily. If this certainty is, as Wittgenstein writes, "so anchored in all my questions and answers, so anchored that I cannot touch it," what sort of scientific evidence could move me to doubt?

As Jacques Bouveresse observes, Wittgenstein teaches that "there are beliefs too fundamental to shake or discredit simply by invoking the fact that they have no serious [scientific] basis."[29] Although science brings forth evidence that may challenge our criteria of male and female, it is unlikely to unsettle (or for that matter verify) our certainty in two sexes because that certainty is not dependent on the evidence. We can perhaps better appreciate why it does not matter (in this specific sense of raising doubt where no doubt exists) whether one discovers five sexes or more: the appeal to this empirical reality in feminist science does not undo sexual dimorphism as part of a passionate system of reference, a system that includes what will count as the truth (or falsity) of empirical propositions about males and females. It is entirely possible to read about the intersexed population and still "know how to go on" with the language-game of two sexes.

The ungrounded ground called certainty "is not *true,* nor yet false" (OC § 205). And thus neither are the deeply imbricated hinge propositions: "There are males and there are females; there are men and there are women." Giving proof for the existence (or nonexistence) of the two sexes and two genders is like giving proof for the existence of God. Sure, you can give it. But, as Wittgenstein observed, it won't matter as far as belief is concerned, because belief in God (or in two sexes or two genders) is not dependent on the evidence. "A proof of God's existence ought really to be something by means of which one could convince oneself that God exists. But I think that what *believers* who have furnished such proofs have wanted to do is give their "belief" an intellectual analysis and foundation, although they themselves would never have come to believe as a result of such proofs" (CV 85).

> It strikes me that a religious belief could only be something like a passionate commitment to a system of reference. Hence, although it's *belief,* it's really a way of living, or of assessing one's life. It's passionately seizing hold of *this* interpretation. Instruction in a religious faith, therefore, would have to take the form of a portrayal, a description, of that system of reference, while at the same time being an appeal to conscience. And this combination would have to result in the pupil himself, of his own accord, passionately taking hold of the system of reference. It would be as though someone were first to let me see the hopelessness of my situation and then show me the means of rescue until, of my own accord, or not at any rate led to it by my *instructor,* I ran to it and grasped it. (CV 64)[30]

What would it mean to see sexual difference as part of a system of reference to which we make a passionate commitment but not in the sense of having weighed the evidence for or against it? Would feminism be about committing oneself, in this passionate (not simply intellectual) way, to another frame of reference? These are questions I cannot adequately pose, let alone answer, here.

Wittgenstein's description of the passionate practice of committing oneself to a system of reference shows how we come to hold certain beliefs by taking hold of them, making them our own, without so much as thinking about a verification. "This direct taking-hold corresponds to a *sureness* [*Sicherheit:* certainty, safety], not to a knowing" (OC § 511). It is the kind of sureness (certainty or safety) that allows me to use all the words in my sentence without giving them a second thought; the sureness that allows me to take hold of a thing's name, to judge, indeed to say things like "I have the ticket in my hand," or "Go ask the woman at the ticket counter." This system of reference to which I commit myself by acting—not because I have good reasons—becomes part of my worldview. "I did not get my picture of the world by satisfying myself of its correctness; nor do I have it because I am satisfied of its correctness. No: it is the inherited background against which I distinguish true and false" (OC § 94). Inherited, yes. But also something I take up as *my* inheritance? A frame of reference that I make a passionate commitment to, but not because I find it convincing? A frame that I might remain committed to even if I found it utterly unconvincing, even if I knew better?

These are the sorts of questions that Wittgenstein provokes. They lead me to ask whether the persistent practice (including my own) of questioning foundations in feminism does not, on one side, conceal its own deep dependence on and embeddedness in the very frame of reference it wants to question, and, on the other side, tend to treat that dependence as a kind of blindness or failure of critical intelligence. To what extent do feminists, especially those of us working under the sign of poststructuralism, assume, first, that the frame is really a foundation—that is, a base of noninferential knowledge—and, second, that, as a foundation, it ought to be interrogated, subjected to doubt? To what extent do feminists, especially those seeking to defend foundations in the face of such interrogation, assume that what grounds language-games is itself grounded, a piece of noninferential knowledge that we can all rationally agree to? What would it mean for feminists to acknowledge what Wittgenstein calls certainty, that is, the conditions of doubt, of (feminist) critical practice? Wittgenstein's claims about the language-game of doubting may strike us as obvious: "If you tried to doubt everything you would not get so far as doubting anything." "Doubt comes after belief." But that, I argue, is an indication of our failure to understand his claims.

If the (feminist) practice of questioning hinge propositions is embedded in a system of reference whose ungrounded ground sets the parameters of judging, it is unlikely that this critical practice will undertake to expose, by means of sheer intellectual force, that which passes as the real, the given, the natural.³¹ Even if one agrees (in theory) that "the real is not a ground on which we might easily rely . . . [but] a postulate that requires a political interrogation,"³² from what place would that interrogation be launched? Won't it always be from a place that, on this definition, passes as the real? Not only is there no outside to any system of reference from which we might dispassionately judge it or objectively interrogate it, there is no inside from which to do so: "this system is not a more or less arbitrary point of departure for all our arguments: no, it belongs to the essence of what we call an argument. The system is not so much the point of departure, as the element in which arguments have their life" (OC § 105). Quite simply: the doubts you can raise—the gender trouble you can create—will depend on a whole series of hinge propositions that you will not touch, and that simply will stand fast for you if you are to trouble gender at all. You may deny your dependence on what stands fast for you, but then you give yourself "a false picture of *doubt*" (OC § 249).

To treat our certainty in a system of reference (like the sex/gender system) as a failure of critical thinking is to misunderstand what is involved. And if the call for critical thinking involves demanding in advance that the system be justified by reality, this demand is impossible for reasons that have nothing to do with credulity, blindness, or haste. "The difficulty is to realize the groundlessness of our believing" (OC § 166), says Wittgenstein. But I do not take that, as a feminist critic of foundationalism might, to be an injunction: "Realize the groundlessness of your believing (e.g., in two sexes)!" The difficulty here is not intellectual: I can well realize, through practices of reasoning and intellection, the groundlessness of my beliefs (especially if I read enough of a certain kind of theory).³³ Rather, the difficulty is a problem of the will: I realize that my belief (in two sexes) is groundless, but I am still captivated by a "picture" in which the existence of two sexes constitutes my worldview, the frame of reference within which I act. What is called for, once again, concerns coming to see differently what has been there all along.

What holds sex/gender in place as a system of reference are not the claims to correspondence and practices of verification with which one attempts to prove that this is a female/woman and this is a male/man by reference to the "facts of reality." For those facts (of anatomy or chromosomes or who does the dishes) turn out to be our criteria. Criteria are supposed to be the means by which the existence of something is objectively established; they are the means by which we judge. We say that empirical propositions can be tested, and that our criteria constitute the objective measure according to which we test. If you say, "This is a female and this is a male," and I say, "How do you know?" you might invoke standard criteria of sex difference like chromosomes and hormones and genitalia. But what if those principles of judgments themselves are judgments? *What* is to be tested by *what* if the standard or yardstick itself is a judgment? At what point do we have an objective means of testing our empirical proposition? (see OC §§ 110, 124–31).

Wittgenstein shows what feminists contend: our criteria always disappoint us, and therein consists the impulse to skepticism. Consider, for example, the Olympic Committee's move, in 1968, from the genitalia test for femaleness to the chromosome test, only to return, in 1992, to the genitalia test. (From parading nude in front of judges female athletes were then asked to submit their DNA, only to parade nude once again.) In each instance there were individuals who did not meet the criteria but could not be discounted as female. There were those who "looked" like females and saw themselves as women, but had male sex chromosomes; those who had female sex chromosomes but due to defects in hormone production had men's muscles and masculinized genitals; those who had two X chromosomes but an extra Y one as well. And so on.

If one wanted to contest the skeptical challenge to sex difference by appealing to the stability of criteria, one would not get very far. There simply are no definitive criteria for sex difference, and that is what a range of feminist theorists have been telling us for years. But that doesn't mean that there are no criteria, or that in ordinary life we will not make a judgment about a person's sex, usually without thinking, certainly without thinking about chromosomes or, for that matter, even genitalia. We do make these judgments, and we make them in a flash, without thinking, on the basis of innumerable particulars that constitute, as it were, a sort of prior agreement in judgments, an agreement that makes it possible to establish criteria in the first place, an agreement in what Wittgenstein calls our "forms of life" (PI § 214). Needless to say, this is not an agreement that any of us actually signed our names to: it is not conventional in that sense.[34] But neither is it natural, if by natural we mean somehow determined and determining of our criteria. As Cavell suggests, it is more like our mutual attunement in language; we normally do know what another person means when he or she uses a word. There is nothing in what Wittgenstein calls "facts of nature" (i.e., "such facts as mostly do not strike us because of their generality" [PI p. 230]) that provides a naturalistic justification of our grammar, criteria, and concepts. Still, just because our criteria for gender difference are contestable and bound to disappoint the desire to know what a woman is and who is a woman, that does not mean that the language-game of gender cannot be played. The framework conditions of that game, after all, are not knowledge but certainty.

"At the foundation of well-founded belief lies belief that is not founded" (OC § 253). It is this utterly groundless belief that persists when our criteria are questioned, and our agreement in judgments seems threatened or lost. The Olympic Committee revised the criteria for femaleness in the face of uncertainty about who counts as female. But the important point to see is this: the frame of such judgments—the two-sex system—can persist despite the instability of the relevant criteria. That is because what stands fast for us does so, not because it is obvious or convincing, but because it is "held fast by what lies around it" (OC § 144). Consequently, every form of representation provides a means for accommodating that which is "deviant" (e.g., the "females" with "male" sex chromosomes) without having to surrender the form of representation. Paraphrasing section 79 of *Philosophical Investigations*, I would put these points like this: Should one of my definitions be called into question—say, a female human being has two X chromosomes—is it not the case that I have, so to speak, a whole series of props in readiness, and am ready to lean on another if one should be taken from me? How much of what I think a female human being is must be proved false for me to give up my definitions as false? The point is that there is no fixed point at which I'd have to abandon my definitions. I use the word "female" without fixed meaning. (But that detracts little from its usefulness, as it detracts little from that of a table that it stands on three legs instead of four and sometimes wobbles.) That is why feminist accounts of those individuals who do not meet the criteria of the two-sex system are not as effective at contesting that system as their authors would like them to be. The table may wobble a bit, but that doesn't mean we won't call it a table; the Olympic Committee changed the test (twice in fact), but it never occurred to anyone that what they were testing for, sex difference, did not exist.

"Giving grounds . . . come[s] to an end sometime. But the end is not an ungrounded presupposition: it is an ungrounded way of acting" (OC § 110). The committee's justification in 1992 for the new test (which was the old test) amounts to: this is what we do. A feminist could question this explanation, but if her questioning proceeds by exposing "the foundational premise [of the criteria for sex difference] as a contingent and contestable presumption," what gets exposed won't be what holds that criteria in place, quite simply because what secures them is not an ungrounded presupposition, a foundation, a knowledge claim.[35]

I cannot unlearn the proposition "There are males and there are females" or "There are men and there are women" if I never learned it as a proposition—that is, if I learned it, not in the form of hypothesis that could be proved or disproved, but as part of a world-picture that I inherited and on the basis of which I judge, that is, act. "The propositions describing this world-picture might be part of a kind of mythology. And their role is like that of rules of a game; and the game can be learned purely practically, without learning any explicit rules." "Children do not learn that books exist, that armchairs exist, etc. etc.—they learn to fetch books, sit in armchairs, etc. etc." (OC §§ 151, 95, 476). Would not the same sort of practical activity apply to how we learn about males and females, men and women?

When I was a child, no one ever pointed toward someone and said to me: "That is a woman and that is a man"—or, if they did, it wouldn't have mattered because that is not how one comes to acquire language and to hold beliefs. To learn what something is by ostensive definition is already to know, among so many other things, what an object is and what it means to point to it. (Besides, an ostensive definition provides not a link between word and world but a sample, which, in turn, provides a standard for the correct use of the word in other contexts.) If "the teaching of language is not explanation, but training" (PI § 5), we acquire our understanding of sex and gender differences in ways that have little to do with explanations, justifications, and definitions.

Piece by piece a system forms, then, in which we come to hold our beliefs in two sexes (male and female) and in two genders (man and woman), beliefs that, because they lend each other mutual support, are far more resistant to doubt than we "gender-troublerians" seem to think: sex supports gender, gender supports sex, and both are supported by what lies around them. Should these hinge propositions turn out to be false, we would lose the background against which we distinguish true and false. What this means, in effect, is that a genuine challenge to the two-sex system—as the literature of that trenchant critic of heterosexuality, Monique Wittig, so powerfully shows[36]—is actually far more radical than we sometimes make it out to be. What we would discover if we could in fact see intersexed bodies (or transsexuals or lesbians or for that matter men and women) outside our frame of reference goes far beyond matters of sex and gender. Imagine discovering that you are a brain in a vat, and you will begin to appreciate what the collapse of our two-sex hinge propositions would look like.

To emphasize the sheer radicality of real change in our form of representation, however, is not to suggest that the problem with our concepts is that they are too determinate to encompass even a sliver of the plurality of human life. Male/female (sex) and man/woman (gender) belong to a system of reference in which, paradoxical as it sounds, their stability derives from their contingency and relative plasticity. I am calling attention to the fact that language is not only stable but also amazingly tolerant. If a word did not contain some amount of indefiniteness, it could not possibly have a place in "the pattern of life, [which is] after all, not one of exact regularity" (LWPPI § 211). I want to question the notion, so pervasive in current feminist theory, that the problem with a concept like woman/women is that we have treated it as essential, unitary, and fixed, and that what we now need to do is to interrogate it, destabilize it, put it into flux. But what if I were to say this: "women" and "woman," as words in our language-games (one of which is feminism), are not nearly as fixed as this feminist critical project makes them out to be. If we paid attention to the ordinary contexts in which these words are used, rather than treating them, in the manner of philosophical abstraction, as a generic object ("the category of women"), we will bring words like "women" and "woman" "back from their metaphysical to their everyday use" (PI § 116), without the cognitive acrobatics that keep us riveted to—indeed obsessed with—searching out and destroying whatever presents itself as foundational, unquestionable.

I suggested at the beginning of the chapter that Woman is a mythology. In that sense it might seem that Woman is akin not to the river but to the riverbed in Wittgenstein's metaphor: not in flux but fixed. But what if our uses of the term "woman" imply both, both bedrock and fluid, as the notion of a language-game suggests? What if, moreover, the word were not the totality that attacks on the "category of women" in feminism make it out to be? We do well to recall that the "category of women" was developed by feminists in order to contest the myth of Woman. The category of women is what Beauvoir had in mind when she tried to distinguish her use of "woman" from the myth that she was criticizing. We are rightly critical of attempts, like Beauvoir's, to articulate that category in terms of "the common basis that underlies every individual feminine existence"; but what we tend to forget is that "the category of women" is an object of feminist theory, precisely a category. When we read those attempts and the more recent critiques of them, we should ask: Is the word "women" ever actually used this way in the language-games, one of which is feminism (the practice), that are its original home? (PI § 116).

If the argument for using "women" strategically strikes me as a curiously Humean solution to a distinctly philosophical sort of problem, it is because I suspect that the problem to which the strategic use of women is put forward as a solution can arise only under very specific conditions: abstraction from the ordinary and a "craving for generality" that borders on worldlessness. Is it not the case that, to the extent that it so much as warrants our undivided critical energies, "women" (the category) must first be construed as if it were unitary, as if it consisted in the (misguided) attempt to bring together a wide range of empirical cases into a coherent theoretical kind? Inasmuch as those cases do not conform to the totality condition that the category imposes on them, so the critique goes, the category is based on a system of classification that is bogus. And not only bogus but politically motivated, because what counts as a woman under this system of classification, this category of women, defines who is entitled to speak in the name of feminism and the nature of the claims that she is entitled to make. But can all the meanings for "women" come before my mind when I actually hear or read that word, even when it is invoked as a category in feminist theory? When I reflect on my understanding of this word, what comes before my mind is the general case. But that case is really a particular one that presents itself as a picture (i.e., the white, middle-class, heterosexual woman). We are right to find problems with this picture, but aren't we too captivated by it when we turn one generality (the category of women) into another generality (*the* problem with the category of women)? What has that picture to do with the particular sense that the word has for me in different contexts? Isn't it a matter, really, of who speaks (when and where) and to whom?[37]

If my assessment of the critique of "the category of women" is correct, what follows? I suggest that the argument that feminism can no longer posit a subject in advance of political action is correct but meaningless. It is correct because when I act politically I bring into existence a subject—"the subject of feminism" (de Lauretis)—that is not given in advance of my actions; it is meaningless because, in order to act at all, I will make claims to community, and others will decide whether to accept or to contest those claims. I will make claims like "We women demand," and there will be others who will say: "For whom do you speak? Not me." To say that every claim to the category of women inevitably excludes the very individuals it is supposed to unite and thus inevitably generates refusals to accept the category is to miss the whole point of politics. Politics consists precisely in the making of claims, which, being claims, are inevitably partial and thus exclusive. Acting politically is about testing the limits of every claim to community; it is about positing agreement and discovering what happens when that agreement breaks down or simply fails to materialize in the first place. That the claim "we women demand *x*" excludes some women turns not on the theoretical insight (in the philosopher's study) into the exclusionary character of the category of women but rather on the political character of making claims (in a public space). Thus to use exclusion as the criterion on which to base one's feminist critique of political claims is already to accept the possibility that there could in fact be a claim that does not exclude.

And herein consists the irony of feminist critiques of the category of women: they are captured by the very fantasy—call it a "picture"—that they explicitly reject: namely, a political claim that would not exclude, that could indeed account for—would correspond to—the empirical reality of differences. We can break the spell of this picture on our view of feminist politics, but only if we acknowledge that to make a claim is to speak for someone and to someone. It is to assert one's power to make claims, to embrace the predicative power of one's words, and say: "This is how I see the world." I may assume or anticipate your agreement, but I expect you will tell me how you see it.

8

On Seeing Liberty As

Jonathan Havercroft

> Now you try and say what is involved in seeing something as something.
> It is not easy. These thoughts I am now working on are as hard as granite.
> —Ludwig Wittgenstein

Between 1947 and 1949 Ludwig Wittgenstein became interested in the phenomenon of being able to see a single image as a number of different images. The paradigmatic example of the phenomenon of *seeing-as*, for Wittgenstein, is Joseph Jastrow's figure known as the duck-rabbit (PI p. 194). One of the reasons Wittgenstein investigated this phenomenon was that it had important consequences for his philosophical *Weltanschauung* (philosophical method):

> It could be said of [Wittgenstein's] philosophical method that its aim is to change the aspect under which certain things are seen—for example to see a mathematical proof not as a sequence of propositions but as a picture, to see a mathematical formula not as a proposition but as a rule, to see first person reports of psychological states ("I am in pain" etc.) not as descriptions but as expressions, and so on. The "understanding that consists in seeing connections," one might say, is the understanding that results from a change of aspect.[1]

Images such as Jastrow's duck-rabbit present a peculiar problem to Wittgenstein's efforts at gaining a "synoptic view" *(Übersicht)*. When someone changes from seeing the image as one gestalt to seeing it as another, the temptation is to find an explanation as to *what* has changed (in either the image or the perception of the image). Wittgenstein, however, "wants to describe the situation in such a way that this question itself does not arise. Like all cases of philosophical confusion it is the question itself that misleads."[2] For Wittgenstein, the real question was not "What has changed in a gestalt shift?" but "What difference does a change in aspect make?"

> Now if some man deviates radically from the norm in his description of [aspectival images] or when he copies them, what difference does it make between him and normal humans that he uses different '*units*' in copying and describing? That is to say, how will such a one go on to differ from normal humans in yet other things? (RPPI § 982)

In this chapter I will argue that Wittgenstein's reformulation of the question about changes in aspects is of special significance to political philosophy because Wittgenstein believes that the discovery of a new aspect in an image is akin to experiencing the meaning of a word in a new way. As such, I believe that Wittgenstein's writings on changes in aspect can be used to illuminate changes in aspect of important words used in political philosophy. Just as confusion emerged with images that can be *seen as* several different things, a similar type of confusion occurs in political theory in debates over the meaning of words, such as "liberty," "justice," and "power," which can be interpreted in a number of different ways. As such, Wittgenstein's remarks on aspectival images are of particular importance to political theorists who often work with aspectival concepts. In order to demonstrate this, I will, in the first section of this chapter, examine Wittgenstein's writings on seeing-as and aspect-dawning in part II, section xi of the *Philosophical Investigations,* in order to get a clear picture of Wittgenstein's reflections on this matter. In the next section, I will survey three different accounts of the meaning of the word "liberty," contained in the writings of Isaiah Berlin, Charles Taylor, and Quentin Skinner, and argue that while each of these theories fails to provide a comprehensive account of liberty, each one does succeed in capturing an aspect of it. On the basis of this survey, I hope to demonstrate that liberty should be seen as an aspectival concept, and rather than trying to find a theory that provides a comprehensive explanation of liberty, political philosophers should try to get an *Übersicht* (a synoptic view) of the uses of the word. In the final section I will offer some brief remarks about how the shift to seeing liberty as an aspectival concept necessarily implies a shift in how concepts such as liberty should be studied.

From "Seeing an Aspect" to "Experiencing the Meaning of a Word"

Upon first inspection, in part II, section xi of the *Investigations* Wittgenstein seems to be attempting to dispel a theory of vision that is associated with explaining the dawning of an aspect. Initially, Wittgenstein characterizes aspect-dawning this way:

> I contemplate a face, and then suddenly notice its likeness to another. I *see* that it has not changed; and yet I see it differently. I call this experience "noticing an aspect." (PI p. 193)

In the following pages, Wittgenstein surveys a number of different examples of aspect-dawning (schematic-drawings, puzzle-pictures, pictures of faces, etc.) This survey reveals that what is special about the dawning of an aspect is its paradoxical nature: when we notice the dawning of an aspect, we see the image differently, *but* we also see that the image has not changed. Wittgenstein examines two theories with his interlocutor that could account for the paradox of noticing an aspect: (1) a physiological event (movement of the eyes) and (2) a change in what we subjectively see—a change in our visual impression rather than the figure itself (PI p. 196). Wittgenstein rejects the first explanation on the grounds that the problem emerges as a conceptual one and not a physiological one. As such, any physiological explanation avoids, rather than solves, the conceptual problem of aspect-dawning.

The second explanation forms the basis of Wittgenstein's main target in part II, section xi of the *Investigations*. This account of noticing an aspect assumes that a set of copies of what we see is stored in our brain, and these copies mediate our perception of things in the external world. It is only because objects we see produce copies in our mind that we are able to describe what we see. These copies exist as objects in our mind, and only the perceiver can experience these "inner copies." They are what we "see" when we notice an aspect in an external picture. As such, as Stephen Mulhall observes, "a description of what is seen which goes beyond references to color, shape, and spatial organization can at best be an indirect result of interpreting what is really seen."[3] Or, as Wittgenstein puts it:

> "What I really *see* must surely be produced in me by the influence of the object"—Then what is produced in me is a sort of copy, something that in turn can be looked at, can be before one; almost something like a *materialization*.
>
> And this materialization is something spatial and it must be possible to describe it in purely spatial terms. For instance (if it is a face) it can smile; the concept of friendliness, however, has no place in an account of it, but is *foreign* to such an account (even though it may subserve it). (PI p. 199)

Wittgenstein attacks the interlocutor's "inner-copies" theory of perception by showing how such a theory cannot effectively account for aspect-dawning. According to this theory, aspect-dawning can either be a result of a change in one's inner copy of the picture or a change in how one interprets that inner copy. First, Wittgenstein looks at the possibility that aspect-perception is a result of a change in the person's inner copy (materialization) of the object being perceived. As a means of refuting this position, Wittgenstein looks at the shifting aspects of a schematic cube (PI p. 193). If the shifting of aspects of the schematic cube could be accounted for within the inner-picture theory of vision, then each shift in aspect of the schematic cube would have to be accounted for by a change in the inner copy. Again, if the inner copy is an exact replica of what is seen there would be no change, but if the inner copy changes with each aspect then the inner copy is not an exact copy of the object being perceived. "Now the only possible expression of our experience is what before perhaps seemed, or even was, a useless specification when once we had the copy" (PI p. 196). The only way to keep the interlocutor's theory intact would be to hypothesize the inner copy of what is being perceived as "a queerly shifting construction." This hypothesis would depend upon the possibility that changes to the inner copy of an object would occur in a way that could not be expressed outside the viewer's mind. Wittgenstein is quick to chastise the interlocutor:

> And above all do *not* say "After all my visual impression isn't the *drawing;* it is *this*—which I can't shew to anyone"—Of course it is not the drawing, but neither is it anything in the same category, which I carry within myself. (PI p. 196)

This means that the interlocutor cannot claim that when someone uses an expression such as "now I am seeing a rabbit" they are not describing a change in perception.

Wittgenstein rejects the interlocutor's theories about aspect-change because they fail to capture the *experience* of noticing a new aspect. He illustrates this point with the following example:

> I look at an animal and am asked: "What do you see?" I answer: "A rabbit."— I see a landscape; suddenly a rabbit runs past. I exclaim "A rabbit!"
>
> Both things, both the report and the exclamation, are expressions of perception and of visual experience. But the exclamation is so in a different sense from the report: it is forced from us.—It is related to the experience as a cry is to pain. (PI p. 197)

The analogy Wittgenstein makes between exclamations of aspect-dawning and exclamations of pain is meant to serve two purposes. First, the exclamation "A rabbit!" is a direct expression (*Äußerung*) of a visual experience, and not the result of an interpretation of what is being seen. Second, this *Äußerung* characterizes the dawning of the aspect. Just as the cry of pain is part of the pain being felt, the *Äußerung* is part of the experience of the dawning of an aspect.[4]

The difference between Wittgenstein's description of aspect-dawning and the theory offered by the interlocutor is that the interlocutor wants to create a rigid theory that can explain seeing. Wittgenstein's point in associating *Äußerungen* with aspect-dawning is that this type of seeing is different from our other conceptions of seeing. The interlocutor's theory of vision reduces all seeing to associating images with inner copies in our mind. By finding a case where this theory of vision cannot account for what is going on, Wittgenstein is pointing out that there are a multiplicity of meanings for the term "seeing":

> The concept of "seeing" makes a tangled impression. Well, it is tangled.—I look at the landscape, my gaze ranges over it, I see all sorts of distinct and indistinct movement; *this* impresses itself sharply on me, *that* is quite hazy. After all, how completely ragged what we see can appear! And now look at all that can be meant by "description of what is seen."—But this just is what is called description of what is seen. There is not *one genuine* proper case of such description—the rest being just vague, something which awaits classification, or which must just be swept aside as rubbish. (PI p. 200)

The fact that there are many different uses of "see" is obviously a call for a perspicuous representation of seeing. This perspicuous representation of seeing would allow us to understand the different ways in which "see" is used, and would help us avoid false theories of vision, such as the interlocutor's inner copies theory, which serve only to confuse our understanding of "seeing." This is what Wittgenstein means when he says: "What we have rather to do is to *accept* the everyday language-game, and to note *false* accounts of the matter *as* false" (PI p. 200).

Mulhall argues that for Wittgenstein "the concept of seeing is forced on us because of our immediate response to the question 'What are you seeing?' when shown a drawing even for a moment."[5] Because Wittgenstein believes that the description an individual offers of what she sees is equivalent to what she is seeing, the answer to the question "What are you seeing?" is the criterion by which we analyze her visual experience. Wittgenstein's distinction between seeing and knowing therefore must rest in the statements people give about their perceptions. Because someone who is asked "What are you seeing?" must give an answer immediately, she is forced to give her first impression. By giving her first reaction to an image, the person is *seeing*. Because it is an *immediate* response, she does not have time to properly analyze the image, and she is not aware of all of its aspects. This use of the word "seeing" implies continuous aspect-perception. The person, in seeing in this way, is continuously seeing only one aspect of the object. According to Mulhall, Wittgenstein's concept of continuous aspect-perception "involves an immediate, spontaneous reaching for the relevant form of description; we employ those words as a simple perceptual report, without any awareness that it is one of several available options."[6] *Knowing*, on the other hand, involves analyzing and interpreting the image. As Mulhall notes, a person knows that the silhouette is an image of an arrow would "need to read the drawing like a blueprint, inferring certain things from its particular properties of color and spatial arrangement."⁷

Wittgenstein describes the other way that a person can relate to an image through the concept of *seeing-as*. This notion is used to describe cases where people describe the pictures they are looking at as if they were the objects the pictures are representing. In these cases, the picture is not open to interpretation; the only description of the picture is the one that describes what the picture is representing. In order to clarify this Mulhall draws a useful parallel between Wittgenstein's idea of *seeing-as* and Heidegger's notion of *readiness-to-hand*. Wittgenstein writes the following about *seeing-as*:

> The focus is rather on the *readiness-to-hand* of the correct form of description; and this *readiness-to-hand* is a manifestation of the perceiver's *taking for granted* the identity of what he perceives—a criterion for the fact that its being a picture, and moreover a particular picture (a picture of something in particular), is simply not at issue for him.⁸

Wittgenstein's idea of *seeing-as* is used to describe a general attitude about the relationship between the picture and what is signified by the picture in cases where what the picture is signifying is not in doubt. It is important to note that when Wittgenstein writes about *seeing-as*, he is not implying that people confuse the picture for what the picture represents. His point is that people in some way interact with the picture as if it were the object it is supposed to represent. This type of behavior lets us know that for the perceiver, what the picture represents is never in question. In other words (to continue with the analogy between Wittgenstein and Heidegger) when someone *sees* an image *as* something, the description of the picture is *ready-to-hand*. There is no attempt to stand back from the picture and analyze it. Instead, the person treats the picture as if it were what it is depicting.

The fact that we can *see* a picture *as* what the picture is representing is what makes aspect-perception possible. Furthermore, it is the ready-to-handness of pictures that we *see as* something else that the interlocutor is struggling to explain in his theory of vision. As Wittgenstein writes:

> If I saw the duck-rabbit as a rabbit, then I saw: these shapes and colours (I give them in detail)—and I saw besides something like this: and here I point to a number of different pictures of rabbits.—This shews the difference between the concepts.
> "Seeing as . . ." is not part of perception. And for this reason it is like seeing and again not like. (PI pp. 196–97)

While it is possible to copy the colors and shapes of the picture-rabbit image, we cannot capture or make a copy of what makes us *see* the picture *as* something. To draw another parallel with Heidegger, this categorical difference is a result of how we interact with the object. The colors and shapes of the objects we perceive are understood through a present-at-hand relationship with the object, where as when we see an object as something else, it is ready-to-hand.

It is this categorical difference in how we perceive an object that explains the paradoxical nature of aspect-dawning. We can see an image differently when a new aspect dawns on us without the image actually changing because there has been a shift in what we *see* the image *as*. If I *see* the duck rabbit *as* a duck, then I interact with the image in some respects as if it were a duck. Because the duck aspect of the duck-rabbit is ready-to-hand, the image for me is for all intents and purposes that of a duck. When the rabbit aspect of the image dawns on me, then the rabbit aspect of the image is ready-to-hand. Because of the peculiar nature of the gestalt images, only one aspect of the image can be ready-to-hand at any given time. This is why, when I see a different aspect of a gestalt image, it feels as though I am looking at a completely different picture. As such, the ability to see a new aspect must be dependent upon the ability to see an aspect continuously. If I cannot experience an aspect as ready-to-hand, then I will not be able to experience the dawning of a new aspect.

In showing that the dawning of a new aspect rests on our ability to see an aspect continuously, Wittgenstein also raises the question of people who are incapable of seeing any aspect at all:

> The question now arises: Could there be human beings lacking in the capacity to see something *as something*—and what would that be like? What sort of consequences would it have?—Would this defect be comparable to colour-blindness or to not having absolute pitch? We will call it "aspect-blindness."
> (PI p. 213)

At the beginning of section xi of the *Investigations* Wittgenstein describes aspect-blindness as simply the inability to experience the dawning of an aspect. Here he is introducing a second aspect to the concept of aspect-blindness: those cases where an individual is unable to regard an image as something. Although it is possible for someone to know that the duck-rabbit contains an image of a duck and a rabbit, the aspect-blind person is unable to regard the image as either a duck or a rabbit. So, *knowing* what an image is and *seeing* that image *as* something are two different aspects of seeing an image.

What do these comments about aspect-dawning and duck-rabbits have to do with *political* philosophy? It was Wittgenstein's contention that aspect-perception was very similar to what happens when someone experiences the meaning of a word:

> The importance of this concept [of aspect-blindness] lies in the connexion between the concepts of 'seeing an aspect' and 'experiencing the meaning of a word.' For we want to ask 'What would you be missing if you did not *experience* the meaning of a word?' (PI p. 214)

When Wittgenstein talks about experiencing the meaning of a word, he is referring to those cases where a word is experienced in isolation (outside of the context of a conversation) as well as those cases when reading a work of poetry, fiction, or, we might add, political philosophy, the reader becomes conscious of specific words being used by the author. In these instances, the word manifests one of a number of possible meanings.

Wittgenstein's reflections on experiencing the meaning of a word are significant for political philosophy, because most political philosophers when reflecting on a concept such as liberty, democracy, or sovereignty tend to experience the meaning of that word in only one way. Entire theories of liberty are built upon experiencing the meaning of a word in one or two ways, and as such, many theories of liberty tend to be aspect-blind. In other words, political theorists who focus their work on only one aspect of the word "liberty" are akin to those who are only able to see the duck in Jastrow's duck-rabbit. In both cases there is no convention, no language-game that determines how the image/word is used and understood. Nevertheless, both the word and the image have a meaning for us. This paradox is a serious threat to the project that Wittgenstein was undertaking in the first part of the *Investigations,* where he argues that the way a word is used in a language-game determines that word's meaning. The way out of this dilemma is the same as that which Wittgenstein used to overcome the impasse between the dawning of an aspect and the interpretation of an image. When discussing gestalt images, Wittgenstein was able to discover an intermediate case between interpreting an image as something and suddenly perceiving an image in a different way. In this instance, Wittgenstein explained that in order for a new aspect to dawn on us, we must have first been continuously seeing a different aspect of this image. As such, our capacity to see an image as something new is entirely dependent on our ability to see the image *as* something in the first place. There is a similar phenomena going on when we experience the meaning of a word.

When a political theorist experiences the meaning of the word "liberty," one meaning of "liberty" is ready-to-hand, but the theorist cannot "see" the other meanings, though he may "know" of them. This phenomenon is significant for political philosophy because many debates revolve around how different political theorists experience the meaning of words such as liberty. Confusion occurs when theorists try to solve these debates by defending one meaning of liberty against other meanings. Quite often, debates can seem like two people arguing over whether Jastrow's duck-rabbit is a duck or a rabbit. Wittgenstein suggested that the solution to these problems of aspect-perception can be solved by changing the question from "What does the picture represent?" to "What difference does a change in what we see the picture as make?" In the next section, I will argue that political theorists must make a similar shift in the questions they ask when they are reflecting on words such as liberty, whose meanings can be experienced in a multiplicity of ways.

Five Aspects of Liberty

Three different twentieth-century political theorists—Isaiah Berlin, Charles Taylor, and Quentin Skinner—have experienced five different aspects (meanings) of the word "liberty": as a negative concept, as a positive concept, as an opportunity concept, as an exercise concept, and as a republican concept. Because each of these thinkers, when reflecting on liberty, focuses only on the word, all are in a certain respect experiencing the meaning of the word in isolation. So, their reflections on the meaning of liberty could be seen as an example of *seeing liberty as*. The debate between these three thinkers emerges as a result of each of their attempts to answer the question, What is liberty?

We can handle these debates in two possible ways. The traditional approach of political theorists—which from here on I will refer to as *political theory*—would be to define one aspect of liberty and then argue that rival theorists are wrong in how they define liberty. This approach rests on the assumption that there must be one or two true meanings of liberty, but the fact that political theorists have defined liberty in multiple ways is evidence that there are many ways of experiencing the meaning of the word, each of which can be correct, but none of which could ever be comprehensive. This understanding forms the basis of the second approach, which I shall call *political philosophy*. In this approach, the purpose is not to prove that one meaning of a concept is better than any other meaning.[9] Instead, the political philosopher's task would be threefold. The philosopher must be able, first, to see and use correctly many different aspects of liberty and challenge different uses of liberty in the appropriate contexts; second, to cure aspect-blindness by allowing others to see liberty as something that they could not see it as before; and third, to suggest in which contexts it is appropriate to use a given aspect of liberty.

In order to illustrate what I mean by this, I will now turn my attention to the debate over the meaning of liberty between Berlin, Taylor, and Skinner. My purpose here will be to demonstrate that while each of these political theorists attempts to put forward a comprehensive theory of liberty, each actually only articulates a single aspect of liberty. Each new account of liberty advanced by these thinkers is actually a dawning of a new aspect of liberty that cured us of blindness to it. As such, rather than reading the liberty debates in an attempt to figure out which meaning of liberty we should adopt, we should read them with the intention of curing our own blindness to aspects of liberty. Through an engagement with Berlin, Taylor, and Skinner, we will be able to shift from *seeing liberty as* something to *knowing* liberty.

In "Two Concepts of Liberty," Berlin—acknowledging the aspectival nature of liberty—argues that there are a hundred different aspects of liberty. He, however, decides to focus on just two aspects, the negative and the positive, because he believes that these uses underlie and are expressed in the great struggles between capitalism and socialism in the twentieth century. In narrowing down these hundred different uses of liberty into competing concepts, Berlin closes off the possibility of seeing liberty as aspectival.[10] Berlin sees negative liberty as the freedom from coercion or interference by others. An individual's negative liberty is the ability by which she can act without having her actions obstructed by someone else. From this perspective, whenever someone attempts to prevent me from acting, they are infringing on my freedom. Conversely, the less others interfere with my actions, the freer I am.

Berlin defines being free in the positive sense as freedom to be one's own master. Berlin's argument is that, although at first glance the difference between these two aspects of liberty may not appear to be too different, the end result of conceiving freedom in the positive sense may be quite different from conceiving it in the negative. From the perspective of positive liberty, it is possible "to coerce men in the name of some goal (let us say, justice or public health) which they would, if they were more enlightened, themselves pursue, but do not because they are blind or ignorant or corrupt."[11] Berlin is quick to point out that there is no reason to assume that positive liberty's principle of self-mastery will not come into conflict with one's negative liberty. Because there is a multiplicity of human goals, Berlin argues that only by privileging negative liberty will we be able to ensure that individuals are free to choose for themselves which goals to choose. As such, Berlin concludes that negative liberty is superior to positive liberty, thereby arguing that only by using liberty in the negative sense are philosophers using the concept correctly.

Taylor responds to Berlin in "What's Wrong with Negative Liberty?" by pointing out that dividing liberty into two categories oversimplifies how political theorists use the word. In his craving for a general theory to explain all uses of liberty through two categories, Berlin misses important aspects of several different theories of liberty. Taylor introduces two other aspects of freedom: freedom as an exercise concept, and freedom as an opportunity concept. Upon first glance, these two sets of distinctions appear to be the same. However, there is a crucial difference to be drawn between Taylor's freedom as an exercise concept and Berlin's positive freedom. For Berlin, theories of positive freedom "are concerned with who or what controls," whereas Taylor defines this type of freedom as "exercising of control over one's life."[12] For Taylor, this exercise concept allows him to differentiate between theories of positive liberty based on *self-realization* (such as Herder's) and theories of positive liberty in which individuals are *forced to be free* (such as Rousseau's).

The differences between Taylor's and Berlin's categorizations of freedom become even more apparent when we consider how the two deal with negative conceptions of liberty. Berlin defines negative liberty as the absence of obstacles to one's ability to act; Taylor argues that negative theories of liberty can rely on either an exercise or an opportunity conception of freedom—"for we have to allow for that part of the gamut of negative theories ... which incorporate some notion of self-realization."[13] By introducing the exercise versus opportunity distinction, Taylor accomplishes two things. First, he is able to explain why defenders of negative liberty reject any conception of freedom that is not identical to the Hobbesian-Benthamite understanding of liberty as totalitarian. Second, he demonstrates that any useful conception of freedom (even a negative one) must incorporate some aspect of freedom as an exercise concept. This is because the opportunity conception of freedom says that freedom is being in a position not to be hindered in doing whatever you wish. Taylor's point is that, according to this view, you are free whether or not you act in a way that accords with your basic objectives. Emphasizing such basic objectives in the understanding of freedom does not justify coercion by external authorities who force you to act in accordance with them, but it does mean that it is possible for you to be described as less free if you do not act in a manner that accords with the basic purposes of your life. The negative view of freedom treats all our possible actions as having an equal amount of significance. As Taylor points out, however, some limits on our freedom, such as traffic lights, are less significant than other limits, such as the state banning religious worship.[14] If freedom is to have any meaningful connotation, it must reflect "the sense of being able to act on one's important purposes."[15]

In order for Taylor to make the shift from the negative/positive aspects of liberty to *seeing* liberty *as* an exercise concept, he must first have Berlin's uses of liberty *ready-to-hand*. Because Taylor's ability to see liberty as an exercise concept relies so heavily on Berlin's negative/positive distinction, it is impossible to treat Taylor's theory of liberty as a comprehensive one. In order to *see* liberty *as* an exercise concept one has to first *see* liberty *as* noninterference. So, in criticizing Berlin, Taylor does not prove that the negative aspect of liberty is wrong; he simply demonstrates that Berlin's negative and positive theories of liberty are not comprehensive. Taylor is also freeing us from *seeing* liberty *as* either negative or positive, and as such he is freeing us from the possible misconception that Berlin's negative/positive schema of liberty is the only way to look at liberty. Taylor accomplishes this by surrounding the word "liberty" with images and similes of self-realization, thereby allowing another aspect of liberty to dawn on us: the opportunity-exercise scheme of liberty that cuts across the negative/positive scheme.

Quentin Skinner makes a similar move when he introduces the republican use of the word "liberty." In seeing the republican aspect of liberty, Skinner already has "negative liberty" and "liberty as an exercise concept" ready-to-hand. In "The Idea of Negative Liberty," "The Republican Ideal of Liberty," and *Liberty before Liberalism* he rejects the positions of both Taylor and Berlin. Skinner argues that both theorists falsely assume that it is impossible to find a coherent theory of liberty that combines both negative and positive liberty. However, rather than theorizing about the form that such a theory of liberty would take, Skinner uses history to show us how such a theory was articulated in Renaissance Republicanism.

Skinner believes that the best articulation of Renaissance Republicanism can be found in Machiavelli's *Discourses on Livy*.[16] Machiavelli's use of the word "freedom" is very similar to the negative meaning of the term. This is because he uses the term to refer to individual freedom. "What he clearly has in mind is that [individuals] are free in the sense of being unobstructed in the pursuit of whatever ends they may choose to set themselves." For Machiavelli, the issue is which society best secures the negative liberty that both the *grandi* (the elites) and the *popolo* (the common citizens) desire. He argues at the start of book II that the only way to secure liberty (in the negative sense) is if one lives in a community that "itself is living 'a free way of life.' "[17] A free community is one that is not controlled by anyone outside it and is free to govern itself and choose its own ends. This community allows the ambitious *grandi* to acquire power and glory, while ensuring that the *popolo* can live securely, without the threat of their property being taken from them.

Machiavelli's defense of Republicanism was extremely influential on Western political theory until the late eighteenth century.[18] Subsequent republican theorists tend to share several common traits with Machiavelli. First, they all believe that the private liberty of individuals rests upon the liberty of the state. Because "these writers take the metaphor of the body politic as seriously as possible," they believe that a political body is free in the same way that a natural body is, "if and only if it is not subject to external constraint."[19] So, a free polity is one that is able to govern itself without interference, according to its own will. Second, republican theorists believe that there are two main benefits that citizens of free republics will enjoy. One benefit is that republican governments are the surest way for a city to be prosperous. The second benefit is that republics are the best way for citizens to ensure their personal freedom. This type of freedom is freedom in the negative sense of the term. The public liberty of a republican government is the best way to ensure that the personal liberty of the citizen of that republic is not infringed upon. Third, following in the tradition of Cicero, most republican theorists argue that a republic's prosperity depends upon its citizens cultivating *virtù*. "The term is used to denote the range of capacities that each one of us as a citizen most needs to possess: the capacities that enable us willingly to serve the common good, thereby to uphold the freedom of our community, and in consequence to ensure its rise to greatness as well as our own individual liberty."[20]

Skinner, just like Taylor, had first to *see* liberty *as* negative liberty and *as* an exercise concept before he could experience the dawning of the republican aspect of liberty. Without having these two other aspects of liberty *ready-to-hand*, he would not have realized that what is unique about the republican aspect of liberty was that it has elements of both the negative and exercise aspects of liberty. Skinner's understanding of liberty, however, is not a comprehensive synthesis of Taylor and Berlin's theories of liberty, because Skinner's concept of liberty is applicable to only a specific case: the liberty of political communities and the 'personal liberty' of individuals within them. As such, Skinner's concept of liberty complements rather than replaces the valuable work of Taylor and Berlin.

To illustrate what I mean when I say that the work of these three theorists is complementary rather than competitive, let us consider briefly contemporary debates about multilateral trade agreements and globalization. In these debates each of the rival parties *see* liberty *as* a different aspect. Let us take two of the many interlocutors in this complex and multifaceted debate. For example, some advocates of global free trade agreements *see* liberty *as* negative liberty. In contrast, some opponents of free trade, whom I will call nationalists, oppose free trade agreements because these deals subordinate the freedom of their state (made manifest in laws passed by their sovereign legislatures regulating labor practices, protecting the environment, and guaranteeing the public funding of essential services) to the rules of international arbitration boards, which are unaccountable to the citizenry of any of the countries party to this agreement. The nationalists, then, *see* liberty *as* a republican concept because they believe that the liberties of individuals depend upon their being citizens of free states. Traditionally, upon noticing such a significant difference between two theories of liberty, political theorists would see their task as determining which of the two accounts was correct, on the assumption that they must be *(a)* comprehensive and *(b)* exclusive, rather than *(a)* partial and *(b)* complementary.[21] It seems to me, however, that implicit in the shift from *seeing* liberty *as* a single comprehensive theory to *seeing* liberty *as* a word with several different aspects, there is also a shift in how political concepts are studied. It is this shift that I would like to examine in the next section.

Political Philosophy as a Cure for Aspect-Blindness

In the introduction to this chapter, I stated that for Wittgenstein the important question concerning changes in aspect-perception is not "What has changed?" but "What difference does a change in aspect make?" Wittgenstein's point is that by focusing on how the image changes in a gestalt shift, we become confused as to what is actually happening. If, however, we focus on how a person acts when experiencing the dawning of an aspect, then we are able to get a perspicuous understanding of aspect-dawning. In order to solve the paradox of aspect-dawning Wittgenstein focuses not on how the images change but rather on the *Äußerungen* that people make when they are experiencing the dawning of an aspect. It seems to me that just as a shift in questions concerning aspect-dawning helped to clarify what is actually occurring in these situations, a similar shift in questions concerning liberty may help to solve some of the confusion that has emerged in debates about the meaning of that term.

Among the writers I surveyed, most pointed out the differences between their theory of liberty and the theory of liberty that they were criticizing, as a means of demonstrating why their account of liberty was the comprehensive one (the exception being Skinner). However, if we are to take seriously the observation that liberty is an aspectival concept, then it makes as little sense to claim that one aspect of liberty is the "true" aspect as it does to claim that the duck in Jastrow's duck-rabbit is what the picture is "really" representing. The fact that there is not one "true" aspect of liberty does not, however, mean that the meaning of liberty is relative. My argument is not that political philosophy is non-normative but that the normative tendency of political philosophy can lead to aspect-blindness. If the political philosopher defends one aspect of liberty as normatively superior in all times and all places, then she or he is aspect-blind. The point of political philosophy is to know which aspect of political philosophy should be used in which circumstance. *Seeing* liberty *as* means more than simply respecting other interpretations of liberty; it means being able to use these different aspects of liberty, and to know which situation calls for which use of liberty. To draw an analogy between political philosophy and golf, each aspect of liberty is like a different golf club. A good golfer should know how to use as many different golf clubs as possible, and should know which golf club to use in which circumstance (for example, she shouldn't use her driver to putt the ball into the hole). Similarly, a political philosopher should strive to be able to use as many different aspects of liberty as possible, and to know which aspect of liberty is best in a given circumstance.

A great deal of confusion in the liberty debates comes from the questions that the theorists have asked about liberty and from the theorists' demand for a comprehensive theory of liberty. By focusing only on what is different between two aspects of liberty, political theorists have fallen into a trap of arguing over which conception of liberty is the correct one. Instead, taking a cue from Wittgenstein, political theorists should be asking what difference a change in the aspect of liberty an individual is using might make in how they think and act. This shift in questions, I believe, would have a serious effect on how political theory would be practiced. In fact, the shift would be so significant that it seems to me that such thinkers would be engaged in an entirely different activity, one that, for the sake of clarity, I have been calling "political philosophy."[22]

To return to the example of debates about multilateral trade agreements I considered in the previous section, political philosophy would approach this debate in three steps. First, the political philosopher would examine what the different participants in a debate *see* liberty *as*. This sketch of the different aspects of liberty being used in the debate would in turn be an aspect shift from *seeing* liberty *as* a participant in the debate does, to *knowing* how liberty is being used in these struggles. To *know* liberty then, "consists . . . in the practical activity of being able to give reasons for and against such-and-such a use" of liberty within the debate being investigated.[23] From here, the political philosopher has a couple of options. She can either, upon comparing the different ways of *seeing* liberty *as,* and asking the question "What difference does a change in how liberty is seen make?" decide that in the given case it is better to *see* liberty *as* something than to see it as something else. Second, the political philosopher, through a perspicuous representation of the different aspects of liberty being used in the debate, might be able to demonstrate how the debate in large part is the result of a confusion between the parties owing to the fact that each side experiences aspect-blindness with respect to the way the other side *sees* liberty *as.* Finally, she could, upon examining the different aspects of liberty, *see* a new way of looking at the debate, and propose an alternate way of *seeing* liberty *as.*

The difference between political theory and political philosophy is a significant one that partially reverses a similar type of shift that occurred in the seventeenth century.[24] The work of thinkers such as Descartes was responsible for a shift in philosophy from a practical activity to a theory-centered one. The theory-centered approach to politics "poses problems, and seeks solutions, stated in timeless, universal terms." Thus, political theorists "assumed that uniquely rational procedures exist for handling the intellectual and practical problems of any field of study."[25] Prior to this shift, philosophy was a practical activity designed to help solve specific moral and political problems on a case-by-case basis. However, inspired in part by the success of Newton's scientific method, philosophers became concerned with discovering universal truths. This intellectual shift in the seventeenth century still influences how political theory is done today, and is behind the need that political theorists feel to find a universal and comprehensive account of concepts such as liberty.

In the twentieth century, however, we have seen a move away from this theory-centered approach to politics. Largely due to the work of philosophers such as Wittgenstein and Heidegger, philosophers have once again begun to see how political philosophy can be a practical activity. For instance, James Tully, drawing on the later work of Michel Foucault, has argued that we should see Foucault's philosophy "not as a theory to be elaborated and defended against its critics but as a practical activity, a permanent and critical exercise of thought on thought."[26] So, it seems to me, that the consequence of a shift in aspect, from looking for a comprehensive account of the word "liberty" to seeing liberty as an aspectival concept, is part of an emerging trajectory in contemporary political philosophy.[27]

Part III

Wittgenstein Applied

9

"But One Day Man Opens His Seeing Eye"

The Politics of Anthropomorphizing Language

Wendy Lynne Lee

> We talk, we utter words, and only later get a picture of their life.
> —Ludwig Wittgenstein, *Philosophical Investigations*

Anthropomorphizing and Oppression

The philosophical endeavor to understand oppression ranges over a wide and varied conceptual topography that includes analyses of how particular forms of language use inform the maintenance of oppressive social practices and institutions. However, at least one such use remains undertheorized, namely, that of *anthropomorphizing language*. While *animalizing* language use has received some attention with respect to the role it plays in racism, sexism, and homophobia, adequate attention has yet to be paid to the anthropomorphizing side of this linguistic coinage. In *Neither Man nor Beast,* for instance, the philosopher Carol Adams shows how animalizing discourse significantly contributes to the maintenance of racist and sexist oppression:

> By viewing African-Americans as black beasts, Euro-American men created two pornographic scenarios, one about rapacious black men lusting for white women, and one about lascivious black women available to anyone, man or beast. Both concepts interacted with the notion of white women as pure, virginal, and sexless.... Black men were seen as beasts, sexually threatening white womanhood, a white womanhood defined to aggrandize the sense of white manhood. Black women were seen as sexed, as not able to be violated, because they would enjoy anything—including sex with animals.... Such representations excused as well as invited sexual exploitation by white men.[1]

Sanctioned through dehumanizing language like "nigger" or "black bitch," the animalizing of African-American men and women forms an entrenched aspect not only of the cultural and political landscape but of the epistemic landscape as well. Such language use casts African Americans as a generic other against which a specific conception of what it is to *be* human, namely, white and male, can be defined. Our very image of what it is to *be* a black man or woman is informed by an animalizing whose conceptual load helps to legitimate and sustain oppression. Black men are conceived as rapacious beasts, black women as "in heat," white men as the rational superhuman whose interests determine what is best for all, white women as the mirrors of the interests of white men.

While analyses of animalizing language are clearly crucial to our understanding of oppression, such endeavors are incomplete without complementary analyses of the less obvious, but equally potent, twin of animalizing language: anthropomorphizing. A similar approach to anthropomorphizing language can, I think, deepen our insight with respect to the reproduction and endurance of oppressive institutions and practices. A clearer picture of the ways in which we treat nonhuman or nonliving things *as if* they exemplified human characteristics is not only conceptually integral to an analysis of oppression but illustrates how the maintenance of oppressive institutions becomes a naturalized, unremarked feature of the epistemic landscape.

A significant difference, in other words, between animalizing and anthropomorphizing language lies in the epistemic conditions under which we use language. We animalize only human beings, but we anthropomorphize both human and nonhuman subjects. The latter act, however, is mostly concealed by our conceptions of race and sex. For instance, were the male beasts of Adams's example not tacitly conceived *as if* they were at least enough like human males to carry out "the act" with an (albeit animalized) human female, rationalizing a discourse to protect white women from black men would lack "moral" force.[2] While our focus is drawn to the animalizing language, the extent to which black men are also anthropomorphized tends to be missed. The animalizing language of the example is, moreover, epistemologically dependent on the anthropomorphizing language in that what makes black men vulnerable to the application of animal traits is precisely that their humanity can be regarded as suspect. Black men are both animalized insofar as they are characterized as beasts and anthropomorphized in that the prospect of their humanity provides the propellant toward such characterization. The relationship between human and animal in such a case is dialectical: black men must be and not be human, be and not be animal.

If our aim, then, is to understand how oppressive practices and institutions are sustained through language, we need to come to grips with this other, less obvious but equally powerful, form of language use. To fully appreciate Adams's example, we need to be able to see that even white women are anthropomorphized in it. For although the humanity of white women is alleged to be attractive to black men by virtue of a self-controlled purity and virginity associated with being human, it remains precariously *as if* for white men who see themselves as humanity's paradigmatic examples. As Ludwig Wittgenstein suggests with respect to the deciphering of unfamiliar script, we need to come to a clearer understanding of the "pictures" or "fictions" that "surround" our interpretations of what counts as, in this case, human behavior (PI p. 210). The white men of Adams's example see the world *as* one created for the realization of their interests; they experience *their* world through a picture within which their status as human being forms a natural feature of the conceptual and linguistic topography. Deciphering how others come to be animalized and anthropomorphized in this picture, however, takes it not as given but as "fiction," that is, as a set of institutions or practices that could be otherwise. As Wittgenstein remarks, "To interpret is to think, to do something; seeing is a state" (PI p. 212). To ask how language use informs the maintenance of institutions is to interpret, to think.

Taking this Wittgensteinian perspective as my guide, I will argue for two claims: First, anthropomorphizing—the treatment of nonhuman living and nonliving things as if they exhibited characteristics and behaviors assumed to be more or less unique to human beings—forms a central and ubiquitous feature of our epistemic situations, and thus of the oppressive practices and institutions that form and are informed by them. Anthropomorphizing is a primary conceptual artery by which social and political privilege is accorded to those who, conceived as paradigmatically human, are empowered at the expense of others whose status as human is presumed to be only *as if.*

Second, given its ubiquity, anthropomorphizing forms a key deposit in the institutional bedrock of anthropocentrism (human-centeredness), androcentrism (male-centeredness), heterosexism, and racism. Adopting a Wittgensteinian approach to the relationship between language use and the maintenance of social institutions and practices, I will argue that if Wittgenstein is correct and the meaning of a language is to be found in its multivalent uses, then its meaning is discoverable in those institutions and practices sustained, altered, reified, or abandoned through the linguistic politics of its usage. While many philosophers might be credited with some version of this insight, it is Wittgenstein's sustained attention to the ways in which anthropomorphizing language informs our epistemic situation that most clearly demonstrates, I suggest, the conceptual and linguistic *intimacy* of the relationship between anthropomorphizing and anthropocentrism.

Warren's Logic of Domination

In an earlier essay I attempted to show that a careful analysis of our use of anthropomorphizing language to describe the actions and behaviors of nonhumans sheds light on how such language informs our concept of gender, and hence how anthropocentrism and androcentrism reinforce each other in and through language use.[3] I argued that such analyses support the contention of the ecological feminist Karen Warren that the interlocking oppressions of nonhuman animals, women, and ecological systems are rooted in a *logic of domination:* an ontology or conceptual schema within which moral, political, and aesthetic values are properties determined by their relation to each other within the schema. According to this logic, whatever is identified as female, nonhuman, natural, and nonrational is arrayed against the male, human, cultural, and rational. This ontology naturalizes a value-dualistic hierarchy of superiority and inferiority, which in turn reinforces both anthropocentric and patriarchal institutions and practices.

I argued, following Warren, that the use of anthropomorphizing language is critical to the maintenance of the epistemic matrices within which value is ascribed. Anthropomorphizing language, like animalizing language, confirms the ontological character of distinctions drawn to differentiate what humans "really have" from what nonhumans have only "as if." Because, however, the use of anthropomorphizing language tends to go more or less unnoticed, its confirmation of such distinctions goes unchecked, such that if what counts as paradigmatically human is defined in terms of male characteristics, such that anthropomorphizing ascriptions of abstract thoughts, moral deliberations, intentional actions, and the like will inevitably be as freighted with androcentric as well as anthropocentric values.

A recent Ricky Martin video, "She Bangs," features, for instance, a veritable harem of dancing and swimming women animalized as mermaids, but also anthropomorphized as the potential sexual mates for Martin, who, fully dressed in various suit and tie arrangements (compared to the scanty scales of his mermaid harem), clearly represents a man whose choice of a "little mermaid" bestows upon her the magical gift of getting to be treated *as if* she were really a human being instead of a mermaid. This vision is both human- and male-centered, and it is instructive to try an alternative in which a woman bestows a similar gift on a man, to imagine Disney's *Beauty and the Beast,* for example. Here the animalized man-beast is cast as the dark other to a virginal white woman, who, less through rationality than through her thoroughly feminized beauty and empathy, brings the beast back to his senses and hence to himself as the rational, white, and dominating man she will become subservient to in marriage.

Beyond their obvious sexism or racism, such examples also suggest that no crisp epistemological criteria distinguish anthropomorphizing from non-anthropomorphizing language. The mermaids of "She Bangs" are literally women and fish; their eroticism emerges from an evocative ambiguity of human and animal, reason and instinct, prohibition and provocation.

The mermaid that Ricky Martin chooses becomes a woman by becoming sexualized for him *as* a woman. Reconfirmed as a member in good standing of a male-centered universe, he cannot fail to anthropomorphize the objects of his sexual desires, for, given the logic of domination, women *are* humanized through the sexual attentions of men who cast them, ironically, as animals.

"She Bangs" functions as a metaphor for the anthropomorphic ubiquity of a social and political universe within which human-centeredness is represented as male-centeredness, where all the little mermaids swim right around *him*. Note, however, that I am not suggesting that there are no criteria for distinguishing anthropomorphic from non-anthropomorphic uses of language; I am claiming that the value of attempts to draw such distinctions must itself be assessed in terms of usefulness, in this case, to the confirmation of the logic. One might imagine, for example, a falling poplar leaf as desiring to enjoy its floating to the forest floor or, by virtue of its shape, as intending (pointing) to land there like an airplane. Or, as Wittgenstein observes, if you see "this leaf as a sample of 'leaf shape in general' you *see* it differently from someone who regards it as, say, a sample of this particular shape. . . . if you *see* the leaf in a particular way, you use it in such-and-such a way or according to such-and-such rules" (PI § 74). We are not prevented from drawing a distinction between anthropomorphizing and non-anthropomorphizing uses of language among these examples, but this is beside the point. The more relevant question is: To what ends does drawing the distinction guide us? What purposes are served?

An analysis of the logic of domination implies that if it is possible to disrupt its asymmetrical dualisms, it may also be possible to disrupt the naturalized epistemic links between anthropomorphizing and the androcentrism and anthropocentrism that fuel oppressive institutions and practices. That anthropomorphizing is ubiquitous does not necessarily imply an anthropocentrism for which domination is the only logic. The task, as Wittgenstein might put it, is to become more perspicuous about how our anthropomorphizing is useful, and to whom. Consider, for example, a passage from Toni Morrison's *Beloved* in which a slaveholder called Schoolteacher instructs his (all male) pupils to line up the slave Sethe's human traits in a column beside her animal traits. He corrects his pupil: "No, no. That's not the way. I told you to put her human characteristics on the left; her animal ones on the right. And don't forget to line them up."[4] The aim of this lesson is both animalizing and anthropomorphizing, in that Schoolteacher encourages his pupils to contemplate a comparison of Sethe's alleged animal traits with her human ones, reinforcing at once her radical ontological difference and his pupils' human superiority. Sethe is "discovered" to be animal in her difference, but it is also essential to the logic that she exhibit just enough humanity to make such a "pedagogical" exercise worthwhile. After all, nonhuman animals are merely owned; domination, however, is born of conquering, and as Hegel foresaw in the master/slave dialectic, only human or humanlike opponents can fortify the identity of the master. Hence, such "discoveries" must always be modeled after whatever counts as a paradigmatic *human* case, not because there is some metaphysical truth about what traits or characteristics things have (or have only anthropomorphically), but because it serves a purpose (or multiple purposes) to ascribe such traits in a fashion that maintains this distinction.

In his 1987 book *The Intentional Stance*, the philosopher Daniel Dennett argues for a similar notion:

> How do we attribute the desires (preferences, goals, interests) on whose basis we will shape the list of beliefs [of a given thing or system]? We attribute the desires the system *ought to have*. That is the fundamental rule. It dictates, on a first pass, that we attribute the familiar list of highest, or most basic, desires to people: survival, absence of pain, food, comfort, procreation, entertainment. Citing any one of these desires typically terminates the "Why?" game of reason giving.... Somewhat more informatively, we attribute desires for those things a system believes to be best means to other ends it desires. The attribution of bizarre and detrimental desires thus requires, like the attribution of false beliefs, special stories.[5]

Dennett goes on to point out that "the next task would seem to be distinguishing those intentional systems that *really* have beliefs and desires from those we may find it handy to treat *as if* they had beliefs and desires." "But that," he argues, "would be a Sisyphean labor, or else would be terminated by fiat," for there are no objects to which the anthropomorphizing attribution of intentions are altogether useless.[6] Consider, for example, the lowly thermostat to which we attribute a variety of intentional states related to its "noticing" of a chilly room that it "wants" to warm up:

> In these cases often the only strategy that is at all practical is the intentional strategy; it gives us predictive power we can get by no other method.... For people of limited mechanical aptitude, the intentional interpretation of a simple thermostat is a handy and largely innocuous crutch, but the engineers among us can fully grasp its internal operation without the aid of this anthropomorphizing.... [Yet] the cleverest engineers find it practically impossible to maintain a clear conception of more complex systems... without lapsing into an intentional stance.... but this is just a more advanced case of human epistemic frailty.[7]

While Dennett gives a compelling argument for the epistemic ubiquity of anthropomorphizing, his view remains well within the logic of domination, in that he fails to ask to what other purposes ascriptions of intention and desire could be put. Ascribing intentional states to Morrison's Sethe is a far less innocuous act than ascribing the desire to heat a room to a thermostat; Schoolteacher encourages his pupils to anthropomorphize Sethe just insofar as she will have the characteristics she *ought to have,* namely, those that insure her status as a comprehending but docile instrument of his will. So too the thermostat. Schoolteacher suffers the same epistemic frailty we all do, but while Dennett rightly recognizes that to distinguish the attributes that things *really have* from those they have only *as if* is a Sisyphean labor, he fails to appreciate that this is as much an opportunity as it is an enigma. For the very reasons that Dennett insists that any system can be described as possessing intentional attributes, the door is left open to motives other than the objective or disinterested. As Dennett puts it: if the behavior of a lectern can be described anthropomorphically as believing itself to be the center of the civilized universe and desiring to stay there, anything can be.[8] And so too Sethe, whose desires, like the thermostat's, must be governed by others.

It appears, then, that there simply are no epistemic limitations with respect to what can become the subject of anthropomorphizing language other than what counts as an attribution of the bizarre or the detrimental, and such is not the case with Schoolteacher, however much we may want to think so. For what Schoolteacher's exercise reinforces in his pupils is precisely the rightness and naturalness of slavery; were Sethe not able to be characterized by her animal qualities as well as her human ones, slavery could not be justified as in the interest of the enslaved who, like animals, are considered unable to fully comprehend such interests themselves. Neither bizarre nor detrimental from the point of view of the deeply interested logic that governs slavery, what such examples show is that ascriptions of what characteristics a thing ought to have are rarely if ever disinterested. Schoolteacher is no less authoritative as a candidate for exercising the power to anthropomorphize or animalize than any similarly situated white man. Both Dennett and Schoolteacher enjoy the largely invisible but unparalleled luxury of being the white male whose claim to objectivity is reinforced through the logic of domination.

Intrinsic versus Instrumental Worth

Even what may constitute the most important of value dualisms, the distinction between intrinsic and instrumental worth, turns out to be subject to the logic of domination. Intrinsic worth inheres in a thing simply by virtue of being that thing. Contrary to this is the worth assigned externally by virtue of a thing's usefulness as the instrument of others. On closer inspection, however, it seems that the beneficiaries of this distinction are the same as those who benefit from other aspects of the logic. Like intentions and desires, intrinsic worth is attributed in accord with its usefulness in, for example, establishing what counts as an appropriate object of moral consideration or what counts as having not moral but, say, labor value. Neither Morrison's Sethe nor Dennett's thermostat count as moral objects because, as Schoolteacher points out in the course of lining up Sethe's characteristics, Sethe is a slave, a living instrument of his will. Even the living/nonliving distinction will not help us to distinguish between Sethe's value and the thermostat's, for the thermostat can be treated *as if* it were alive, and Sethe can be treated *as if* she were simply an extension of a plow or harness.

If Sethe and the thermostat can be assigned value through that authority naturalized by the logic, then worth must itself constitute a form of anthropomorphizing. Because we assume that the white and the male represent the archetype of intrinsic worth, all other worth must be derived or *as if* by definition. This, however, is hardly a surprising find: as feminist research demonstrates, identifying women, non-Europeans, and nonhuman nature with instrumental value is not only ontologically but materially prerequisite to the maintenance of heteropatriarchal and racist institutions. How else could we rationalize slavery or misogyny, not to mention fur wearing and animal consumption? Indeed, while many ecological philosophers, feminist and nonfeminist alike, disparage the attribution of instrumental worth to a thing as neglectful of its intrinsic value, such disparagement can only occur at the cost of tacitly promoting a concept of "intrinsic" that, locating itself on the human, white, male, and superior side of the logic's value-dualistic ontology, reinforces the marriage of anthropocentrism to androcentrism and racism.

Given an analysis of how such dualisms function to sustain the logic of domination, it's not surprising that in the interest of rejecting racism and heterosexism, feminist philosophers of ecology would seek to reject anthropocentrism as well. It would not seem that, as feminists and philosophers, we could coherently do otherwise. Hence we face a dilemma: either we discover some nondualistic way to escape our anthropocentrism or we seek to rupture the mutually implicative links between anthropocentrism, heterosexism, and racism. Given both the ubiquity of anthropomorphizing and the implications of the logic, the first option is at least unrealistic. The second option, I suggest, is not only viable but important to ongoing ecofeminist critique of the relationship between the domination of women and that of nonhuman animals and systems.

Anthropocentric ubiquity need not imply the reproduction of the heterosexism and racism associated with the logic of domination. To the extent that we can critically evaluate the relationships among these isms, we can become clearer about *how* they become naturalized through the use of anthropomorphizing language. We cannot *not* anthropomorphize, but we can comprehend how it informs the character of our anthropocentrism in hopes of developing a more self-critical centrism whose epistemic integrity stems not from ignoring the ubiquitous but from embracing a human-centeredness that takes such ubiquity seriously as an epistemic constraint on both knowledge and moral judgment.

The Masculine *as* Generic

The epistemically relevant difference between anthropomorphizing and anthropocentrism is that while the former constitutes a critical aspect of our efforts to explain and describe what things are and do, the latter merely follows. That we treat nonhuman entities as if their behavior exhibited human qualities is a ubiquitous feature of our human-centeredness. But this does not imply that anthropomorphizing has any particular implications for anthropocentrism other than that it is the only point of view available to human language users who are themselves epistemically, socially, and politically situated. That some are socially and politically situated such that their epistemic status becomes identified with what it means to *be* a knower is a function, not of anthropomorphizing per se, but rather of place within the logic of domination; in this picture, epistemic credibility is naturalized as "man." As Wittgenstein remarks in *Philosophical Investigations*:

> The evolution of the higher animals and of man, and the awakening of consciousness at a particular level. The picture is something like this: Though the ether is filled with vibrations the world is dark. But one day man opens his seeing eye, and there is light.
> What this language primarily describes is a picture. What is to be done with this picture, how it is to be used, is still obscure. Quite clearly, however, it must be explored if we want to understand the sense of what we are saying. But the picture seems to spare us this work; it already points to a particular use. *This is how it takes us in.* (PI p. 184, emphasis added)

The picture that Wittgenstein describes is suggestive of the intimate relationship between anthropomorphizing and anthropocentrism. Its world is dark until "one day man opens his seeing eye" and casts his gaze about, filling the world with the light of his awakening consciousness. This world *is* anthropomorphic in that its light represents consciousness, his seeing eye its newfound knowability. This world is as known as this man sees, and his application to it of qualities he takes to be his own are as natural as his assumption that the world is in fact *as* he sees it.

That this correspondence might be faulty or mistaken fails to occur to him, for the picture is as seamless as it is made comprehensible through his anthropomorphizing of it; "he" is "man."⁹ By this same token, it fails to occur to him that his epistemic situation is specifically anthropocentric, for no other view of the world seems either possible or different given this seamlessness. He could no more have failed to anthropomorphize than he could have kept his seeing eye closed; still, the picture's seamlessness is the product of a correspondence, not between his seeing and the way the world really is, but rather between his seeing and the usefulness of the picture that confirms him as a knower. *This is how it takes us in;* anthropomorphizing forms no additional step to knowing, but is rather incorporated into it as an unremarkable feature of the act itself.

The picture also "takes us in" by assuming a standard of valuation premised on a specific image conjured for the reader, namely, an image of a man who, representing generic humankind, identifies the very conditions of knowing—the awakening of consciousness—as masculine. It is only through *his* seeing eye that there is light and, as Naomi Scheman points out, such uses are no more generic than uses of feminine pronouns fail to designate a variety of "other." "Masculine nouns and pronouns," writes Scheman, "do not . . . have genuinely generic senses. Rather, in designating the masculine *as* generic, they designate the feminine as different."¹⁰ The meaning of "but one woman opens her seeing eye" elicits a particularity neither anthropocentric nor gynocentric but merely discordant, in that the attempt to locate "her" as generic threatens to expose the picture for what it is—a picture—grounded in a use of language that, by defining the masculine *as* generic, defines the androcentric *as* the anthropocentric.

Consider, for example, the following picture of thinking:

> Suppose that our picture of thinking was a human being, leaning his head on his hand while he talks to himself. Our question is not "Is that a correct picture?" But "How is this picture employed as a picture of thinking?"
>
> Say, not: "We have formed a wrong picture of thinking"—but: "We don't know our way about in the use of our picture, or of our pictures." And hence we don't know our way about in the use of our word. (RPPI § 549)

In this picture, thinking is squarely imagined in terms of the masculine *as* generic. An image of a man leaning his head on his hand while he talks to himself is readily "employed as a picture of thinking" precisely because it exemplifies the unremarkably paradigmatic case. The substitution of a woman could not serve the same purpose because the picture's usefulness is premised on the very seamlessness that introducing "she" would disrupt. It is, in other words, a picture of thinking because its anthropocentrism is bolstered by the androcentrism that characterizes the patriarchal ontology within which such pictures are useful. That androcentric "pictures" of rationality, intention, or deliberation inform the use of psychological language more generally is not surprising; anthropomorphizing is as deeply woven into our understanding of the behavior and actions of basset hounds and macromolecules as it is woven into our understanding of that of human beings.

Consider, for instance, the sentence "the chair is thinking to itself:"

> WHERE? In one of its parts? Or outside its body; in the air around it? Or not *anywhere* at all? But then what is the difference between this chair's saying something to itself and another one's doing so, next to it?—But then how is it with man: where does *he* say things to himself? How does it come about that this question seems senseless; and that no specification of a place is necessary except just that this man is saying something to himself? Whereas the question *where* the chair talks to itself seems to demand an answer—The reason is: we want to know *how* the chair is supposed to be like a human being; whether, for instance, the head is at the top of the back and so on. (PI § 361)

In this picture, determining how the chair could be like a human being is identical to determining how it could be like "man." Largely effaced by the inquiry into what it means to say that something is "thinking to itself," the masculine as generic operates as a tacitly given feature defining the paradigmatic case. Even so, it remains no clearer in the case of "man" than in that of the chair what it means to say *where* something is thinking to itself. We can readily imagine a chair in a children's story thinking to itself: furrowing its brow, rubbing its chin, staring out into space, and so on. We imagine it, in other words, as if it were like a human being precisely because we take it for granted that such notions make sense in the latter case.

But herein lies what Wittgenstein might call the conjuring trick. For like the man who has but to open his seeing eye, the picture boasts a kind of naturalized epistemic cache. That is, we readily recognize that its meaning spares us the hard work of determining what "thinking" means applied to our own case. The question "Where is 'man' thinking?" simply does not occur to us; hence we fail to notice that while "thinking" may be applied more usefully to human beings than to chairs, this does not mean it is applied less anthropomorphically. To see this, one might try imagining the following alternative pictures of thinking: ducks flying in perfect formation or the Borg cube from Star Trek. Questions like "where is the duck formation or the Borg cube thinking?" seem almost absurd, yet not unimaginable. Such is the stuff, after all, of good science fiction. The case of "man" only seems more obvious because what is useful in such language just is his confirmation as the paradigm case.

What follows from a consideration of such cases, however, is not a call to repudiate the use of anthropomorphizing language but the need for a more lucid distinction between what such cases illustrate—that anthropomorphizing is a ubiquitous feature of our epistemic situations—and what such cases reinforce—the androcentric forms taken by the anthropocentrism that follows. We cannot, for example, simply throw up our hands and declare anthropomorphizing useless. It is difficult to overestimate the value of a language that allows us to query whether it is possible to *harm* an ecological system, *respect* a body in preparation for burial, or *teach* a gorilla American Sign Language, although each case involves treating the thing in question *as if* it could experience harm, respect, or teaching *as such*. It is, moreover, difficult to imagine a science that could progress without the use of anthropomorphizing language to describe, for instance, the "intentions" of macromolecules or the "beliefs" of dynamic systems.

Failing, however, to draw the distinction between the ubiquitous and the culturally and historically variable commits us to the assumption that no other anthropocentrism is possible given the usefulness (for some) and the sheer pervasiveness of the anthropomorphizing language we *do* use. Anthropomorphic ubiquity need not, however, imply this, for treating things—whatever they are—*as if* they exemplified qualities identified as distinctively human does not necessarily imply identifying these qualities as male. What's needed is a denaturalizing analysis of *how* such language contributes to a logic within which some men continue to be invisibly empowered as the imprimatur of all humanity.

Denaturalizing "Man"

Just as the attempt to imagine just where a formation of ducks or the Borg cube could be thinking to themselves serves by comparison to denaturalize "man" as the paradigm case of thinking, so too we can easily imagine other uses of "thinking" whose meanings reflect the privileged status accorded to the masculine as generic. Consider, for example, the following: "Where is woman thinking to herself? In one or all of her parts? Or not anywhere at all?" Whatever interpretation we might offer, one feature seems clear enough: "woman" cannot be substituted for "man" without a disruptive alteration of meaning which, depending on the context, could range from ridicule (a joke told by a man in a sports bar) to spiritual insight (read or sung at a women's music festival). By comparison, the use of "man" appears both natural and ordinary; its force derives from the epistemic seamlessness sustained through those social relations that confirm and empower men as paradigmatic human beings. Note that this is not to say that we merely use language in heteropatriarchal ways, but rather that language *is* as heteropatriarchal as are the social relations naturalized through it; it is through language that oppression becomes ordinary.

The man who opens his seeing eye is thus blind to the possibilities raised by duck formations, Borg Cubes, women, and so on; he cannot be otherwise without disrupting the epistemic correspondence between his "seeing" and the "reality" "seen" that defines his claim to embody the paradigmatically human. Disruptions, in other words, denaturalize; the issue for us is merely *how*. Consider for example, bell hooks's autobiographical account of her experience growing up in Kentucky in *Wounds of Passion:*

> Memories of being told to stay away from white men stayed with me. But like those metal detectors, I learned early which white men were low-down—looking for hot black pussy—looking to get some from anything black wearing a skirt, and those white men who minded their own business, who could look at you without sex on their mind. If only I had a dollar for every white man that tried to lure us to take a ride. Growing up southern was to know race and sex were always mixed—always present even without the "other." Everything about race had shaped black desire. We had to learn it young because southern white men couldn't tell the difference between girl and woman—not if her color was black. And everything black could be bought, had, taken, owned.[11]

Despite its intimation of sexual violence, or perhaps even by virtue of it, what hooks captures here is one moment of male prerogative understood to be so ordinary that it forms an aspect of the moral educations of black girls. Little different than being warned away from, say, a volcano or a cliff, the danger posed by "man" requires the development of good instincts, which, like metal detectors, seek not to end but rather to evade the "low-down." Such men are like the weather; they form a feature of hooks's girlhood reality disrupted only by the telling of its story, that is, only by the questioning tone suggested by hooks's first-person narrative.

From the point of view of this "I," however, we can begin to see the outline of a more disruptive reading, for the power authorized to "man" is confirmed by hooks's deference to warning *and* divested of its claim to represent the generic by her first-person particularizing of an ethnically, culturally, politically, historically, economically, and geographically specific relationship of white men to black women and girls. Indeed, power here is not authorized to "man" or even to men at all, but rather only to those white men who are "looking to get some from anything black wearing a skirt." In hooks's text, the masculine operates only as generically as does the social and sexual domination of white men whose prerogative to objectify and animalize black women is confirmed in a logic that sanctions the actions of the "low-down" at the same time it promotes white maleness as the human ideal. In either case, power derives not from any generic humanity in fact represented, but simply from the *presumed right to claim it*. The introduction of race further reinforces *and* denaturalizes "man" by defining what black women and girls are expected to know while divesting this knowledge of its metaphysical pretensions, leaving in its place some men's prerogative to initiate specific social relations naturalized through the animalizing language of "pussy" or "woman," or the objectifying language of "bought, had, taken, owned."

By the same token, however, that the first-person nature of hooks's account of the low-down serves to denaturalize the generic, it also discloses the extent to which "man" is itself an anthropomorphism applied *as if* legitimate authority were merely recognized in its use. This cannot, of course, be the case, for to the extent that "man" is defined within the logic of domination in opposition to "woman," the authority its use endorses is not merely recognized but instantiated in the form of a particular social relation. Indeed, this authority could not be "recognized" under any circumstances other than heteropatriarchal *regardless of who appropriates it,* a point well exemplified by hooks's position as a writer. In relation to her text as autobiography, her position is highly conflicted: she is located both as "she" who represents precisely that which is not "man," and yet, *qua* writer, as that "man" whose presumed authorial distance from the text signals the generic.

Hooks is both animalized and anthropomorphized in that, cast within the text as black and female, she is defined not merely as a fuckable object but as that through which white men define themselves as human. In the context of a social relationship determined by the logic of domination, a mere object will not do because it cannot be defined in opposition to white male humanity; for this task, something "hot and black" is required. Hooks is thus animalized to the same extent as the "black beasts" of Carol Adams's example, namely, to whatever extent the logic is reinforced by references to that black female animal whose representatives, women and girls, are conceived to be like animals: ready to copulate with anything. Hooks, however, also anthropomorphizes herself, in that she situates herself within the text in direct opposition to the epistemic position she occupies outside it. For by staking a claim in her own authority as a writer, she effectively treats herself *as if* she were a representative of generic humanity. Yet, because hooks is neither male nor white, her writing persistently disrupts any invitation to interpret her this way, for her text remains autobiographical.

At once the writing animal and the animalized writer, hooks's words disrupt the logic's ontological stability. For unlike the leap required to imagine the Borg cube or a formation of ducks thinking to themselves, no such imagination is required to comprehend that hooks is writing to empower herself *as* a black woman. Such readings are nothing if not a danger to the institutions that rely on the logic. Far from the "comfy" disposal of science fiction, hooks *is* a black woman writer who, "thinking to herself," could "really have" qualities associated exclusively with the masculine as generic. Her words put the lie not only to the material conditions of racism and sexism but to the very conceptual edifice that supports it. So too, Toni Morrison's Sethe, who, in an act at once horrifying and liberating, animalizing and humanizing, kills her baby to keep the child from becoming appropriated by the slaveholders:

> When she got back from the jail house, she was glad the fence was gone. That's where they had hitched their horses—where she saw, floating above the railing as she squatted in the garden, Schoolteacher's hat. By the time she faced him, looked him dead in the eye, she had something in her arms that stopped him dead in his tracks. He took a backward step with each jump of the baby heart until finally there was none. "I stopped him," she said, staring at the place where the fence used to be. "I took out my babies where they'd be safe."[12]

The same Schoolteacher who treated it as a pedagogical exercise to line up Sethe's animal characteristics next to her human ones is stopped as dead in his tracks, as we are when we realize the staggering meaning of this act of infanticide. Sethe's act puts the lie to any such easy distinction between what humans really have—and do and what nonhuman animals have and do only *as if.* Sethe could not be more human, or humane, than to keep her baby from slavery, nor could she have been thinking less to herself when she "just flew": "If she thought anything it was No. No. Nonono. Simple. . . . This here Sethe talked about safety with a handsaw."[13]

Sethe's "words" so threaten to destabilize the logic of domination that its claim to ontological status becomes denaturalized. According to the logic, Sethe should no more be able to claim the freedom of her children than hooks should be able to claim the authority to write. *Neither should have access to the words of their own emancipation.* The conflict is that they *do* have access, and they are black and female. Hooks not only recognizes this conflict, but exploits it in prose that captures both its scope and its very real potential consequences. In the third person she writes: "She had not been able to understand, then, in her girlhood why being smart with books and words was dangerous, but she knew that it was making her into something no man would want as a wife. . . . being smart might make you become something men might desire but never something in his right mind any man could love." And then in the first person: "He acted as though it was only natural that I was smart, not anything strange or unusual. He made me feel as though it was only natural that I wanted to be a writer. He was the same as me or so it seemed. With him the part of me that longed to think and think had found a place. I was no longer in hiding."[14]

In the first passage, hooks effectively creates herself as a credible witness to her own experience as smart through the appropriation of an epistemic posture whose generic credentials define the third person. Cast as unnatural within the text, hooks lays bare the meaning of her appropriation via its potential consequences: to claim the generic is, in effect, to betray women. As the writer, hooks cannot but disrupt the third-person claim to a seamless correspondence between the generic gaze and the picture cast before the reader. For when hooks opens her "seeing eye" there is not the uninterrupted light anthropomorphically born of her consciousness, but rather a more jarring light interrupted by shadows cast by hooks herself. The reader is left to read anthropomorphically, that is, *as if* a black woman writer could represent the "man who opens his seeing eye" even though she is simultaneously "never something in his right mind any man could love." Yet the recognition of such a reading also animalizes hooks, for by anthropomorphizing her, one must first see her as not "man," and hence not human.

In the second passage, hooks is recreated as "smart, not anything strange or unusual" by a male lover who recognizes her desire to be a writer. It is as if in and by him she is outfitted for the discovery of her own intrinsic worth, her own natural ability as a writer. Through his "seeing eye" she is disclosed as "the same," that is, as "man" thinking to herself such that the question "Where?" is as senseless for her as it is for him. But just as hooks's longing "to think and think" is endorsed and promoted in the passage, so it is also denaturalized by the very surprise with which it is greeted by the narrating "I." She has not expected this recognition, yet she experiences it as the discovery of an intrinsically valuable feature of her self. She can know herself through him to be a writer, yet at the same time what she knows is already undone by the "I" whose imposition on the text effects a reminder to the reader that she is no more "man" than his creation of her as an extension of himself.

His representation of "man" remains unremarked to her; her representation not only disrupts the text but unravels his claim to the masculine as generic by locating him as "the same as me." Again, she is both animalized and anthropomorphized through the first-person narrative, for to whatever extent hooks discovers herself to be as smart as her lover, she does so against the backdrop of a logic that locates black women as not "man"—a logic whose rejection is attended by consequences that can only serve to remind her of her status as the potential prey of the low-down. By this same token, however, hooks's claim to be a writer whose worth as such is recognized by a legitimate authority is itself unraveled by the text's inability to sustain a distinction between intrinsic and instrumental worth. That is, hooks's worth is defined in terms of her instrumental worth to those white men who would lure her into cars or, as in Sethe's case, would line up her animal traits next to her human ones. But neither Sethe's or hooks's claim to be of worth can be understood as an affirmation of their intrinsic worth over their instrumental worth. Rather, it signifies a collapse of the distinction itself; for claims are not intrinsic, they are made through words and actions.

The tacit claim that hooks, *qua* writer, makes to represent generic "man" locates hooks along that axis of the logic of domination identified with intrinsic worth, yet this same claim is unraveled by hooks's own recognition that this worth is discoverable only to the extent that she fulfills her instrumental worth to her lover. For given that her smartness stands in direct opposition to her value as a woman, she cannot otherwise assume herself to be something any man could love. The recognition of her worth as smart, as that which identifies her with the fully human, is, in other words, premised on precisely that to which it is opposed, namely, her instrumental value to men as an animal, as something that can be bought, taken, or sold, as a woman. That her lover appears to represent something better than, say, the white men who lure little black girls into cars only serves to enhance the conflict, for it reminds us that his epistemic position is as discordant as hers in that both are black. He, then, is identified like her with the instrumental worth rejected by both in hooks's claim to be "the same as me."

Ecofeminist Critique and a Self-Critical Centrism

Anthropomorphizing forms a subtle but critically important aspect of the conceptual construction of sex and race. In *Wounds of Passion,* hooks articulates an autobiographical narrative of her experience of growing up black and female in a 1950s America steeped in cultural and political practices whose aim was, in effect, to ensure the maintenance of an anthropocentrism whose paradigmatic representatives were primarily white affluent males. What an analysis of hooks's narrative—as well as Morrison's, Adams's, and Dennett's—can help to illustrate is how anthropocentrism codes not only the masculine but also the white as generic. Hooks's conflicted position in the text exemplifies how sex and race are coded as deviant through the use of language that takes as its unremarkable point of departure a conception of "man" that not only empowers some—namely, white men—at the expense of others, but does so in conformity with a logic whose constitutively hierarchical and oppositional order serves to naturalize domination.

Sexed and raced through language, hooks is not only cast as "other" but defined in opposition to the paradigmatic case through a language that, animalizing on the surface, relies on the epistemic ubiquity of anthropomorphizing to insure the ontological order. The autobiographical character of her text serves not only to disrupt our assumptions about black women as writers but to denaturalize the impulse to read in conformity with the logic. For through her use of "I" as well as her jarring juxtaposition of the first and third person, hooks interrogates what "one man sees"; not taken in by the picture, her prose ruptures the mutually supportive links between androcentrism, anthropocentrism, and racism.

From the anti-anthropocentric perspective favored by many ecological feminists,[15] the most that such analyses can show is that because anthropocentrism is so clearly mired in an ontology that supports androcentric privilege, it can offer no philosophical footing for the development of an ecologically responsible moral posture. I suggest, however, that drawing this conclusion is premature, and that a closer examination of the position hooks adopts in *Wounds of Passion* may hint at exactly the footing we need. Far from anti-anthropocentric, hooks occupies an acutely centric epistemic, historical, social, and material position in that, by moving back and forth between first and third person, she reminds us of her particularity, and she takes responsibility for it in the very questioning of that position. This centrism is achieved not merely because her text is autobiographical but because in both style and content she examines what it means to exemplify the contradiction of being both a black woman and a writer—what it means to find her way about in words not intended for her use.

Hooks claims to be a credible witness to her own experience as black, as a woman, as thinking to, for, and about herself; and, however contradictory her centrism may be, it is neither egocentric nor self-effacing but rather highly self-critical as well as defiant. Hooks does not flinch, but takes her epistemic situation seriously, actively disparaging the pretense to a seamless correspondence between her knowing and the reality supplied by experience. Such a centrism understands itself not as the center but rather as that experientially credible, relationally defined, always revisable, point of departure whose identity derives not from a notion of essence, but rather from the more forthright recognition that no other than *this* epistemic situation is possible, and *it* is a human one.

In *Wounds of Passion,* hooks stakes a claim to humanity, evoking profoundly human desires, sufferings, and foibles in the very project of dismantling the claim to privilege accorded to the male and the white. Such a centrism does not then condemn us to reproduce the heterosexism and racism that currently pervade the ways in which we animalize and anthropomorphize through language. It does, however, demand that we dispense with conceptual distinctions that are more likely to contribute to the maintenance of oppressive social institutions than to a sound critique. This aptly characterizes the distinction between intrinsic and instrumental worth, in that, however well intentioned, our attempts to apply it only reinforce a logic within which the right to dominate is secured by the unquestioned assumption of intrinsic worth.

The energy spent in defense of this distinction could be better invested in the exploration of ways in which the use of anthropomorphizing language contributes to the maintenance of the logic of domination across other axes of domination. How, for example, do such analyses bear on the animalizing and anthropomorphizing ways in which we conceive nature, affectivity, or homosexual identity? In this chapter, I have barely scratched the surface of such issues.[16] Still, if the meanings of words are to be found in their uses, nowhere is there more telling a place to stake a claim than where oppression finds its most powerful allies. I have tried to demonstrate that one such place is anthropomorphizing. Wittgenstein remarks,

> If the formation of concepts can be explained by the facts of nature, should we not be interested, not in grammar, but rather in that in nature which is the basis of grammar?—Our interest certainly includes the correspondence between concepts and very general facts of nature. . . . But our interest does not fall back upon these possible causes of the formation of concepts; we are not doing natural science; nor yet natural history—since we can also invent fictitious natural history for our purposes. (PI p. 230)

Perhaps "nature" is itself a word whose meaning lies in its use, that is, in its usefulness to very human projects. In this light "natural history" might be best conceived as that ontology or "fiction" within which staking a claim to humanity is best conceived not as a project of domination but rather as an always revisable project of critical self-reflection.[17]

10

Does Your Patient Have a Beetle in His Box?

Language-Games and the Spread of Psychopathology

Carl Elliott

These are strange times for psychiatry. Each month brings news of a newly popular mental disorder. Some of these disorders have just been discovered. Many others are old but are said to be spreading at unprecedented rates. Depression, panic disorder, obsessive-compulsive disorder, social phobia, post-traumatic stress disorder, attention-deficit hyperactivity disorder, multiple personality disorder, gender identity disorder, chronic fatigue syndrome, fibromyalgia: fifty years ago, most of these disorders did not exist, and those that did exist were thought to be very rare. Yet at some point in recent decades each of them has emerged as a force to be reckoned with, both in psychiatric clinics and in the pages of medical journals. In the 1950s depression was thought to be such a rare problem that no pharmaceutical company wanted to invest money into a treatment.[1] Yet by the early 1990s, the antidepressant Prozac had become the second most prescribed drug in the United States.

The emergence of so much psychopathology might suggest that the psychiatrist's office has become a very busy place. Instead, however, psychiatrists have found themselves under attack. Many intellectuals refuse to believe that all these mental disorders are real. Health insurers and government bodies are declining to pay for lengthy psychotherapy. Patient advocate groups line up on both sides of the barricades, one side claiming to defend vulnerable people from psychiatrists too enthusiastic about dispensing psychoactive drugs, the other claiming to defend sick people from skeptics who do not take their suffering seriously. Right-wing critics accuse psychiatrists of medicalizing sin and weakness, while left-wing critics accuse them of medicalizing legitimate lifestyle choices. A recent book attacking the *DSM-IV*, the psychiatric manual of diagnosis, is titled *Making Us Crazy*.[2]

The stakes in this debate are not merely academic. Any health system must make choices about which medical treatments it will fund. Most systems will pay for treatments that are medically necessary but not for those that are merely cosmetic or do not work. Many will pay for reconstructive plastic surgery, for example, but draw the line at cosmetic surgery. How should policy makers think about psychiatric treatment? Which newly emerging disorders should be counted as legitimate candidates for third-party payment? If mental disorders really are expanding at the rates at which many psychiatrists suggest, many health systems could soon be facing a crisis.

Philosophers have responded to this issue predictably. They have defined the problem in this way: "What counts as a mental illness?" The answer, they have suggested, lies in coming up with a satisfactory definition. If we can just set up necessary and sufficient conditions for what counts as mental illness, we can then use these conditions to whittle away at the edges of the concept of mental illness, discarding the pretenders to legitimacy and including only those we deem worthy. This is the approach, for example, of the psychiatrist and philosopher Lawrie Reznek, who writes that a condition is a mental illness "if and only if it is an abnormal and involuntary process that does (mental) harm and should best be treated by medical means."[3] His purpose here is to exclude from the domain of mental illness such pretenders as sexual excess (it is not involuntary) or drug addictions (they are not best treated by medical means) while including core conditions such as schizophrenia or bipolar affective disorder.

The role of the philosopher, on this view, is to codify a language that has fallen into disorder. Mental illnesses have a reality apart from our descriptions of them, and philosophers make sure that our vocabulary matches up to that reality while at the same time avoiding fuzziness, sloppiness, or contradiction. The philosopher thus serves as a kind of language czar, deciding for the linguistic community the ways in which words can be legitimately used. It is this kind of role, of course, that Wittgenstein explicitly rejected. "It is not our aim to refine or complete the system of rules for the use of our words in unheard-of ways" (PI § 133). The job of the philosopher, according to Wittgenstein, is not to build philosophical theories, not to explain, not to systematize the language. "We must do away with all *explanation*, and description alone must take its place" (PI § 109).

In Wittgenstein's view, not only is linguistic rule-writing an illegitimate job for the philosopher, it is not even an especially interesting job. To look at this extraordinary proliferation of mental disorders and see only an opportunity for rule-writing is like looking at a tropical rain forest and seeing only the opportunity to use a lawn mower. The more interesting question is: How has all this extraordinary complexity come about? I don't want to suggest that policy questions are immaterial, of course. It matters to all of us which psychiatric treatments our health systems fund, and under what circumstances. But we will never get a handle on these questions without understanding just what it is about mental illness that allows it to expand and contract in such remarkable ways. The answer to this question, I want to suggest, is partly philosophical and partly empirical. What allows mental illness to expand and contract is a function not only of the nature of the mind but of the particular ways in which our own North American societies have developed.

The Beetle in the Box

In a well-known passage of the *Investigations,* Wittgenstein tells a philosophical parable. "Suppose everyone had a box with something in it: we call it a 'beetle.' No one can look into anyone else's box, and everyone says he knows what a beetle is only by looking at *his* beetle" (PI § 293). It would be quite possible, Wittgenstein points out, for each person to have something different in his box. It might even be possible for whatever a person has in his box to be constantly changing. Yet the word "beetle" could still have a place in the language-game. Even if all the boxes were empty, these people could still talk to one another using the word "beetle." There need not be any actual beetles in the boxes for the language-game to be played.

What is Wittgenstein getting at here? For one thing, he is suggesting that this particular language-game does not depend on the existence of any actual object to which the words refer. Beetle or no beetle, people can still play the game. The meaning of these words depends not on the existence of objects to which they refer but on the rules of this particular game (PI § 43). Words like "pain" or "red"—or to offer examples closer to home, "panic attack" or "social phobia" or "fibromyalgia"—do not get their meaning from some internal condition of the mind to which the words refer but from the rules of the particular language-game that is being played.

Does this mean that when people use words like "pain" or "panic attack" or "anxiety" they are not describing any private experience? No, of course not. Wittgenstein is not claiming that there is no difference between actually being in pain and pretending to be in pain, or that there is no difference between pain-behavior that is accompanied by pain and pain-behavior that is not (PI § 304). That claim would be absurd. And in fact, we do in fact have a complex vocabulary to distinguish these sorts of things (pretending to be in pain, acting as if you are pretending, and pretending not to pretend, etc.) (see LWPPI §§ 861–77). Wittgenstein's point is just that the words we use to describe these internal mental states get their meaning from the social context in which they are used. We use these words to describe our private mental states, but the words get their *meaning* from a public language-game.

Wittgenstein is trying to show us here that the grammar of this particular language-game is not like the grammar of naming objects. We learn the language-game not by looking inward and naming what we see there—not by looking into the box and describing its contents—but by being initiated into the game by others. In the same way that a person learns the beetle-box game from more experienced players, we learn how to describe our inner states from language users more experienced in the use of a particular set of words. In the case of mental disorders, we learn the language from psychiatrists, psychologists, current and former patients, novels, plays, the popular media, the courts, and, increasingly, television advertisements aimed directly at potential buyers of psychoactive drugs.

Wittgenstein's beetle-box story helps us understand why mental disorders are so flexible in their application, and so apt to expand and contract, depending on the language-game in which they are applied. In the case of most mental disorders, psychiatrists have no concrete, objective way of verifying whether or not the person has the disorder: no blood test, no medical imaging device, not even a characteristic finding upon physical examination. Psychiatrists do not listen to heart sounds or percuss chests; they cannot open up the box and look at the beetle. They diagnose mental disorders based on what people tell them and how they behave. The grammar of diagnosis, however, is not like the grammar of naming: psychiatrists are not trying to pinpoint and name a private sensation inside a patient's head. The diagnoses they give to patients are determined by the rules of the language-game. These rules are in turn influenced by a vast array of larger forces and pressures, from market forces to identity politics to the bureaucracy of third-party payers.

Wittgenstein suggests that the words we use to describe pain are connected to primitive, natural expressions of the sensation. When we are children, we are taught to replace these primitive expressions with expressions of more complexity. "A child has hurt himself and he cries; and then adults talk to him and teach him exclamations, and later, sentences. They teach the child new pain-behavior" (PI § 244). But while pain is universal, mental disorders are not. Unlike pain, mental disorders are not (as Wittgenstein would put it) part of the natural history of human beings. Everyone has felt sad, but very few of us descend into full-blown clinical depression. Everyone has felt self-conscious, but few of us are so anxious and inhibited that we cannot raise a glass of water in front of another person without our hand trembling. Everyone has sexual desires, but few people have a sexual desire for small children. Elementary physical pain is one thing; any medical student studying physical diagnosis will learn the various ways in which a person can describe physical pain: stabbing pain, burning pain, aching pain, and so on. But the ways in which psychic distress can be expressed and described is a far messier, more complex, historically and locally contingent affair.

The meaning of a word, Wittgenstein suggests, is its use in the language-game. And in this language-game, one of the key elements is uncertainty—

uncertainty about what others have in their boxes, uncertainty about what to call it, even uncertainty about what is in your own box. This kind of uncertainty is what makes it possible to have such a complex set of concepts to refer even to physical pain, much less psychic distress. (Just look, as Wittgenstein does, at the concepts of mimicry, sincerity, fakery, hypocrisy, pretense, and so on.) Uncertainty, he says, "is an (essential) trait of all these language-games. But this does not mean that everyone is hopelessly in doubt about what other people feel" (LWPPI § 877).

In the case of psychic distress, in fact, it is probably more accurate to say that we have no single language-game. Instead, we have many language-games, each overlapping with the others: one specialized vocabulary used by psychiatrists, another vocabulary used by the courts, yet another vocabulary used by pharmaceutical companies to sell psychoactive drugs, still another used in the popular media, and so on. In each of these overlapping games, the vocabulary of mental illness has particular uses, and these uses are often very specialized. A single word may have many different uses in many different language-games, and these language-games are themselves constantly changing: new language-games are constantly coming into existence, while others become obsolete (PI § 23).

This overlap leads to a high degree of complexity. The notion of "mental disorder" may mean one thing when it comes to the law (you are excused from legal responsibility if you are mentally ill, but accountable if you are not), another when it comes to surgical or medical treatment (you qualify for sex-change surgery if you have the right mental disorder, but not if you simply want your genitalia removed or altered), yet another when it comes to third-party payment (your health plan may cover treatment for physical illness but not mental illness), and yet another in ordinary conversation (you do not want to be called mentally ill because that suggests you are crazy). These are the kinds of complexities that many philosophers try to sort out and correct by defining an essential set of features that all mental illnesses share.

But must all mental disorders necessarily share a set of defining features? Wittgenstein would suggest not. Merely because we call a range of conditions "mental disorders" does not mean that any single feature is common to them all. Wittgenstein points to a concept like "game" (PI § 66). Look at all the different kinds of proceedings we call games—board games, card games, ball games, Olympic games, and so on. Is there any feature they all share? For example, do all games involve winning and losing? No, says Wittgenstein; look at the game of "patience." Do they all involve skill? No, some are a matter of luck. Do they all involve more than one person? No, look at a boy throwing a ball against a wall. As we pass from one kind of game to another, we find that some features of games drop out, while others appear. Board games are like card games in some respects, but in other respects they are more like ball games; card games in turn are like ball games in some respects, but in other respects they are more like solitary games, and so on. In the same way, a given mental disorder may resemble one disorder fairly closely, while differing from another disorder in important ways. We see a complex network of similarities that crisscross and overlap (PI § 66).

Wittgenstein compares this sort of overlap and crisscross to "family resemblances" (PI § 67). Some resemblances run in families, but are not common to every single member of the family. Eye color, hair color, height, gait, temperament: any given feature may be shared by some members of a family without being shared by all of them. The fact that there is no single feature shared by all members of the family does not mean that family members do not resemble one another. It simply means that the resemblances crisscross and overlap, like the features of games—or, as I am suggesting, like the features of mental disorders.

This does not mean that it never makes sense to limit what counts as a mental disorder. It may be important for policy reasons to decide that some conditions count as mental disorders while others do not. If you do not think that alcoholism should count as an excuse from legal responsibility, then it makes sense to exclude it from counting as a mental disorder in the eyes of the law. If you do not think that gay people should be encouraged to undergo psychiatric treatment in order to become heterosexual, then it makes sense to eliminate homosexuality from the *DSM*. The point here is that these kinds of limits and definitions are justified, not because they correspond to some kind of extra-linguistic reality, but because they function pragmatically in human activities. We are not trying to identify and name the beetle in the box. We are merely trying to play a particular kind of language-game.

Forms of Life

"If a lion could talk, we could not understand him," writes Wittgenstein in his characteristically cryptic fashion (PI p. 223). The reason we would not be able to understand a lion, suggests Wittgenstein, is not because a lion would speak another language. It is because that language would arise from a form of life that is largely alien to ours. A lion's language would be tied to a lion's way of living, a lion's concerns and activities, a lion's way of seeing the world. Language does not stand on its own. Nor is it a solely private matter. It is an activity tied to particular ways of seeing and relating to the world. To understand what Wittgenstein's lion was saying, we would need to understand the lion's form of life (see also PI § 19).

When Wittgenstein writes that "to imagine a language is to imagine a form of life," at least part of what he is getting at is that language is a practical activity. We use words in certain ways for certain purposes, and those purposes are tied up in cultural forms that are temporally and geographically variable. In the same way that we cannot understand the word "checkmate" without understanding something about the game of chess, neither can we understand words like "social phobia" or "gender identity disorder" or "post-traumatic stress disorder" without knowing something about the form of life in which those words have arisen. If we wish to understand the language of psychopathology, we cannot simply look at a person's private inner states. We cannot look for the beetle in the box. Instead, we must look at the form of life in which the language is embedded.

This is exactly what the philosopher Ian Hacking has done in a striking series of books and articles on the emergence of psychopathologies such as dissociative fugue and multiple personality disorder.[4] As way of understanding the forms of life in which these psychopathologies have arisen, Hacking has developed an explanatory concept called an "ecological niche." In the same way that biologists use the concept of an ecological niche to explain how the alligator is adapted to the Florida everglades or the yellow-eyed penguin to the South Island of New Zealand, Hacking uses the notion of a niche to explain the conditions that make it possible for a particular mental disorder to emerge and thrive in a particular time and place. Why is it, for example, that some Asian men (but not European men) develop *koro*, the absolute conviction that their penis is shrinking into their bodies and that this is going to kill them? What was it about nineteenth-century Bordeaux that made it possible for young men to lapse into amnesic fugue states and begin wandering the European continent? Why was the fugue state common in France but rare in North America? Any kind of psychopathology can have many causal mechanisms, of course: neurochemical dysfunction, childhood trauma, environmental toxins, infectious disease, etc. Hacking's point is that a single causal mechanism is rarely sufficient to explain all the particular manifestations of a mental disorder. For that, you must take a much wider view.

Hacking's major books have been on dissociative disorders: one on the fugue state in nineteenth-century France, the other on multiple personality disorder in late twentieth-century America. Neither disorder can be fully understood, he suggests, without an understanding of the particular cultural and historical moment at which it arose. The epidemic of amnesic wandering known as dissociative fugue, for example, arose during the first flowering of mass tourism in Europe: the age of Thomas Cook travel agencies, Baedaker travel guides, and the novels of Jules Verne. Prior to the mid-nineteenth century, travel had been limited to two segments of French society: the upper classes, who had the money and time to travel, and vagrants, who subsisted on the fringes of a criminal underworld. When mass tourism began to flourish, leisure travel became available for the first time to the middle classes. Soon thereafter came the epidemic of dissociative fugue. As Hacking points out, the epidemic occurred mainly in men for whom conventional travel was unavailable: rural pipe-fitters, skilled craftsmen and artisans, low-ranking military personnel—young French men trapped in a life of boredom and longing. Given these circumstances, it is not surprising that such men began to lapse into amnesia and wander off to Moscow or Algeria.[5]

In the complex ecosystem of psychopathology, psychiatrists occupy an important niche themselves. Psychiatrists do not simply stand apart from the ecosystem, observing and diagnosing mental disorders. They are a part of the ecosystem itself. They make certain disorders possible, and influence the shape they take. The particular shape that any disorder takes will depend on the way persons with that disorder are situated in the world—the way they see their past, their identity, their temperament, their sexual desires, the many ways in which their future is open or closed. Psychiatrists suggest to them new ways of seeing the world and their place in it. By looking at patients through the lens of a particular set of diagnostic categories, by offering patients a certain kind of treatment, by asking them a particular set of questions, by offering them a particular way of understanding their past, psychiatrists allow patients to interpret their lives in new ways.

Hacking argues that the shape a particular mental disorder takes will depend on what Wittgenstein might call a form of life—the culture, the historical moment, the particular ways in which it is possible for a people to see the world. I believe Hacking is right. My aim here is similar to his but also slightly different. I do not want to ask the question, Why this particular mental disorder? so much as, Why mental disorder at all? The striking thing about the way we North Americans live now is not simply that so many people see themselves as having gender identity disorder or social phobia or panic disorder, but that so many people see themselves as having any mental disorder at all. What is it about our particular cultural and historical moment that makes psychopathology such an attractive way of explaining human life?

I don't want to suggest that the question has a simple answer, of course. Nor do I want to suggest that mental disorders have no biological substrate, or that mental disorders are somehow not "real." What I want to do instead is briefly to sketch out some identifiable cultural forces that I believe have made the diagnosis of mental disorder such a common and plausible way of explaining psychic distress.

Technology and the Market

The first force pushing toward the expansion of psychopathology today is medical technology. The second force is the market. Medical technology produces medical treatments; medical treatments turn unpleasantness into medical problems; the market puts these treatments up for sale.

Something like this can happen with any kind of medical technology. Before the invention of the lens, as Willard Gaylin has pointed out, poor eyesight used to be an ordinary part of getting old. Now that it can be fixed with glasses, it is a medical problem called "presbyopia," to be treated by an ophthalmologist. The inability to become pregnant and have children used to be a part of ordinary human unhappiness. Today, new reproductive technologies have turned it into a medical problem called "infertility." We ordinarily think that diseases exist out in the world and researchers look for treatment. But often the reverse is true. Researchers develop a treatment, and a disease emerges in response.[6]

The clearest examples of this process have occurred in psychiatry. Gender identity disorder developed only after the development of the surgical and endocrinological interventions to make sex-change possible. The concept of neurosis developed only after the development of psychotherapy. Of the psychiatric disorders that have expanded so rapidly in recent years, a fair proportion spiked in popularity almost immediately after the development of a drug treatment for the disorder. Depression, social phobia, panic disorder, obsessive-compulsive disorder: in each case, rates of diagnosis have shot up dramatically shortly after it became evident that the disorder responded to a psychoactive drug.[7]

Take social phobia, for example. Social phobia, according to the *DSM-IV*, is the fear of acting in a way that will be humiliating or embarrassing. People with social phobia are often desperately fearful that their hands will tremble while they are signing their names in a public place, or that they will tense up in a public lavatory and be unable to urinate, or that they will sweat and blush during a public presentation and humiliate themselves. Just the anxiety of anticipating such situations may lead them to avoid social situations obsessively, so that they will go to great lengths to avoid writing checks or giving public speeches or making small talk. Social phobia is distinguished from shyness mainly by degree: the diagnostic criteria for social phobia stipulate that the distress of social phobia must be so severe that it interferes with a person's job, social activities, or everyday routine.

In the psychiatric literature, social phobia is commonly said to be the third most common mental disorder in the United States (after depression and substance abuse). Studies show that over 13 percent of Americans will suffer from it at some point in their lives, and it is still frequently called an under-recognized disorder.[8] Yet fifteen years ago, social phobia was seen as a rare problem. It was hardly ever mentioned in the psychiatric literature. In response to the keyword "social phobia," for example, the medical database Medline lists only 16 articles published from 1966 to 1984. But the same search run from 1984 to 1998 turned up 653 articles. The disparity is even more striking on Psychinfo, a psychological literature database: from 1967 to 1983 the database lists only 17 articles, but from 1984 to 1998 the number was 1137.

Two events of the mid-1980s are largely responsible for this upsurge of interest in social phobia. The first event was the publication of the *DSM-III-R*, the American Psychiatric Association's official manual of psychiatric diagnoses. For the first time, it included a diagnosis of social phobia. The inclusion of social phobia in the *DSM-III-R* gave shape to what was previously an amorphous and poorly defined diagnosis. The second (and more important) event was evidence that social phobia responded to antidepressants. Initially, studies showed that social phobia responded to phenelzine or Nardil.[9] These studies were published as early as 1986. Later came evidence that social phobia responded to a new class of antidepressants: the serotonin reuptake inhibitors (of which Prozac remains the most famous example). The most convincing evidence was for Paxil, or paroxetine. The serotonin reuptake inhibitors also proved safer than previous treatments, easier to use, and more likely to be free of side effects.[10] Psychiatrists began to use the serotonin reuptake inhibitors for social phobia; researchers began to publish their data on social phobia in the medical literature; and GlaxoSmithKline began an aggressive, direct-to-consumer marketing campaign in glossy magazines and on television.

What is important to understand here is the way that psychiatric treatment drives psychiatric diagnosis. If a person responds to a drug approved for social phobia, it is taken as evidence that the person is socially phobic. If a person responds to a drug for depression, it is taken as evidence that the person is depressed. If a person responds to a drug for obsessive-compulsive disorder, it is taken as evidence that the person is obsessive or compulsive. In fact, the very concepts of social phobia or depression or obsessive-compulsive disorder change over time as a result of this kind of feedback. Psychiatrists try antidepressants on patients who look anxious or shy or obsessive; the patients respond to the antidepressants; as a result, the concept of depression is gradually widened to include anxiety or shyness or obsessiveness.

There is nothing mysterious or illegitimate about this process. It is simply a consequence of the way psychiatric disorders are classified and diagnosed. Psychiatrists do not really know the causes of most psychiatric disorders, or even their pathophysiology. What they do know is how their patients speak and behave. Thus they classify and diagnose patients by virtue of that patient's speech and behavior. The class of socially phobic patients simply comprises those who manifest the cluster of signs and symptoms called social phobia; the class of depressed patients comprises those who manifest the cluster of signs and symptoms called depression. If the class of patients previously classified as "socially phobic" experiences improvement when they are given a drug previously used to treat "depression," then it makes a certain amount of pragmatic sense to think that the classifications of "social phobia" and "depression" are somehow related.

The problem comes when the classes of "depression" or "social phobia" overlap not with each other but with the kind of behavior or character traits otherwise thought to lie within the range of ordinary variation. If ordinary shyness improves with Paxil, does this mean that the person really had social phobia? If ordinary unhappiness improves with Prozac, does this mean that the person was really depressed? If an ordinary desire for order and neatness improves with Anafranil, does this mean that the person really had obsessive-compulsive disorder?

Wittgenstein would question the grounds for asking such a question, of course—the assumption that there really is a fact of the matter, the existence or nonexistence of a mental disorder, which a person's response to a drug can reveal. The question to be asked is not "Does she really have major depression?"—not "Does she have a beetle in her box?"—but rather, perhaps, "In whose interests is it to pose such a question? And why pose it in just this way?"

Here is where market capitalism comes into play. Like any ordinary business selling its products, pharmaceutical companies have an interest is expanding their sales to as many people as possible. Unlike ordinary businesses, however, pharmaceutical companies must sell their products through doctors. Doctors make the diagnoses and write the prescriptions. The more people doctors diagnose with social phobia, the more paroxetine they will prescribe, and the more money GlaxoSmithKline will make. In order to sell a drug, the company must first sell a diagnosis.

How do you sell a diagnosis? Clinical depression is an interesting case in point. As David Healy points out in his history of the antidepressants, depression was once thought to be an extremely rare disorder. In the 1950s, in fact, drug companies thought that depression was too rare for an antidepressant to be profitable. Thus when Merck started to produce amytriptaline, a tricyclic antidepressant, in the early 1960s, they realized that in order to sell their antidepressant they needed to sell the diagnosis of depression. Consequently they bought and distributed 50,000 copies of a book by Frank Ayd called *Recognizing the Depressed Patient*. This book instructed general practitioners how to diagnose depression. Merck's strategy worked. Doctors began to diagnose depression, and prescriptions for amytriptaline started to rise. The rise had little to do with the merits of amytriptaline itself. Amytriptaline was not even the first antidepressant on the market. Imipramine, another tricyclic antidepressant, had been available since the mid-1950s.[11]

The act of diagnosis, as Merck realized, is not just a matter of giving the patient's inner state a name. It is not even just a way of deciding on a patient's treatment. Diagnosis is a crucial element in a much larger language-game. When drugs are approved by the U.S. Food and Drug Administration or the Canadian Health Protection Branch, they are approved for particular diagnoses. When researchers conduct clinical trials, they test drugs for particular diagnoses. When clinicians file for reimbursement by third-party payers for a patients treatment, they must give that patient a particular diagnosis. Scientific communications, keywords in computer databases, diagnostic measurement scales, medical textbooks, diagnostic manuals, outcome measurement studies: all use (and thus reinforce) a language-game of which psychiatric diagnosis is a crucial part. If a pharmaceutical company can insert a particular diagnosis into this bureaucratic web—by sponsoring conference sessions, distributing scientific articles to clinicians, paying for thematic journal supplements, and advertising the diagnosis to potential patients—their diagnosis has a much better chance to flourish.

Identity and Community

In the 1960s the anthropologist Victor Turner coined the term "cults of affliction." Turner did his fieldwork in Zambia, among a group called the Ndembu. In the Ndembu cosmology, sickness and misfortune are caused by sorcerers, witches, or ancestor spirits. When people fall sick, it is because a spirit has caught them in some misdemeanor or another. The Ndembu deal with sickness by performing what Turner calls a "ritual of affliction." Different ancestor spirits cause different afflictions: one will cause leprosy, another will cause menstrual problems, another will cause twin births. Sometimes, if the cause of the affliction is not obvious, people need diviners to tell them which spirit is causing their problems.[12]

What interested Turner about these rituals of affliction was the people who take part in them. The afflicted person needs a doctor, but the doctor has to gather together a group of people who have also been afflicted with the sickness. This group of people then perform a ritual on behalf of the sick person. The significant thing about these groups is the way they transcend any other sort of grouping. Members of the group do not all come from the same family, the same tribe, the same village, or the same clan. The only thing they have in common is that they have suffered from the same sickness and have been treated by the same kind of group. Hence what Turner calls "cults of affliction": groups of people bound together by common experience of illness.

Without trying to draw too tight a parallel here, anthropologists such as Paul Brodwin and Paul Rabinow see something similar going on in North American culture today.[13] People are coming together in support groups, self-help groups, and activist groups, all of which are organized solely around a particular illness or disability. These groups have different purposes, of course—different from one another and different from Turner's cults of affliction. But there is one important parallel, and that is the composition of the group. The members of these groups are not from the same family, do not work together, do not all come from the same town or region, do not necessarily share a common ethnicity or religious background. What they do share is a common experience of illness or disability (or in some cases, a biological characteristic they insist is not an illness or disability): AIDS, breast cancer, intersexuality, transgenderism, deafness, alcoholism, or attention deficit disorder, to mention only a few disorders on a large and growing list.

These contemporary illness groups fill a gap left by mainstream society: they provide emotional support in the face of social stigma. In his classic book on stigma, Irving Goffman points out the way that members of most stigmatized categories of people, even as they are set apart from mainstream society, will find a group of people who share their particular standpoint in the world.[14] So that at the same time that the stigmatized person is cut off from the world of so-called normal people, who see the stigmatized person as deviant or subnormal or irremediably different, this group of sympathetic others reassure him that he is essentially human and normal despite his own self-doubts. We generally applaud such groups if the stigma is membership in an ethnic minority, or being deaf, or suffering from AIDS. But we worry about them if the stigma comes from something like criminality.

Psychiatric disorders present a problem for such illness groups. There is no doubt that such groups serve as a needed barrier against social stigma, especially when the disorder itself is seen as so shameful that it cannot be openly admitted. Yet the groups also nourish the psychiatric disorders themselves. By putting like-minded people in touch with one another, they reinforce the notion that the disorder they share is socially acceptable or morally legitimate. By encouraging people on the outside to become a part of the group, they encourage people to reconceptualize their identities. By joining the group you conceptualize your shyness as social phobia, your poor concentration as attention deficit disorder, your troubled sexual past as gender identity disorder. The expansion of such groups may not be terribly worrying if the disorder in question is relatively harmless. But it becomes more worrying when it is, say, pedophilia. Of course, the extent to which a person's identity, temperament, and desires can be shaped by such groupings is still an open question. But for so many Americans who feel the absence of more traditional kinds of community, such groups fill a noticeable gap.

The Internet is adding an additional layer of complexity to such groups. Websites, listservs, and chat rooms are putting far-flung but like-minded people in electronic contact with one another. Often these are people who discovered others like them only when they logged on to the Internet. They thought they were alone, thought they were crazy, thought they were perverse until they punched a keyword into an electronic search engine and discovered a community of sympathetic strangers who shared their physiological anomaly, their sexual fetish, their experience of abuse, alienation, or shame. Some writers call such electronic groups "virtual communities." But they are communities of a very odd kind. They are really more like clubs. Like Turner's cults of affliction, the members are bound to one another by virtue of a particular experience and come together for a particular purpose.

The Internet does a couple of things for such groups that could not be easily done before. First, because many of the characteristics shared by members of such groups are so rare, it is unlikely that the members of the group would be able to gather physically in a single place. But the Internet brings them together on-line. Second, the Internet allows members to take part in secret. Many people participate in these virtual illness groups anonymously. Thus people get the comfort and satisfaction of being part of a group, of knowing they are not alone in the world, while avoiding the potential shame of actually having to reveal themselves to anyone else face-to-face.

There is nothing deterministic about these social groupings, of course. They can contest medicalization as well as nourish it. Something like this has happened in the transgender community. In the early days of sex reassignment surgery, candidates for surgery embraced (or at least did not resist) the diagnosis of mental disorder, not least because a disorder was a necessary condition for surgical and medical treatment. Today, many transgendered people object to the medical label. In 1993, for example, the Second International Conference on Transgender Law and Employment Policy adopted a set of criteria for sex reassignment surgery called the Health Law Standards, which were explicitly designed as an alternative to the medical model set out in the Harry Benjamin Standards. These criteria characterize transgendered people not as mentally disordered but as a minority within a broad range of human sexual diversity. The relationship between doctors and candidates for sex reassignment surgery in the Health Law Standards is not like a doctor-patient relationship at all. It is like a commercial relationship between buyers and sellers of services.[15]

Many such groups, both virtual and real, can be exploited for commercial means. Pharmaceutical corporations realize this, and many are donating money to illness support groups. For instance, GlaxoSmithKline, the maker of Paxil, donates money to support groups for social phobia, while Ciba-Geigy, the maker of Ritalin, donates to Children and Adults with Attention Deficit Disorder. These donations may well help patients with the disorders in question. But they also help sell the psychiatric diagnoses that the groups in question support.

The Importance of Psychopathology

In the *Last Writings on the Philosophy of Psychology,* Wittgenstein imagines a tribe unfamiliar with the concept of simulated pain (LWPPI § 203). Members of the tribe feel pain, but they do not pretend to be in pain. So when they come across anyone who appears to be in pain, it never occurs to them that he might be pretending. A traveler from our culture will often see a member of this tribe complaining that he is in pain and think that his complaint is exaggerated, or that he is just looking for pity. But this thought never occurs to members of the tribe.

Then imagine, writes Wittgenstein, that a missionary comes to this tribe and teaches these people our language. Under his tutelage, the members of the tribe learn the expressions for "to feel pain" and "to simulate pain." They also learn how to distinguish between genuine expressions of pain and those that are simulated. The question, says Wittgenstein is this: Have these people been taught a new concept of pain?

It is a difficult question. Certainly they have not just learned what "pain" is. In fact, it would not even sound quite right to say that they have only just learned what "simulated pain" is. This would suggest that before the missionary came, they did not recognize the difference between actually being in pain and simulating pain. This can't be right: surely a member of the tribe who sometimes complained while he was in pain and sometimes complained while he was not in pain has not always thought that the two things were the same (LWPPI § 205).

Wittgenstein then asks: "But why not say: the difference wasn't important to them?" (LWPPI § 205). The notion of "importance" strikes me as the best way to understand what the members of the tribe have learned. It is not that by learning a new concept the members of the tribe have learned something that they never knew before. It is that the new concept has called their attention to something that previously had no importance for them. Imagine, for example, that Wittgenstein's missionary, in addition to teaching the tribe the distinction between "pain" and "simulated pain," has also brought to the tribe new practices that made the distinction between "pain" and "simulated pain" much more important. He might have established a church, for example, which teaches that God disapproves of people who simulate pain. This new practice might well make the concept of "simulated pain" far more important. The members of the tribe might learn to notice things they had not previously noticed, make distinctions they had not previously made, and even come to understand their own behavior in a way they never had.

This may be what new concepts of psychopathology do as well. One way of understanding the spread of psychopathology in our own time is by asking what these new concepts bring to people that they did not have before. For many people today, it matters (in a way that it might not have mattered before) to have a diagnosis of social phobia. Why? Because you can be treated successfully with a drug; because your treatment will be paid for by a third-party payer; because social phobia is a useful way of understanding something about yourself that you had never understood before; because it is a passport to a community of sympathetic people who are like you. These are not, by any stretch, the only reasons it is important; there are many more reasons, practical as well as more abstract. (One should not overlook America's long history of enthusiasm for technology, for instance, or the social conditions that contribute to the longing for community.) The point is simply that what is called "social phobia" is not, as philosophers tend to assume, just a matter of the characteristics of social phobia itself. It is a matter of the language-game in which it is embedded, and the form of life that makes the concept important.

"Does your patient have a beetle in his box?" Wittgenstein shows us that the question is meaningless. Claims about the reality of the beetle are idle in this language-game: the box might be empty, and the game can still be played. The question to be asked is not whether the beetle is really in the box, not whether a given mental disorder is real, but what role these mental disorders play in the various language-games in which they are used. If, rather than asking, "Is there a beetle in the box?" we were to ask instead, "In whose interests is it to talk about beetles in boxes?" we will come closer to finding a useful answer.

11

Wittgenstein on Bodily Feelings

Explanation and Melioration in Philosophy of Mind, Art, and Politics

Richard Shusterman

I

In his *Vermischte Bemerkungen,* in the course of a political discussion concerning nationalism, anti-Semitism, power, and property, Wittgenstein speaks of one's having an "aesthetic feeling for one's body [*aesthetische Gefühl für seinen Körper*]" (CV 21).[1] This phrase attracted my attention because of my interest in developing a philosophical notion I call somaesthetics, which I conceive as a discipline dedicated to improving the understanding, use, and experience of the body as a locus of sensory-aesthetic appreciation *(aisthesis)* and creative self-fashioning.[2] But Wittgenstein's phrase particularly intrigued me because his philosophy is famous for refuting the centrality of bodily feelings in explaining the key concepts of philosophy for which those feelings are often invoked: concepts of action, emotion, will, and aesthetic judgment. He thinks that philosophers invent them as primitive explanations for the complexities of mental life. "When we do philosophy, we should like to hypostatize feelings where there are none. They serve to explain our thoughts to us. '*Here* explanation of our thinking demands a feeling!' It is as if our conviction were simply consequent upon this requirement" (PI § 598).

In contrast to traditional theories that have used feelings or sensations (whether corporeal or allegedly more purely mental) to explain the causes and meanings of our psychological and aesthetic concepts, Wittgenstein argued that such complex concepts are better understood in terms of their use. They are grounded and expressed in the sedimented social practices or consensual forms of life of a community of language-users. "*Practice* gives the words their meaning" (CV 85), and such practice involves "agreement . . . in form of life" (PI § 241).

Because Wittgenstein provides powerful arguments for rejecting theories of sensationalism and psychologism with respect to mental concepts and aesthetic judgment, there is a tendency or a temptation to conclude that he thought bodily sensations were cognitively insignificant and unworthy of philosophical attention. In this chapter I argue that this temptation should be resisted. Despite his devastating critiques of sensationalism, Wittgenstein recognizes the role of somaesthetic feelings in fields as varied as philosophy of mind, aesthetics, ethics, and politics. The fact that such feelings cannot provide an adequate conceptual analysis of our concepts does not entail that they lack other cognitive value and are therefore irrelevant for philosophy. We may be tempted to make this inference if we equate philosophy narrowly with conceptual analysis. But like Wittgenstein, I think otherwise. Philosophy has a much wider meaning; it concerns what Wittgenstein called "the problem of life" and the self-critical task of improving the self: "Working in philosophy—like work in architecture in many respects—is really more working on one's self" (CV 4, 16).[3]

If philosophy involves the tasks of self-improvement and of self-knowledge (which seems necessary for self-improvement), then we should find an important role for somaesthetic perceptions. While examining the various ways Wittgenstein recognizes the positive role of somaesthetic feelings, I will go beyond Wittgenstein to argue how such feelings should be more widely and powerfully employed. To understand these positive uses properly, we need to distinguish them from Wittgenstein's sharp critique of the use of somatic feelings for explaining central concepts of aesthetics, politics, and philosophy of mind. But first, it may be necessary to explain how key concepts and issues in these different philosophical disciplines are in fact closely related. Modernity's logic of professionalization and specialization tends to compartmentalize aesthetics, politics, and philosophy of mind and thus obscures their fundamental connection in philosophy's pursuit of better thinking and living, a connection that was powerfully affirmed and cultivated in ancient times.

To appreciate how strongly philosophy once tied aesthetics and philosophy of mind to political theory, we need only recall the paradigmatic text that largely established political philosophy and still helps define it today—Plato's dialogue *The Republic*, or *Politeia*, one of the most widely read of philosophical texts and one that in late antiquity bore the subtitle "On Justice." In this seminal work, Socrates argues that justice is essentially a virtue, that is, a special psychological achievement and disposition rather than a mere external social contract (as his interlocutors argue against him in the dialogue). A good part of *The Republic* is therefore devoted to philosophy of mind, analyzing the soul's basic faculties, needs, and desires in order to see whether the psychological underpinnings of Socrates' political theory or those of his rivals are more correct. Arguing that justice as a mental virtue is essentially the ruling of the proper order in the human soul, Socrates projects that view of the right ruling order onto the public order of the state. A just state, then, is ruled by the proper order of its different kinds of citizens, each group doing what it can do best for the better benefit of the whole community; the philosophers are charged with the highest role of governing guidance, teaching the ruling group of guardians.

But to secure the proper education of the guardians and ensure more generally the proper order of mind that constitutes the virtue of justice in the individual, Socrates insists that we must address aesthetic issues. Not only our intellects but our feelings and desires must be educated to recognize and appreciate the right order, so that we will desire and love it. The harmonies of beauty are therefore advocated as crucially instrumental in such education. Conversely, Plato's condemnation of art is similarly motivated by his moral psychology and political theory. Art is politically dangerous, he argues, not only because it purveys imitative falsehoods, but because it appeals to the baser parts of the soul and overstimulates those unruly emotions that disturb right order in the mind of the individual and the polis in general.

This integral connection of aesthetics, politics, and philosophy of mind is reaffirmed by Friedrich Schiller, who argues that art is the necessary key to improving both mental and political order. In his *On the Aesthetic Education of Man,* written after the French revolution had turned into the Reign of Terror, Schiller posed the dilemma that a just society requires "the ennobling of character" to create more virtuous people; yet how can we ennoble character without already relying on a just political society to educate people toward virtue? Schiller's famous answer is "aesthetic education"; the "instrument is Fine Art," whose exemplars of beauty and perfection inspire and elevate our characters. Art's educational value for virtue and justice is again explained in terms of human psychology. If man's mind is torn between an earthy, sensual, material drive *(Stofftrieb)* and an intellectual, transcendental formal drive *(Formtrieb),* then art's expression of a mediating play drive *(Spieltrieb)* provides a crucial reconciling force, since in this drive "both the others work in concert." "Taste alone brings harmony in society, because it fosters harmony in the individual. . . . only the aesthetic mode of communication unites society because it relates that which is common to all."[4]

The same nexus of moral psychology, aesthetics, and politics could also be traced in later thinkers like Dewey and Adorno. But I trust that the linkage between these disciplines is now sufficiently clear to warrant examining the theme of bodily feelings in Wittgenstein's aesthetics and philosophy of mind before turning to their role in his ethics and political thought, the topic with which this volume is more closely concerned. Since Wittgenstein repudiates the view that bodily feelings can explain the meaning of our central mental and aesthetic concepts, let us begin with his critique of this view before considering the positive roles he allows for bodily feelings.

II

In critiquing the use of somatic feelings for explaining crucial mental concepts like emotion and will, Wittgenstein takes the pragmatist philosopher William James as his prime target. James influenced Wittgenstein more than any of the other classical pragmatists did, and we know that Wittgenstein greatly appreciated James's thought on religious issues.[5] But here Wittgenstein uses the somatic sensationalism of James's psychology as a critical foil to develop his own theories. James is famous for his corporeal explanation of emotion: Not only are "the general causes of the emotions . . . indubitably physiological," but the emotions themselves are identified with the feelings we have of these physiological excitations. When we perceive something exciting, "*bodily changes follow directly the perception of the exciting fact, and . . . our feeling of the same changes as they occur IS the emotion;* . . . we feel sorry because we cry, angry because we strike, afraid because we tremble, and not that we cry, strike, or tremble, because we are sorry, angry, or fearful, as the case may be. Without the bodily states following on the perception, the latter would be purely cognitive in form, pale, colorless, destitute of emotional warmth."[6]

If James one-sidedly identifies emotions with bodily sensations (and a charitable reading of James could deny this by distinguishing sensations from feelings and linking the latter to the cognitive content of the exciting perception), then Wittgenstein's response is emphatically to reject this identification by insisting that emotions "are not sensations" of the body, since they are neither localized nor diffuse, and always have an object (which is different than a bodily cause). Emotions are "in the mind," "expressed in thoughts," and experienced and aroused by thought, "not body pain." In contrast to James, Wittgenstein "should almost like to say: One no more feels sorrow in one's body than one feels seeing in one's eyes" (Z § 495). My fear of the dark may sometimes manifest itself in my consciousness of shallowness in my breathing and of a clenching of the jaw and face muscles, but sometimes it may not be so manifested. Even if such bodily feeling is always present, this does not mean that it is the cause of my fear, nor its object. I am not afraid of shallow breathing or of these muscle contractions, but instead of the dark. "If fear is frightful and if while it goes on I am conscious of my breathing and of a tension in my face—is that to say I feel *these feelings* frightful? Might they not even be a mitigation?" (Z 484–99). Wittgenstein is surely right that our emotions are not reducible to bodily feelings nor to any mere sensation; emotions instead involve a whole context of behavior and a background of language-games, a whole form of life in which the emotion plays a part.

Bodily feelings, Wittgenstein argued, are also incapable of explaining will. Here again James is the target of critique. In the chapter on will in *Principles of Psychology,* James argues that our voluntary movements rely on more primary bodily functions and are guided by "kinaesthetic impressions" of our proprioceptive system that have sedimented into a "kinaesthetic idea" or "memory image": "whether or no there be anything else in the mind at the moment when we consciously will a certain act, a mental conception made up of the memory-images of these sensations, defining which special act it is, must be there." James goes on to insist that "there need be nothing else, and that in perfectly simple voluntary acts there is nothing else, in the mind, but the kinaesthetic idea, thus defined, of what the act is to be."[7]

Though James's kinaesthetic theory might be criticized as "inflationary" in positing the need for a special conscious feeling to explain and accompany every act of will, he actually intended his theory to be a deflationary challenge to the more bloated account of will proposed by Wundt, Helmholz, and Mach. These philosopher-scientists posited, in addition to kinaesthetic feelings, a special active "feeling of innervation," that accompanies "the special current of energy going out from the brain to the appropriate muscles during the act" of will, while James maintained that the more passive "kinaesthetic images" he described were enough to induce the action.[8]

Though appreciative of James's efforts of theoretical economy, I prefer to take the reductive path further by endorsing Wittgenstein's claim that specific kinaesthetic ideas or other conscious visceral feelings constitute neither the sufficient nor necessary cause of voluntary action and cannot adequately explain the will. Recall Wittgenstein's famous posing of the problem in *Philosophical Investigations* (which clearly evokes James): "what is left over if I subtract the fact that my arm goes up from the fact that I raise my arm? ((Are the kinaesthetic sensations my willing?)) . . . When I raise my arm I do not usually *try* to raise it" (PI §§ 621–22).

Voluntary action does not typically involve any conscious effort of "trying" or any related conscious kinaesthetic impressions of "willing," whether actual or remembered. Most voluntary action is produced spontaneously or automatically from our intentions without any attention at all to any visceral feelings or bodily processes that could occur when initiating the action.

> Writing is certainly a voluntary movement, and yet an automatic one. And of course there is no question of a feeling of each movement in writing. One feels something, but could not possibly analyse the feeling. One's hand writes; it does not write because one wills, but one wills what it writes.

One does not watch it in astonishment or with interest while writing; does not think "What will it write now?" (Z § 586)

In fact, Wittgenstein adds, such attention to one's movements and feelings can hinder the smooth execution of willed action: "self-observation makes my action, my movements, uncertain" (Z § 592).

Like our emotions, then, acts of the will cannot be explained by or identified with the particular kinaesthetic feelings that may occasionally accompany them. Voluntary action (just like emotion) can only be explained in terms of a whole surrounding context of life, aims, and practices, "the whole hurly-burly of human actions, the background against which we see any action." "What is voluntary is certain movements with their normal *surrounding* of intention, learning, trying, action" (Z §§ 567, 577).

There is also a third important area where Wittgenstein challenges the use of visceral feelings as essential to understanding key concepts of our mental life: this area concerns the concept of self and self-knowledge of one's bodily state or position. Once again, James is the explicit target. He is attacked for identifying the self with basic somatic sensations that can be discerned by introspection, for "the idea that the 'self' consisted mainly of 'peculiar motions in the head and between the head and throat'" (PI § 413).[9] This, unfortunately, is an ungenerous distortion of James's concept of self, which indeed includes a vast variety of dimensions—from the body parts, clothes, property, and diverse social relations that form our material and social selves to the various mental faculties of what he calls our "spiritual self."

What James described in terms of bodily feelings in the head (ascertained through his own personal introspection) is only *one*, though allegedly the most basic, part of the self, which he called "the central active self," "the nuclear self," or "the Self of selves." The full concept of self, as both James and Wittgenstein realized, is not reducible to any kind of basic sensations in the head or anywhere else. A whole background of social life and practices is needed to define it. Most of the time, as James himself asserts, we are entirely unaware of these "head feelings"—which typically "are swallowed up in [the] larger mass" of other things that claim more conscious attention than these primitive background feelings of the self[10]—yet we are not therefore most of the time unaware of ourselves or unconscious of where we are and what we do. Wittgenstein, however, is far clearer than James about this, and he wisely avoids the positing of a nuclear self that would be identified with or identifiable by particular head sensations, for such homuncular theories can encourage many essentialist confusions. One is much more than one's head, and even one's mental life extends far beyond one's head sensations.

Wittgenstein, moreover, emphatically insists (much like Merleau-Ponty) that our knowledge of our bodily position does not require our paying special attention to feelings of our body parts and then inferring from them the particular location and orientation of our body and its limbs. Instead we have an immediate sense of our somatic position. "One *knows* the position of one's limbs and their movements . . . [with] no local sign about the sensation" (Z § 483). In performing ordinary tasks like washing or feeding ourselves, climbing stairs, riding a bicycle, or driving a car, we do not usually need to consult the separate feelings of our body parts in order to calculate the necessary movements to achieve the action we will (e.g., what parts need to be moved, in which direction, distance, speed, articulation, and degree of muscle contraction).[11] Wittgenstein refutes the thesis that "My kinaesthetic sensations advise me of the movement and position of my limbs" (PI p. 185) by engaging in some somaesthetic introspection of his own:

> I let my index finger make an easy pendulum movement of small amplitude. I either hardly feel it, or don't feel it at all. Perhaps a little in the tip of the finger, as a slight tension. (Not at all in the joint.) And this sensation advises me of the movement?—for I can describe the movement exactly.
>
> "But after all, you must feel it, otherwise you wouldn't know (without looking) how your finger was moving." But "knowing" it only means: being able to describe it.—I may be able to tell the direction from which a sound comes only because it affects one ear more strongly than the other, but I don't feel this in my ears; yet it has its effect: I *know* the direction from which the sound comes; for instance, I look in that direction.
>
> It is the same with the idea that it must be some feature of our pain that advises us of the whereabouts of the pain in the body, and some feature of our memory image that tells us the time to which it belongs. (PI p. 185)

In short, our knowledge of bodily location and movement is typically immediate and nonreflective. It is not always accompanied by conscious kinaesthetic feelings that we attend to; nor is it usually derived from such feelings when they are present. Nor does successful voluntary action require the mediation of attention to somaesthetic feelings. Such feelings may also be absent from much of our experience of will, emotion, and self. It is tempting, therefore, to conclude that they are unimportant for these topics of philosophy of mind and that a behaviorist skepticism about their role in mental life might be appropriate.

But that would be a mistake, even in Wittgenstein's view. Such feelings, despite their inadequacy for explaining mental concepts, remain a real part of the phenomenology of mental life that philosophy should describe. Kinaesthetic sensations are not theoretical nothings like phlogiston, but elements of experience that can be properly or improperly described. "We feel our movements. Yes, we really *feel* them; the sensation is similar, not to a sensation of taste or heat, but to one of touch; to the sensation when skin and muscles are squeezed, pulled, displaced." And we can also, though we don't always have to, feel the position of our limbs through a distinct "body-feeling" (*"Körpergefühl"*), for example, "the 'body-feeling' of the arm ... [in] such-and-such a *position*" (Z §§ 479, 481). Indeed, in certain circumstances we can even learn of our movements and position through the mediation of feelings, as when a perceived tension in the neck informs us that our shoulders are hunched up near our ears. Though Wittgenstein rightly insists that we typically neither require nor use such somaesthetic clues to know about our bodily position, he recognizes that they can, on occasion, provide such knowledge, and he provides his own characteristically "painful" example: "A sensation *can* advise us of the movement or position of a limb. (For example, if you do not know, as a normal person does, whether your arm is stretched out, you might find out by a piercing pain in the elbow.)—In the same way the character of a pain can tell us where the injury is" (PI p. 185).

I want to go farther by insisting that, in the same way, attention to somaesthetic feelings can sometimes usefully inform us about our emotions and our will. It is a commonplace that a person may be angry, upset, anxious, fearful, etc. before he is consciously aware of it. He often, however, becomes aware of it when someone else, noticing his movements, gestures, breathing, tone of voice, inquires whether there is something bothering him. Behaviorism finds support in this phenomenon for claiming that emotions are not defined by what we are aware of feeling and that introspection is not the true arbiter of our emotional state. Observers from "the outside" can inform us of an emotional state of which we are not yet consciously aware. But we should realize that introspective attention to our somaesthetic feelings (shortness of breath, clenching in the chest or jaws) can also provide us with such observation.

In certain situations, where I am not initially aware of my anxiety or fear and when I am still unconscious of its having a specific object, I can learn that I am anxious or fearful by noticing my shallow, rapid breathing and the heightened muscle contraction in my neck, shoulders, and pelvis. Of course, different people have somewhat different patterns of muscular contraction and of breathing rhythm when undergoing emotional stress. But this does not negate the fact that an individual can know her own pattern and infer from it that she is in a heightened emotional state (and often know which emotional state it is), even before she is conscious of that state having a specific object—that is, some particular thing about which she is angry or anxious or fearful. Wittgenstein admits: "My own behaviour is sometimes—but *rarely*—the object of my own observation" (Z § 591). Somaesthetic feelings provide us with helpful tools for such self-observation, through which we can better attain philosophy's classic goal of self-knowledge. Of course, one often needs a sustained effort of training and practice to learn how properly to read one's own somaesthetics signs, but somatic education disciplines like the Feldenkrais Method or yoga can provide such training.

The role of somaesthetic feelings and discipline goes still further, once we realize that attention to these feelings can give us not only knowledge of our emotional states but, through that knowledge, a means for coping with them better. Once emotions are thematized in consciousness, we can take a critical distance and thus understand and manage them with greater mastery (which does not mean with greater repression). Moreover, because emotions are (at least empirically) closely linked with certain somatic states and feelings, we can influence our emotions indirectly by transforming our somatic sensations through conscious exercise of somaesthetic control. We can regulate our breathing to become deeper and slower, just as we can learn to relax certain muscle tensions that reinforce a feeling of nervousness because of their long-conditioned association with states of nervousness. These strategies are familiar from ancient practices of meditation, but are also exercised in modern strategies of stress management.

The effective understanding of the will and voluntary action can also be enhanced through disciplined attention to somaesthetic feelings. Successful willed action depends on somatic efficacy, which in turn depends on accurate somaesthetic perception. A struggling golfer may have the desire to perform the voluntary action of keeping her head down and eyes on the ball when swinging the club to hit the ball properly, yet nonetheless always lift her head and fail in her swing. She will not even notice that she is lifting her head and therefore cannot correct the problem because she is insufficiently attentive to her head movement and eye position, which she could sense if she were more somaesthetically disciplined and skilled. This golfer lifts her head against her will. But no one is forcing her to lift it, nor is there any wired-in instinct or physiological compulsion that makes her lift it. So her lifting is not involuntary in these senses; yet it is not what she consciously wills to perform and what she could perform if she had a better grasp of her body position and movement through more attention to somaesthetic sensations. The same kind of impotence of will is evident in the insomniac who wants to relax but whose efforts only increase his state of tension because he does not know how to relax his muscles and breathing, since he cannot feel how they are tight and tense.

But doesn't such attention to bodily feelings distract the golfer from hitting the ball and the insomniac from fully relaxing? Experience (with proper training) shows the contrary, and, in any case, somaesthetic attention certainly need not be a permanent distraction. Once the feelings of faulty movements are attended to, the movements can be corrected and replaced by proper ones accompanied by other somaesthetic feelings that can be habituated and then be allowed to slip into unreflective but intelligent habit. If philosophy involves not merely knowledge of one's mind, but ameliorative self-mastery (as Wittgenstein fervently believed), then attention to somaesthetic feelings should be crucial to philosophy's task of "working on one's self." This task of self-mastery brings us to the central questions of ethics, but let me first turn to aesthetics, since Wittgenstein closely identified these two domains of value, even to the point of regarding the quest of the good life in largely aesthetic terms.[12]

III

Like his philosophy of mind, Wittgenstein's aesthetics presents a critique of sensation-based psychologism. Aesthetic explanations are not causal ones and, like the aesthetic judgments they explain, "have nothing to do with psychological experiments." As with emotions and other mental states, aesthetic judgments and experiences cannot be explained in terms of the artist's or audience's somatic sensations, "their organic feelings—tension of the muscles in their chest."[13] We can explain aesthetic experiences and judgments much better by describing the particular artworks that are being judged and experienced, as well as describing the behavior of the artists and audience, including ourselves. Gestures are also very effective in conveying how the artwork makes us feel.

In any case, our appreciation of art is not an appreciation of any separable somatic sensations that art can give us (just as it is not an appreciation of associations that are independent of the artwork). Otherwise we could imagine foregoing any interest in the artwork simply to get the sensations (or associations) more directly through some other means (say, some drug). But we cannot separate our aesthetic experience of art from the object of that experience; and that object is art, not our somatic sensations. Finally, the appeal to "kinaesthetic feelings" to explain our aesthetic judgments is logically unsatisfactory, since these feelings themselves are not adequately describable or individuated without appealing either to the artwork itself or to some set of gestures that we feel expresses them. For Wittgenstein, there seemed to be no "technique of describing kinaesthetic sensations" of aesthetic experience more accurately than by our gestures. Moreover, he argued, even if we did devise a new system of describing "kinaesthetic sensations" in order to determine what would count as "the same kinaesthetic impressions," it is not clear that its results would correspond with our current aesthetic judgments and their gestural expression.[14]

But if somatic feelings are neither the object nor the explanation of our judgments and experience of art, this does not entail that such feelings are not aesthetically important. Wittgenstein, as we have seen, is clearly attentive to somatic feelings, and he acknowledges their aesthetic value in a number of ways. First, they form the mediating focus (if not also the precise object) of aesthetic satisfactions derived from experiencing our bodies. Wittgenstein highlights "the delightful way the parts of a human body differ in temperature" (CV 11). Secondly, kinaesthetic feelings may help us derive a greater fullness, intensity, or precision in our experience of art, because (at least for some of us) aesthetic imagination or attention is facilitated or heightened by certain bodily movements that somehow feel as if they correspond to the work. Wittgenstein provides his own example:

> When I imagine a piece of music, as I often do every day, I always, so I believe, grind my upper and lower teeth together rhythmically. I have noticed this before though I usually do this unconsciously. What's more, it's as though the notes I am imagining are produced by this movement. I believe this may be a very common way of imagining music internally. Of course, I can imagine without moving my teeth too, but in that case the notes are much ghostlier, more blurred and less pronounced.[15] (CV 28)

"If art serves 'to arouse feelings,'" Wittgenstein later asks, "is, in the end, perceiving it sensually [*ihre sinnliche Wahrnehmung*] to be included amongst these feelings?" (CV 36). This cryptic, apparently rhetorical, question reminds us that aesthetic perceptions must always be achieved through the bodily senses, and it could be recommending a more embodied and sensually attentive use of art. In other words, we might sharpen our appreciation of art through more attention to our somaesthetic feelings involved in perceiving art instead of narrowly identifying artistic feelings with the familiar kind of emotions (such as sadness, joy, melancholy, regret, etc.) that often make art appreciation degenerate into a gushy, vague romanticism. Wittgenstein's remark is not at all clear, and my interpretation may be more or other than what he intended. But independent of Wittgenstein, the point can be validly made. If better somaesthetic awareness and discipline can improve our perception in general by giving us better control of the sense organs through which we perceive, then it can also, *ceteris paribus*, give us better perception in aesthetic contexts.

For Wittgenstein, the body may have a crucial aesthetic role that goes deeper than any conscious somaesthetic feeling or expression. As with Merleau-Ponty, the body serves Wittgenstein as a central instance and symbol of what forms the crucial, silent, mysterious background for all that can be expressed in language or in art, the unreflective source for all that can be consciously grasped in reflective thought or representation. "The purely corporeal can be uncanny." "Perhaps what is inexpressible (what I find mysterious and am not able to express) is the background against which whatever I could express has its meaning" (CV 50, 16). Music's inexpressible depth of meaning and its grand, mysterious power derive from the body's silent role as creative ground and intensifying background. That is how a surface of ephemeral sounds can touch the very depths of human experience. "Music, with its few notes & rhythms, seems to some people a primitive art. But only its surface [its foreground] is simple, while the body which makes possible the interpretation of this manifest content has all the infinite complexity that is suggested in the external forms of other arts & which music conceals. In a certain sense it is the most sophisticated art of all" (RCV 11).[16]

Here again, I think Wittgenstein's recognition of the body's crucial role needs to be taken a step further in a pragmatic direction. More than guitars or violins or pianos or even drums, our bodies are the primary instrument for the making of music. And more than records, radios, tapes, or CDs, bodies are the basic, irreplaceable medium for its appreciation. If our bodies are the ultimate and necessary instrument for music, if one's body—in its senses, feelings, and movements—is capable of being more finely tuned to perceive, respond, and perform aesthetically, then is it not a reasonable idea to learn and train this "instrument of instruments" by more careful attention to somaesthetic feelings?

The value of such somaesthetic training (as I argue in *Practicing Philosophy* and *Performing Live*) extends far beyond the realm of fine art, enriching our cognition and our global art of living. Improved perception of our somatic feelings not only gives us greater knowledge of ourselves but also enables greater somatic skill, facility, and range of movement, which can provide our sensory organs greater scope in giving us knowledge of the world. Besides augmenting our own possibilities of pleasure, such improved somatic functioning and awareness can give us greater power in performing virtuous acts for the benefit of others, since all action depends on the efficacy of our bodily instrument.

Earlier in this chapter, I noted how ideas of proper mental order and the proper aesthetic education of taste to appreciate right order have traditionally been very important for ethics and political philosophy. If bodily feelings have a meaningful place in Wittgenstein's philosophy of mind and aesthetics, do they play a corresponding role in his ethical and political thought?

IV

Wittgenstein's discussion of somatic feelings with respect to politics is rather limited, but the notion still has a noteworthy role. First, our sense of the body, he argues, provides the ground and often the symbol for our concept of what it means to be human. Our basic existential situation, as embodied beings, implies how we are limited by the constraints and weakness of our mortal flesh: "We are prisoners of our skin."[17] But the sense of body (as the Greeks and even idealists like Hegel recognized) is also crucial to our sense of human dignity and integrity and value. Our bodies give us substance and form without which our mental life could not enjoy such a varied, robust, nuanced, and noble expression. "It is humiliating to have to appear like an empty tube which is simply inflated by a mind" (CV 11). Our ethical concepts of human rights, the sanctity of life, our high ideals of moral worth and of philosophical and aesthetic achievement all depend, Wittgenstein argues, on a form of life that takes as a premise the way we experience our bodies and the way that others treat them. Consider this strikingly brutal passage from his Cambridge notebooks, whose evocation of violence reminds one of Foucault (though without Foucault's apparent relish and utopian hope for the positive transformations that bodily disfigurement can bring):

> Mutilate completely a man, cut off his arms & legs, nose & ears, & then see what remains of his self-respect and his dignity, and to what point his concepts of these things are still the same. We don't suspect at all, how these concepts depend on the habitual, normal state of our bodies. What would happen to them if we were led by a leash attached to a ring through our tongues? How much then still remains of a man in him? Into what state does such a man sink? We don't know that we are standing on a high narrow rock & surrounded by precipices, in which everything looks different.[18]

If the familiar forms and normal feelings of our body ground our form of life, which in turn grounds our ethical concepts and attitudes toward others, then we can perhaps better understand some of our irrational political enmities. The fanatical kind of hatred or fear that some people have for certain foreign races, cultures, classes, and nations does display a deep visceral quality, which suggests that such enmity may reflect profound concerns about the integrity and purity of the familiar body in a given culture. Such anxieties can be unconsciously translated into hostility toward foreigners who challenge that familiar body and threaten to corrupt it through ethnic and cultural mixing that can alter the body in both external appearance and behavior.

Wittgenstein may be suggesting something like this as an explanation for the stubborn persistence of rabid anti-Semitism in the apparently most rational countries of Europe. This seemingly irrational hatred of the Jews may in fact have a deep compelling logic of its own that seems to operate on a visceral model or analogy. The Jews, in this unhappily familiar analogy, are a diseased tumor *(Beule)* in Europe, though Wittgenstein is prudent enough not to call this tumor a fatal cancer.

"Look on this tumor as a perfectly normal part of your body!" Can one do that, to order? Do I have the power to decide at will to have, or not to have, an ideal conception of my body?

Within the history of the peoples of Europe the history of the Jews is not treated as circumstantially as their intervention in European affairs would actually merit, because within this history they are experienced as a sort of disease, and anomaly, and no one wants to put a disease on the same level as normal life [and no one wants to speak of a disease as if it had the same rights as healthy bodily processes (even painful ones)]. We may say: people can only regard this tumor as a natural part of the body if their whole feeling for the body changes (or if the whole national feeling for the body changes). Otherwise the best they can do is *put up with* it.

You can expect an individual man to display this sort of tolerance, or else to disregard such things; but you cannot expect this of a nation, because it is precisely not disregarding such things that make it a nation. I.e. there is a contradiction in expecting someone *both* to retain his former aesthetic feeling for his body [*aesthetische Gefühl für seinen Körper*] and *also* to make the tumor welcome. (CV 20–21)

After a half-century of efforts to overcome the horrors of the holocaust with arguments for multicultural tolerance, should we simply endorse the apparent political implications of this alleged contradiction and argue that it is unreasonable for European nations to tolerate the Jews or other alien minorities that are experienced as tumors? If we respect Wittgenstein's intelligence and ethical integrity (and how could we not!), should we read this private notebook entry from 1931 as Wittgenstein's final view on the Jewish question, asserting that a nation's essential function or duty is to preserve the ethnic purity of its body politic? We can reject this purist conclusion without denying the explanatory links between political enmity against the Other and the concern for our familiar body feelings and practices. Instead Wittgenstein's remarks on the politics of aesthetic bodily feelings can be given a much richer and more politically progressive interpretation.

It is a commonplace of anthropology that maintaining the intact boundaries and purity of the body are essential symbols of preserving the unity, strength, and survival of the social group. Thus, for example, in trying to ensure the social identity of the young Hebrew nation the early books of the Old Testament are full of meticulous injunctions for the Hebrews about body purity with respect to diet, sexual behavior, and the cleanliness of intact body boundaries. Bodily "issues" like bleeding, pus, spit, semen, vomit, and menstrual discharge defile all those who come in contact with them, and the unclean need to be separated and cleansed. "Thus shall ye separate the children of Israel from their uncleanness" (Leviticus 15). Incest, bestiality, homosexuality, adultery, and the eating of foods declared unclean are similar defilements. "Defile not ye yourselves in any of these things for in all these the nations are defiled which I cast out before you" (Leviticus 18). Foreign nations are portrayed as unclean dangers of contamination that threaten the purity and health of the Hebrew people. As Wittgenstein's tumor analogy suggests, the same metaphorical logic of unclean disease has been turned *against* the Jews in the symbolic unconsciousness of Europe. Jews are stereotyped as dark, hairy, malodorous, unclean, and unhealthy, yet nonetheless mysteriously thriving in their filthy darkness like a tumor, while the true nation or folk is idealized as essentially pure or unmixed. And the ugly tumor of anti-Semitism similarly thrives through the dark power of such symbolism rather than through the critical light of rational analysis.

It is precisely because anti-Semitism (like other forms of ethnic hatred) has this compellingly sinister symbolism—a picture that holds whole nations captive—that rational arguments for multicultural tolerance always seem to fail, since the hatred is acquired not by rational means but by the captivating aesthetic power of images. Yet, as Schiller long ago claimed, aesthetic education may be able to achieve ethical-political transformation where rational arguments find no purchase. So if Wittgenstein is right that it is contradictory to expect a person to welcome a tumor while retaining his former aesthetic feeling for the body, this does not mean that the tumor must be exterminated. An alternative would be to modify that person's aesthetic feeling for the body and the body politic.

In such ethical and political matters, the discipline of somaesthetics can offer once again a productive pragmatic step. If much racial and ethnic enmity resists resolution through logical means of verbal persuasion because it has a visceral basis of discomforting unfamiliarity, then as long as we do not consciously attend to these deep visceral feelings we can neither overcome them nor the enmity they foster. So somaesthetic discipline, involving a focused, systematic scanning of our bodily feelings, is first helpful in identifying these disturbing somatic sensations so that we can better control, neutralize, or overcome them. If we can do no more than simply "put up with" them, in Wittgenstein's words, we will at least have the ability to identify and isolate them in our consciousness, which better enables us to take a critical distance from them and avert their infecting our political judgments.

But somaesthetic efforts could go further than the remedy of diagnosis and isolation by actually transforming the undesirable, "intolerant" bodily feelings. Somatic feelings can be transformed through training because they are already the product of training. One's normal feelings and tastes are almost entirely the results of learning rather than innate instinct; as habits derived from our experience and sociocultural formation, they are malleable and responsive to efforts of reformation.[19] Disciplines of somaesthetic training can therefore reconstruct our attitudes or habits of feeling and also give us greater flexibility and tolerance to different kinds of feeling and bodily behavior. This is a commonplace of gastronomy, athletics, and somatic therapies; but modern philosophical ethics and political theory have not given it enough attention.

Part of the problem may be that philosophers who do suggest that greater tolerance can be achieved through disciplines of somatic transformation—figures like Wilhelm Reich or Michel Foucault (and many of Foucault's followers in queer theory)—focus their sociopolitical advocacy of somatic discipline on the radical transformation of sexual practice. However useful and needed their reformatory proposals may be, their concentration on the sensitive issue of sex and transgression creates a cloud of controversy and polemics that distracts most mainstream philosophers (and the general public) from the broader notion and value of transformative somaesthetic discipline. The whole promise of improving social tolerance and political understanding through somaesthetic means should not be so narrowly tied to the sensationally charged but still rather limited issue of sexual behavior.[20] For all the joys of sex (and despite the brilliant insights of Freud), there is a great deal more of interest and of value in our bodily life than our experience of sexual activity and desire. This is something that Wittgenstein must have known, since sexuality hardly seems to constitute the preoccupying center of his life and work.

If the seductive image of bodily-ethnic-political purity lurks as the deep prejudice that incites fear and hatred toward alien groups, then one strategy for overcoming the problem would be to make vividly clear and visible the impure and mixed nature of all human bodies, including one's own. Somaesthetic disciplines can give us such a heightened, lived awareness of the impure mixture of bodily constitution and remind us that our body boundaries are never absolute but rather porous. The body is a messy container of all sorts of solids, liquids, and gases; it is always being penetrated by things coming from the outside in the air we breathe and the food we eat, just as we continuously expel materials from within our bodies. The somaesthetic strategy of focusing on our impure bodily mixture can already be found in the Buddha's sermon advocating heightened mindfulness of body: "a *bhikkhu* [monk] reflects on this very body enveloped by the skin and full of manifold impurity, from the sole up and the hair down, thinking thus: 'There are in this body hair of the head, hair of the body, nails, teeth, skin, flesh, sinews, bones, marrow, kidneys, heart, liver, midriff, spleen, lungs, intestines, mesentery, stomach, faeces, bile, phlegm, pus, blood, seat, fat, tears, grease, saliva, nasal mucus, synovial fluid, urine.' . . . Thus, he lives observing the body."[21]

Having indicated my general arguments for the ethical and political potential of somaesthetic disciplines, I shall not try to provide here a more detailed account of the concrete pragmatics of these practices.[22] That would take us too far from the topic of Wittgenstein, who provides no real analysis of programmatic somaesthetic disciplines, ancient or modern. So let me conclude this essay by considering a Wittgensteinian theme that may help underline the pertinence of somaesthetics, not just for the integrated branches of philosophy we have so far examined, but for philosophy as a whole.

V

Wittgenstein frequently insists on the crucial importance of slowness for properly doing philosophy. Philosophers often err by jumping to wrong conclusions by misinterpreting the gross surface structure of language in terms of some primitive scheme and then inferring something that seems at once necessary and impossible. Instead of rushing "like savages, primitive people" to "put a false interpretation" on language "and then draw the queerest conclusions from it" (PI § 194), the key to good philosophical work is taking the time to carefully untangle the knots of conceptual confusion caused by such hasty conclusions from language. We do this by patiently "clearing up" the complexities of our language-games, "by arranging what we have always known," by "assembling reminders" so as "to bring words back from their metaphysical to their everyday use" and thus "uncovering . . . one or another piece of plain nonsense and . . . bumps that the understanding has got by running its head up against the limits of language" (PI §§ 118, 109, 127, 116, 119). This work of painstaking linguistic analysis requires slow, patient labor and thus demands a sort of practiced, disciplined slowness. Wittgenstein therefore cautions that "someone unpractised in philosophy passes by all the spots where difficulties are hidden in the grass, whereas the practiced [philosopher] will pause and sense that there is a difficulty close by even though he cannot see it yet" (CV 29).

Hence Wittgenstein's appreciation of slowness: "The salutation of philosophers to each other should be: 'Take your time!' " Wittgenstein's manner of reading and writing aim at attaining this slowness. "I really want my copious punctuation marks to slow down the speed of reading. Because I should like to be read slowly. (As I myself read.)" "My sentences are all supposed to be read slowly" (CV 80, 68, 57). We know, however, that Wittgenstein's temperament was the opposite of patient. Exceedingly quick of mind and movement, he had great difficulty in either sitting or standing still.[23] Fiery and quick-tempered, he nonetheless insisted, "My ideal is a certain coolness," a state of tranquillity where "conflict is dissipated" and one achieves "peace in one's thoughts" (CV 2, 9, 43).

But how can we achieve a better mastery of slowness and tranquillity without drugging ourselves with mind-deadening tranquilizers? Self-isolation in a quiet, foreign place that is far from familiar and unwanted distractions is one traditional method, and Wittgenstein indeed applied it in his periods of hermit life far up on the Sogna Fjord in Norway. But another ancient answer has been a focused attention to and consequent regulation of our breathing. Since breathing has a profound effect on our entire nervous system, by slowing or calming our breathing, we can bring greater slowness and tranquillity to our minds. In the same way, by noticing and then relaxing certain muscle contractions that are not only unnecessary but distractive to thinking because of the pain or fatigue they create, we can strengthen our mental concentration and build its patient endurance for sustained philosophical meditations. We can then afford to take our time.

Attention to bodily feelings cannot explain our thinking, our emotions, or our will. But it can improve them. Somaesthetic sensations neither explain nor justify our aesthetic judgments, but they can help us enhance our aesthetic capacities and even our ethical powers. Sensation is not the mysterious explanatory *"something"* that defines the fundamental mechanism of all mental life, but, as Wittgenstein recognizes, it "is not a *nothing* either!" (PI § 304). However much somaesthetic feeling counts for Wittgenstein, I hope to have shown that it should count for something more, at least for a pragmatism that seeks to improve the quality of our thought and life, including the thoughtful lives we lead as active political animals.

Notes

INTRODUCTION

1. RCV 69; Norman Malcolm, *Ludwig Wittgenstein: A Memoir* (Oxford: Oxford University Press, 1958), 98.
2. Maurice Drury, "Some Notes on Conversations with Wittgenstein," in *Recollections of Wittgenstein*, ed. Rush Rhees (Oxford: Oxford University Press, 1984), 116.
3. My thanks to Michael Hymers for reminding me of these incidents and their significance by juxtaposing several of them in his paper "Wittgenstein, Pessimism, and Politics," *Dalhousie Review* 80, no. 2 (2000).
4. Ray Monk, *Ludwig Wittgenstein: The Duty of Genius* (London: Vintage, 1990), 211.
5. Monk, *Duty of Genius*, 72–73. Reconciling this remark with intellectual friendships with such distinguished philosophers as Elizabeth Anscombe or Alice Ambrose required some convoluted reasoning on Wittgenstein's part. Monk reports that on one occasion he declared to Anscombe, upon realizing that there were no (other) female students in the lecture room, "Thank God we've got rid of all the women!" (498).
6. This notwithstanding the claims of W. W. Bartley in his notorious biography *Wittgenstein* (Chicago: Open Court, 1985), in which he suggests that a promiscuous spate of anonymous sexual encounters with Viennese flaneurs had a profound impact on the trajectory of Wittgenstein's thought. See Monk's cautious rebuttal in "Appendix: Bartley's Wittgenstein and the Coded Remarks," in *Duty of Genius*, 581–86.
7. If anything, Wittgenstein was oblivious to the politically objectionable theses of this text, preferring instead to focus on Weininger's insights into duty, genius, and death. See Monk, *Duty of Genius*, especially 19–25; Allan Janik, *Essays on Wittgenstein and Weininger* (Amsterdam: Rodopi, 1985); Bela Szabados, "Wittgenstein's Women: The Philosophical Significance of Wittgenstein's Misogyny," *Journal of Philosophical Research* 22 (1997).
8. Monk, *Duty of Genius*, 347–54.
9. See Terry Eagleton, "Wittgenstein's Friends," *New Left Review*, no. 135 (1982).
10. See *Wittgenstein: Biography and Philosophy*, ed. James Klagge (Cambridge: Cambridge University Press, 2001).

11. Quoted in Monk, *Duty of Genius*, 73.
12. Quoted in ibid., 17–18.
13. As, for example, Andrew Lugg argues in "Wittgenstein on Politics: Not Left, Right, or Center," *International Studies in Philosophy* (forthcoming).
14. J. C. Nyíri, "Wittgenstein's Later Work in Relation to Conservatism," in *Wittgenstein and His Time*, ed. B. McGuiness (Oxford: Blackwell, 1981), 44.
15. Nyíri, "Wittgenstein's Later Work," especially 48–57; Eagleton, "Wittgenstein's Friends."
16. Allan Janik and Stephen Toulmin, *Wittgenstein's Vienna* (New York: Touchstone, 1973).
17. Nyíri, "Wittgenstein's Later Work," 58.
18. Ibid., 58–59.
19. Ernest Gellner, *Reason and Culture* (Oxford: Blackwell, 1992), 120.
20. David Bloor, *Wittgenstein: A Social Theory of Knowledge* (London: Macmillan, 1983), 161. See 160–81 for Bloor's larger analysis of Wittgenstein *qua* conservative, and his critique of Winch's reading.
21. Peter Winch, "Understanding a Primitive Society," in *Ethics and Action* (London: Routledge and Kegan Paul, 1972).
22. Ibid., 82.
23. See K. Jones, "Is Wittgenstein a Conservative Philosopher?" *Philosophical Investigations* 9, no. 4 (1986); Andrew Lugg, "Was Wittgenstein a Conservative Thinker?" *Southern Journal of Philosophy* 23, no. 4 (1985); Joachim Schulte, "Wittgenstein and Conservatism," *Ratio* 25 (1983).
24. Hanna Fenichel Pitkin, *Wittgenstein and Justice: On the Significance of Ludwig Wittgenstein for Social and Political Thought* (Berkeley: University of California Press, 1972), 325.
25. Pitkin's suggestion here is the main Wittgensteinian tenet of Cressida J. Heyes, *Line Drawings: Defining Women through Feminist Practice* (Ithaca, N.Y.: Cornell University Press, 2000), and is also central to James Tully, *Strange Multiplicity: Constitutionalism in an Age of Diversity* (Cambridge: Cambridge University Press, 1995).
26. These arguments are developed by Cavell in an extensive corpus. For germinal texts, see Stanley Cavell, *Must We Mean What We Say?* (Cambridge: Cambridge University Press, 1976); *The Claim of Reason: Wittgenstein, Skepticism, Morality, and Tragedy* (Oxford: Oxford University Press, 1979); *Conditions Handsome and Unhandsome: The Constitution of Emersonian Perfectionism* (Chicago: University of Chicago Press, 1990).
27. For an interpretation of the significance of this literature, see Gaile Pohlhaus and John Wright, "Using Wittgenstein Critically: A Political Approach to Philosophy," *Political Theory* 30, no. 6 (2002).
28. James Tully, "Political Philosophy as a Critical Activity," *Political Theory* 30, no. 4 (2002).
29. For a fascinating extended treatment of this material, with many political implications, see Judith Genova, *Wittgenstein: A Way of Seeing* (New York: Routledge, 1995).
30. Richard Shusterman, *Practicing Philosophy: Pragmatism and the Philosophical Life* (New York: Routledge, 1997), 17–64.
31. The former view is, of course, articulated in Nyíri, "Wittgenstein's Later Work," 57–64; a version of the latter can be found in Naomi Scheman, "Forms of Life: Mapping the Rough Ground," in *The Cambridge Companion to Wittgenstein*, ed. Hans Sluga and David Stern (New York: Cambridge University Press, 1996). This controversy

has often turned on conflicting interpretations of Wittgenstein's "Sketch for a Foreword" (to his *Philosophical Remarks*), eventually published in *Culture and Value*, in which he states: "This book is written for those who are in sympathy with the spirit in which it is written. This spirit is, I believe, different from that of the prevailing European and American civilization. The spirit of this civilization, the expression of which is the industry, architecture, music of present day fascism & socialism, is a spirit that is alien and uncongenial to the author" (RCV 8).

1. WITTGENSTEIN AND POLITICAL PHILOSOPHY

1. See Charles Taylor, "Overcoming Epistemology," *Philosophical Arguments* (Cambridge: Harvard University Press, 1995), 1–20.
2. Martin Heidegger, *Being and Time*, trans. Joan Stambaugh (Albany: State University of New York Press, 1996), 7–12.
3. Jean-Paul Sartre, *Being and Nothingness*, trans. Hazel E. Barnes (New York: Washington Square, 1966), 76.
4. According to Wittgenstein, it will be in my use and applications of his techniques and conceptual tools that I will show I understand or misunderstand them, and not in (another) interpretation of or commentary on them (PI §§ 199–201). It is a remarkable fact that Wittgenstein's interpreters have not reflected on this, his central teaching.
5. A "survey" or "perspicuous representation" *(übersichtliche Darstellung)*, "objects of comparison" *(Vergleichsobjekte)*, and philosophical "methods" *(Methoden)*, like "different therapies," are terms of art Wittgenstein uses (PI §§ 122, 130, 133). The importance of his discovery of these methods in 1930 for his later philosophy is discussed by Ray Monk in *Ludwig Wittgenstein: The Duty of Genius* (London: Vintage, 1990), 298–327. The best introductions are Gordon Baker, "*Philosophical Investigations* Section 122: Neglected Aspects," in *Wittgenstein's Philosophical Investigations*, ed. Robert L. Arrington and Hans-Johann Glock (London: Routledge, 1991), 35–69; and G.P. Baker and P.M.S. Hacker, *Wittgenstein: Understanding and Meaning: An Analytical Commentary on the Philosophical Investigations* (Oxford: Basil Blackwell, 1980).
6. For Habermas's distinction between these two types of critical reflection, see Richard J. Bernstein, "Introduction," in *Habermas and Modernity* (Cambridge: MIT Press, 1995), 12–13. Habermas accepts this clarification by Bernstein in *Habermas: Autonomy and Solidarity*, ed. Peter Dews (London: Verso, 1986), 153. For his development of these two types of critical reflection since 1989, see especially Jürgen Habermas, "Discourse Ethics: Notes on a Program of Philosophical Justification," in *Moral Consciousness and Communicative Action*, trans. Christian Lenhardt and Shierry Nicholsen (Cambridge: MIT Press, 1995), 43–116. For the application of his discourse ethics to democratic theory, see Habermas, *Between Facts and Norms: Contributions to a Discourse Theory of Law and Democracy*, trans. William Rehg (Cambridge: MIT Press, 1996).
7. Jürgen Habermas, *The Theory of Communicative Action*, vol. 1, *Reason and the Rationalization of Society*, trans. Thomas McCarthy (Boston: Beacon Press, 1984), 397. (TCA1 hereafter.)
8. Jürgen Habermas, "What Is Universal Pragmatics?" in *Communication and the Evolution of Society*, trans. Thomas McCarthy (Boston: Beacon Press, 1979), 1–69, 2 n. 2, 208–10.

9. Habermas, TCA1, 86.
10. Habermas's contribution to *Transzendentalphilophische Normenbegrundungen*, ed. Willi Oelmuller (Paderborn, Germany: Schoingh, 1978), 156, cited in Thomas McCarthy, "Rationality and Relativism: Habermas's Overcoming of Hermeneutics," in *Habermas: Critical Debates*, ed. John Thompson and David Held (Cambridge: MIT Press, 1982), 57–79, 63. Compare TCA1, 115–16; Habermas, "A Reply to My Critics," in *Habermas: Critical Debates*, ed. John Thompson and David Held (Cambridge: MIT Press, 1982), 270–71.
11. Habermas, cited in McCarthy, "Rationality and Relativism," 63.
12. Habermas, TCA1, 297.
13. Habermas, TCA1, 307–8; and "Reply to My Critics," 271–72.
14. Habermas, TCA1, 308. Compare ibid., 329; and "Philosophy as Stand-in and Interpreter," in Lehnhardt and Nicholsen, eds. *Moral Consciousness*, 1–21.
15. Habermas, "Reply to My Critics," 272. Compare Habermas, *The Theory of Communicative Action*, vol. 2, *Lifeworld and System: A Critique of Functionalist Reason*, trans. Thomas McCarthy (Boston: Beacon Press, 1987), 119–52. (TCA2 hereafter.)
16. Habermas, TCA1, 17; see 317.
17. This paragraph incorporates the changes Habermas has made since TCA1 to the rules governing the three forms of argumentation. "Discourse Ethics" is the best discussion of these changes and the new principles D and U. For an introduction to these developments, see Maeve Cooke, *Language and Reason: A Study of Habermas's Pragmatics* (Cambridge: MIT Press, 1994), 29–51; and William Rehg, *Insight and Solidarity: The Discourse Ethics of Jürgen Habermas* (Berkeley: University of California Press, 1994), 1–88. This paragraph draws on my discussion of discourse ethics: "To Think and Act Differently: Foucault's Four Reciprocal Objections to Habermas' Theory," in *Foucault contra Habermas: Recasting the Dialogue between Genealogy and Critical Theory*, ed. Samantha Ashenden and David Owen (London: Sage Publications, 1999), 90–142, 100–107.
18. Habermas, "Philosophy as Stand-in and Interpreter," 19–20. Compare TCA1, 42; and Habermas, *Justification and Application: Remarks on Discourse Ethics*, trans. Ciaran P. Cronin (Cambridge: MIT Press, 1993), 29.
19. Habermas, "Philosophy as Stand-in and Interpreter," 19. Compare TCA1, 95.
20. Habermas, TCA2, 150–51, and further, 283–94, 396–403.
21. Habermas, "Reply to My Critics," 262; TCA2, 396–403; *Justification and Application*, 51, 151; McCarthy, "Introduction," in TCA1, xxiii–xxiv, 404 n. 12; Cooke, *Language and Reason*, 1.
22. I have discussed "reasonable disagreement" (as developed by Rawls) in relation to Habermas's ideal of consensus in "To Think and Act Differently," 122–24. Compare Jeremy Waldron, *Law and Disagreement* (Cambridge: Cambridge University Press, 1999), 102–6.
23. Habermas, TCA1, 307. For doubts about "reaching understanding/agreement" as the standard form, see John Thompson, "Universal Pragmatics," in *Habermas: Critical Debates*, ed. John Thompson and David Held (Cambridge: MIT Press, 1982), 125–26. The attempt to eliminate "non-serious" forms of speech is questioned in Rudiger Bubner, "Habermas's Concept of Critical Theory," in the same volume, 42–57. The works of Hannah Arendt and Jacques Derrida contain well-known criticisms of this Platonic tendency in political philosophy.
24. For Wittgenstein's dissent from the community-agreement theory of justification see Z §§ 428–31. See G. P. Baker and P. M. S. Hacker, *An Analytical Commentary*

on the Philosophical Investigations, vol. 2, *Wittgenstein: Rules, Grammar and Necessity* (Oxford: Basil Blackwell, 1985), 228–51; and Baker and Hacker, *Scepticism, Rules and Language* (Oxford: Basil Blackwell, 1984), 71–80.

25. See the text at note 16 above.
26. Habermas, TCA1, 95; "Philosophy as Stand-in and Interpreter," 19.
27. Habermas, TCA1, 18–25, 96.
28. Wittgenstein, PI §§ 7, 23, 150, 182, 198, 199, 202. See section 3.1 below and Baker and Hacker, *Rules, Grammar and Necessity*, 159–65.
29. Stephen Hilmy, *The Later Wittgenstein* (Oxford: Basil Blackwell, 1987), 98–137.
30. Wittgenstein states that his aim is to survey and clarify these nonreflective uses of words because they tend to lead us astray and give rise to philosophical problems (PI §§ 90, 107, 109–11, 116, 122, 125).
31. Compare: "I really want to say that a language-game is only possible if one trusts something (I did not say 'can trust something')" (OC § 509).
32. Compare OC §§ 96–99.
33. William Connolly, *The Terms of Political Discourse*, 2d ed. (Princeton, N.J.: Princeton University Press, 1983).
34. For the freedom and indeterminacy of language use, see PI §§ 65–84; section 3.3 below; Henry Staten, *Wittgenstein and Derrida* (Omaha: University of Nebraska Press, 1986), 64–110; and Hilmy, *The Later Wittgenstein*, 180–89.
35. Quentin Skinner, "Some Problems in the Analysis of Political Thought and Action," and "Language and Social Change," in *Meaning and Context: Quentin Skinner and His Critics*, ed. James Tully (Cambridge: Polity Press, 1988), 97–134. For the history of the critical reflection on the indeterminacy of political concepts and Hobbes's attempt to transcend it, see Quentin Skinner, *Reason and Rhetoric in the Philosophy of Hobbes* (Cambridge: Cambridge University Press, 1996), especially 138–80; Richard Rorty, *Contingency, Irony, and Solidarity* (Cambridge: Cambridge University Press, 1989), 3–22.
36. Habermas, "Discourse Ethics," 87. He presents R. Alexy's rules as examples of the kind of logical and semantic rules he has in mind. Rules 1.2 and 1.3 require determinacy of criteria and application. For a discussion of this limitation, see Tully, "To Think and Act Differently," 118–24.
37. For the civic humanist's priority of the good, see Charles Taylor, *Sources of the Self* (Cambridge: Harvard University Press, 1989), 3–110. For the ecologist's objection to the priority of rightness, see Tully, "An Ecological Ethic for the Present," in *Governing for the Environment: Global Problems, Ethics and Democracy*, ed. Brendan Gleeson and Nicholas Low (London: Palgrave, 2000), 147–65, 148–53.
38. For a critical discussion of Habermas's transcendental-pragmatic argument, and of his two logic-of-development arguments in support of his framework of three validity claims and types of argumentation, see Tully, "To Think and Act Differently," 105–7, 109–18. For the limits of the juridical tradition, see ibid., 124–30; John Pocock, "Virtues, Rights and Manners," in *Virtue, Commerce and History* (Cambridge: Cambridge University Press, 1985), 37–51; Quentin Skinner, "The Idea of Negative Liberty: Philosophical and Historical Perspectives," in *Philosophy in History*, ed. Richard Rorty, J. B. Schneewind, and Quentin Skinner (Cambridge: Cambridge University Press, 1984), 193–223; and Michael Sandel, *Liberalism and the Limits of Justice* (Cambridge: Cambridge University Press, 1982).
39. Seyla Benhabib and Simone Chambers, for example, argue, contrary to Habermas, that argumentation in terms of the three validity claims is not transcendental

and thus that participants in a practical discourse should be free to question it. Seyla Benhabib, *Situating the Self: Gender, Community and Postmodernism in Contemporary Ethics* (London: Routledge, 1992), 29–38; Simone Chambers, *Reasonable Democracy: Jürgen Habermas and the Politics of Discourse* (Ithaca, N.Y.: Cornell University Press, 1996), 158–59.

40. See David Owen, "Orientation and Enlightenment: An Essay on Critique and Genealogy," in *Foucault contra Habermas: Recasting the Dialogue between Genealogy and Critical Theory*, ed. Samantha Ashenden and David Owen (London: Sage Publications, 1999), 21–44.

41. Habermas, "Discourse Ethics," 80. For the inconclusiveness of this argument, see Tully, "To Think and Act Differently," 118–24.

42. Wittgenstein discusses the drawing of conditional and non-transcendental boundaries for particular purposes with an interlocutor who believes we require unconditional and transcendental boundaries at PI § 68. For the implications of this line of argument for feminist political philosophy, see Heyes, *Line Drawings*.

43. Michel Foucault, "What Is Enlightenment?" in *Michel Foucault: Ethics, Subjectivity and Truth*, ed. Paul Rabinow (New York: The New Press, 1997), 303–21.

44. For the role of this section in Wittgenstein's philosophy, see James C. Edwards, *Ethics without Philosophy: Wittgenstein and the Moral Life* (Tampa: University Presses of Florida, 1985), 103–60.

45. For this kind of critique by Foucault of the presumed universality of the juridical traditions of reasoning, see Tully, "To Think and Act Differently," 124–30.

46. For the complex history of "rightness" and its cognates, see Richard Tuck, *Natural Rights Theories: Their Origin and Development* (Cambridge: Cambridge University Press, 1979); Richard Tuck, *Philosophy and Government: 1572–1651* (Cambridge: Cambridge University Press, 1993); T. J. Hochstrasser, *Natural Law Theories in the Early Enlightenment* (Cambridge: Cambridge University Press, 2000).

47. For an analysis, see Skinner, "Language and Social Change," 119–34.

48. For the way historical genealogies can be used as "objects of comparison" to free us from conventional consensus, see the chapter by David Owen in this volume, and Quentin Skinner, *Liberty before Liberalism* (Cambridge: Cambridge University Press, 1998), 101–20.

49. For the role of "hinge" propositions, see OC § 341: "That is to say, the *questions* that we raise and our *doubts* depend on the fact that some propositions are exempt from doubt, are as it were like hinges on which those turn" (compare §§ 342–43). See the chapter by Linda Zerilli in this volume.

50. This reconception is set out by Wittgenstein in the *Philosophical Investigations*, §§ 65–84. I have illustrated one way it might be employed in political philosophy in *Strange Multiplicity: Constitutionalism in an Age of Diversity* (Cambridge: Cambridge University Press, 1995), 103–16, and compared it to other approaches in "Political Philosophy as a Critical Activity," *Political Theory* 30, no. 4 (2002).

51. For his relationship to Wittgenstein, see Taylor, *Philosophical Arguments*: 1–20, 61–79, 165–80; and Richard Eldridge, *Leading a Human Life: Wittgenstein, Intentionality and Romanticism* (Chicago: University of Chicago Press, 1997). For Taylor's defense of this tradition, see *Philosophy in an Age of Pluralism: The Philosophy of Charles Taylor in Question*, ed. James Tully (Cambridge: Cambridge University Press, 1994).

52. Taylor's account of understanding in "Overcoming Epistemology" and "To Follow a Rule" in *Philosophical Arguments* is in accord with the account given by Wittgenstein.

53. Charles Taylor, *Philosophical Papers* (Cambridge: Cambridge University Press, 1985), 1:45.
54. Ibid., 1:15, 2:15–45.
55. Ibid., 1:72.
56. Ibid., 75.
57. Taylor, "Philosophy and Its History," in *Philosophy in History*, ed. Richard Rorty, J. B. Schneewind, and Quentin Skinner (Cambridge: Cambridge University Press, 1984), 17–31, 18.
58. For example, Taylor, *Philosophical Papers*, 2:15–57; and Hans-Georg Gadamer, *Truth and Method*, trans. William Glen-Doepel, 2d ed. (London: Sheed and Ward, 1979), 433.
59. Wittgenstein himself succumbed to this widespread inclination to take understanding to be a kind of interpretation and is correcting his own misunderstanding in these sections. See *Wittgenstein's Lectures, Cambridge 1930–1932*, ed. Desmond Lee, from the notes of John King and Desmond Lee (Oxford: Basil Blackwell, 1974), 24; and Baker and Hacker, *Rules, Grammar and Necessity*, 150.
60. For a succinct commentary on sections 198–201, see Baker and Hacker, *Rules, Grammar, and Necessity*, 132–50.
61. Cited in Baker and Hacker, *Rules, Grammar, and Necessity*, 136. For Wittgenstein's idea of understanding as analogous to an immediate grasp, compare *On Certainty*: "It is just like directly taking hold of something, as I take hold of my towel without having doubts" (§ 510).
62. This is the primary ability the reader is meant to acquire by working through the examples in the *Philosophical Investigations* (§ 71). See Baker, "*Philosophical Investigations* Section 122," and the chapter by Jonathan Havercroft in this volume.
63. Friedrich Nietzsche, *The Will to Power*, trans. Walter Kaufmann and R. J. Hollingdale (New York: Vintage, 1968), §§ 283, 522.
64. See Wittgenstein's remarks on the analogous phenomenon of "seeing as" (visual interpretation) in *Philosophical Investigations*, §§ 377–81, and pp. 183–208.
65. Taylor, *Philosophical Papers*, 1:75, quoted above at note 56.
66. This human, all too human *tension* between understanding and interpretation is explored in the works of Stanley Cavell and in Eldridge, *Leading a Human Life*.
67. The history of this form of self-interpretation is the theme of Charles Taylor, *Sources of the Self: The Making of the Modern Identity* (Cambridge: Harvard University Press, 1989), and Michel Foucault, *The History of Sexuality*, vol. 1 (London: Penguin, 1978).
68. Michel Foucault, *Fearless Speech*, ed. Joseph Pearson (Los Angeles: Semiotext(e), 2001), 170–71. Foucault started this kind of historical "survey" of practices of the "critical attitude" in the last years of his life. *Fearless Speech* is a collection of student notes of his lectures at Berkeley in 1983 on this theme in Greek and early Roman thought. The first outline of this form of historical survey is a lecture given to the French Society of Philosophy in May 1978, "Qu'est-ce que la critique?" *Bulletin de la Société française de philosophie* 84 (1990): 35–63; translated as "What Is Critique?" in *The Politics of Truth*, ed. Sylvère Ltoringer (Los Angeles: Semiotext(e), 1997), 23–82. As Cressida Heyes mentions in the introduction, I believe that Wittgenstein's methods can be extended and deepened by adding historical applications to them, such as this work of Foucault and the historical approaches of Quentin Skinner and Charles Taylor, and, as Edward Said has always insisted, by establishing a dialogue with similar scholars and studies in non-Western societies.

69. For a complementary analysis by the leading Wittgensteinian philosopher of the human sciences, see Stephen Toulmin, *Return to Reason* (Cambridge: Harvard University Press, 2001).

70. For a comparison of Wittgenstein's philosophical methods with Nietzsche and Foucault, see the chapter by David Owen in this volume.

An earlier version of this chapter was published in *Political Theory* in 1989. The editor of this volume kindly offered to include an updated version. I have made several changes while retaining the main line of argument, which is to show how Wittgenstein's philosophical methods can be used to clarify the role of concepts and practices of critical reflection in political philosophy. The sections on Habermas's form of critical reflection ("practical discourses of validation") have been rewritten to take into account the considerable changes he has made over the last decade in response to objections similar to the ones I raised in 1989. In addition, I have discussed these changes in a recent publication, to which I refer in the notes. Notwithstanding these improvements and the concession that his arguments are fallible, I argue that he continues to assign a foundational and quasi-transcendental role to his three forms of argumentation to redeem validity claims—his "decentered understanding of the world"—that cannot be sustained. The section on interpretation has been rewritten to acknowledge that Taylor and I are now in agreement on Wittgenstein's distinction between interpretation and understanding, which I initially took to be a point of disagreement. I am greatly indebted to Seyla Benhabib, Peta Bowden, Natalie Brender, William Connolly, Jonathan Havercroft, Cressida Heyes, Susan James, Chantal Mouffe, David Owen, Quentin Skinner, Charles Taylor, Dale Turner, and Linda Zerilli for discussions of the themes of this chapter and of the importance of Wittgenstein for political philosophy.

2. THE LIMITS OF CONSERVATISM

1. Cora Diamond, *The Realistic Spirit: Wittgenstein, Philosophy, and the Mind* (Cambridge: MIT Press, 1991), 34.

2. I am not alone in objecting to conservative readings of Wittgenstein, though none that I have seen explores the line of objection I am recommending. This is not to say, though, that I have not learned from what others have written. See Andrew Lugg, "Was Wittgenstein a Conservative Thinker?" *Southern Journal of Philosophy* 23, no. 4 (1985); and Joachim Schulte, "Wittgenstein and Conservatism," *Ratio* 25 (1983). Closest in outlook to my own is Alice Crary, "Wittgenstein's Philosophy in Relation to Political Thought," in *The New Wittgenstein*, ed. Alice Crary and Rupert Read (London: Routledge, 2000). A principal merit of Crary's paper is her diagnosis of both conservative and activist readings of Wittgenstein as ultimately turning on kindred misreadings of his conceptions of meaning, nonsense, and philosophy. I am also following Crary in distinguishing between Wittgenstein's biography and his philosophy when considering questions of political implications, and, like Crary, I will only be concerned with the latter.

3. The ambiguity of the biographical data has been emphasized by Lugg, "Was Wittgenstein a Conservative Thinker?" (see especially 465–66), as well as by Crary, "Wittgenstein's Philosophy" (see 141–42 n. 1).

4. David Bloor, *Wittgenstein: A Social Theory of Knowledge* (New York: Columbia University Press, 1983).

5. Ernest Gellner, *Language and Solitude: Wittgenstein, Malinowski, and the Hapsburg Dilemma* (Cambridge: Cambridge University Press, 1998). I place "reading" in scarequotes to signal how little Gellner's remarks seem actually to engage with Wittgenstein's writings. Over the course of well over a hundred pages, there are only a handful of citations, and these are usually only a sentence or two, cited without any attention to their original context and without any worry that their meaning is anything other than obvious.
6. Bloor, *Wittgenstein*, 2.
7. Ibid., 83.
8. David Bloor, *Knowledge and Social Imagery*, rev. ed. (Chicago: University of Chicago Press, 1991).
9. Ibid., 105, 106.
10. Bloor, *Wittgenstein*, 93.
11. Ibid., 117.
12. This idea of "other arrangements" raises another difficulty for Bloor's picture, since it is not at all clear that, given the terms of his account, such an idea can be sustained. That is, Bloor appeals to social structure to account for the differences in conceptual repertoire among various groups. However, anything we say about another group is mediated by our (socially determined) perspective. Thus, for us to say that there is another group, which views things differently, is itself conditioned by the perspective from which it is said. Given this, we can only say how the difference appears to us, and so we cannot say what the difference really is. In trying to countenance the existence of another group, we fail to get beyond the limitations of our own. These sorts of considerations are raised by Hilary Putnam in his discussion of cultural relativism. Putnam points out that the trouble arises for the would-be cultural relativist from his desire to say both "When I say something is true, I mean that it is correct according to the norms of my culture" and "When a member of a different culture says that something is true, what he means . . . is that it is in conformity with the norms of his culture." Putnam's point is that since the cultural relativist stands within one culture, his judgments concerning the conformity of a statement made by a member of another culture with the norms of that person's culture are made in accord with the norms of his own (i.e., the relativist's) culture. Putnam's conclusion is that "other cultures become, so to speak, logical constructions out of the procedures and practices" of the culture in which the would-be relativist stands. But this form of "methodological solipsism" runs precisely contrary to what the relativist has wanted to claim, since what he has claimed is that there are a plurality of cultures with their respective truth-determining norms. See Putnam, "Why Reason Can't Be Naturalized," in *Philosophical Papers*, vol. 3 (Cambridge: Cambridge University Press, 1983), especially 234–38.
13. A pressing question, though, is just why it is that Wittgenstein is talking about "the facts of human natural history" at all, if his aim is not to make the kind of point Bloor ascribes to him. Exactly what Wittgenstein means by "natural history," and the import he ascribes to its description, is not easy to specify, in part because he is deliberately vague about its scope. The difficulties are compounded by his occasional appeals to "fictitious natural history," for example in *Philosophical Investigations* II, § xii, discussed below. When Wittgenstein provides examples of "the facts of human natural history," they are usually quite general and uncontroversial, e.g., the list of *Philosophical Investigations* § 25 ("Commanding, questioning, recounting, chatting, are as much a part of our natural history as walking, eating, drinking, playing"). As

I suggest below, Wittgenstein's aim in "reminding" us of such facts is largely critical. That is, such reminders are not contributions to any kind of hypothesis about our relation to the world, but part of a diagnosis of what goes wrong in philosophy when such hypotheses are proposed and disputed.

14. Thomas Nagel, *The View from Nowhere* (Oxford: Oxford University Press, 1986), 105.
15. Gellner, *Language and Solitude*, 77.
16. Ibid., 160.
17. J. C. Nyíri, "Wittgenstein's Later Work in Relation to Conservatism," in *Wittgenstein and His Time*, ed. B. McGuiness (Oxford: Blackwell, 1981), 58–59.
18. Gellner, *Language and Solitude*, 168.
19. I return to this remark, and its image of acceptance, in the concluding section of the chapter. I suggest there that Wittgenstein's talk of acceptance need not be understood as endorsing conservatism.
20. Ernest Gellner, "Relativism and Universals," in *Rationality and Relativism*, ed. Martin Hollis and Stephen Lukes (Cambridge: MIT Press, 1982), 188–89.
21. Part of the defense would be, of course, to reject the charges, at least in the terms they are posed. The particular way in which Gellner raises the problem of "cross-cultural validation," and so voices his demand for the justification of "our" concepts, takes for granted the kind of mutually exclusive closure of cultural-conceptual systems that I take Wittgenstein ultimately to be criticizing.
22. In coming to understand Wittgenstein as concerned to investigate, and ultimately reject, this imagery of confinement, I am deeply indebted to the work of Edward Minar, in particular his paper "Wittgenstein and the 'Contingency' of Community," *Pacific Philosophical Quarterly* 72 (1991).
23. Nyíri, "Wittgenstein's Later Work," 59, emphasis added.
24. In saying this, I do not wish to suggest that Wittgenstein's observation does not report something extremely peculiar: just what it would be like to inhabit that situation is no doubt quite difficult to think all the way through. Would the people in this situation also be rapidly coming into being and passing away? Would they have the concept of an object at all?
25. Indeed, Rush Rhees calls *Investigations* II, § xii "the most important short statement for understanding" Wittgenstein's later philosophy. See Rhees, "The Philosophy of Wittgenstein," in *Discussions of Wittgenstein* (New York: Schocken Books, 1970), 54.
26. Here I use "realistic" following Cora Diamond's characterization of Wittgenstein's later philosophy as manifesting "the realistic spirit," that is, an attitude that rejects metaphysical pictures and demands. See Diamond, *The Realistic Spirit*, especially the essay "Realism and the Realistic Spirit."
27. James Baldwin, "Everybody's Protest Novel," reprinted in the Norton Critical Edition of Harriet Beecher Stowe, *Uncle Tom's Cabin*, ed. Elizabeth Ammons (New York: W. W. Norton, 1994). First published in *Partisan Review*, no. 16 (June 1949).
28. *Uncle Tom's Cabin* was first published in 1852. One measure of its importance is the note on the back of my edition: "In the nineteenth century Uncle Tom's Cabin sold more copies than any book in the world except the Bible."
29. Baldwin, "Everybody's Protest Novel," 499.
30. Ibid., 497.
31. Ibid., 496.
32. Ibid., 499.

33. Ibid., 501.

34. Lawrie Balfour's book *The Evidence of Things Not Said: James Baldwin and the Promise of American Democracy* (Ithaca, N.Y.: Cornell University Press, 2001), likewise emphasizes the notion of acceptance in Baldwin's work, and the (ultimately unfair) accusations of conservatism it invites; see especially 115–17. With respect to Wittgenstein, my remarks in these concluding paragraphs owe a considerable debt to the writings of Stanley Cavell, especially *This New Yet Unapproachable America: Lectures after Emerson after Wittgenstein* (Albuquerque: Living Batch Press, 1989). Cavell sees Wittgenstein's imagery of acceptance as opening him to the charge of conservatism, but to level that charge is to misread that imagery: "In being asked to accept this [human form of life], or suffer it, as given for ourselves, we are not asked to accept, let us say, private property, but separateness; not a particular fact of power but the fact that I am a man, therefore of this (range or scale of) capacity for work, for understanding, for wish, for will, for teaching, for suffering. The precise range or scale is not knowable a priori, any more than the precise range or scale of a word is to be known a priori. Of course you can fix the range; so you can confine a man or a woman, and not all the way or senses of confinement are knowable a priori" (44).

35. I would like to thank Steven Affeldt, Alice Crary, Randall Havas, Cressida Heyes, Edward Minar, and David Stern for comments, criticisms, suggestions, and encouragement at various stages of this project.

3. WITTGENSTEIN, FETISHISM, AND NONSENSE IN PRACTICE

1. Cf. e.g., "What makes sense in language and thought is dependent on and derived from the nature of objects" (Norman Malcolm, *Nothing Is Hidden* [Oxford: Blackwell, 1986], 14); "Language enjoys certain options on the surface, but deeper down it is founded on the intrinsic nature of objects, which is not our creation but is set over against us in mysterious independence" (David Pears, *The False Prison*, vol. 1 [Oxford: Clarendon, 1987], 8); "The propositions of language must reflect the nature of things, and . . . the logico-metaphysical nature of things is objective and language-independent" (P. M. S. Hacker, *Wittgenstein's Place in Twentieth Century Analytic Philosophy* [Oxford: Blackwell, 1996], 80).

2. Peter Winch, "Understanding a Primitive Society," in *Ethics and Action* (London: Routledge and Kegan Paul, 1972). See also Winch, *The Idea of a Social Science and Its Relation to Philosophy* (London: Routledge and Kegan Paul, 1958).

3. Winch, "Understanding a Primitive Society," 12.

4. Scott Gordon, *The History and Philosophy of Social Science* (London: Routledge, 1991), 638.

5. I use scare-quotes in referring to "its color" and to that color "changing" precisely because, in connection with such a creature, it makes no sense to talk of "its color" or of "its color changing."

6. Whether we are still dealing merely with arithmetic is obviously questionable but not an issue I will worry over here.

7. This has taken some work, an elaborate stage-setting (as Wittgenstein might put it). Through the "technology" of measuring cups, of snapshots, etc., we have reconceptualized what it is that we are applying arithmetic to—in the water case, introducing a refined sense in which we are dealing with "volumes" of water—and thereby put ourselves in a position to derive regular arithmetic results and intelligi-

ble deviance. On this "practical" or "creative" aspect of the application of mathematics, see note 10 below.

8. Recall the question of whether, in the chaotic color world, we *cannot* use our color terms or we *do not*.

9. Friedrich Nietzsche, *Human, All Too Human*, trans. R. J. Hollingdale (Cambridge: Cambridge University Press, 1986), 22.

10. My discussion also has Heideggerian echoes in its emphasis on the practical or creative aspect of the application of mathematics. (Cf., e.g., Heidegger, *Phenomenological Interpretation of the* Critique of Pure Reason (Bloomington: Indiana University Press, 1997), sec. 2, and "Modern Science, Metaphysics and Mathematics," in *Basic Writings* (New York: Harper Collins, 1977). The above discussion suggests a more nuanced and, I would argue, more faithful reading of Heidegger on mathematics and its technological application than that which the generally negative tenor of Heidegger's writings on these topics encourages. My discussion suggests that mathematics and technology can indeed embody productive and illuminating "disclosures" of reality and that they cease to do so only when we forget that they are particular disclosures, presupposing a particular "projection" of reality. It is only when they "take on a life of their own," when they are, as I put it below, fetishized, and are treated as *the* way in which reality discloses itself, that they constitute a threat to us.

11. Galileo's dictum "Measure what is measurable, and make measurable what is not so" is quoted in H. Weyl, "Mathematics and the Laws of Nature," in *The Armchair Science Reader*, ed. I. Gordon and S. Sorkin (New York: Simon and Schuster, 1959).

12. What if, one might ask, one cannot trust any member of the profession in question? What if it is systematically or institutionally "corrupt"? One possibility is that one *cannot* evaluate such a profession, on the Winchian grounds that *no one* can tell one when its practice is successful.

13. Compare Wittgenstein's remarks on exactitude in PI §§ 69–70.

14. Above I referred to "formal measures" without defining "formal." I suspect that, if not handled carefully, praise or criticism of "formality" (like praise of "determinacy") could also turn out to be empty.

15. The work of Elias, with some of the work of Quentin Skinner, also suggests a certain fetishism in our understanding of our own history. In order to tell certain stories about ourselves as the outcome of a process of progression, we may need to conceal from ourselves the fact that the use of certain key concepts may span long periods of history in only a rather superficial way. The life of these terms may have been far more eventful than our story of progress requires, articulating lives and interests that, over the course of that history, have changed more profoundly than our linear story allows.

16. Again, part of the force behind the invocation of rights may be precisely to rule out debate on the positive grounds that we are dealing with something that is inviolate, my possession, and not fit for comment or evaluation by someone else.

17. As the Wittgenstein of the *Tractatus* would put it, a set of signs, not a set of symbols (3.326).

18. Analogous responses can be seen in reaction to behaviorism and utilitarianism. Philosophical debate happens here just because it isn't obvious which of these responses is appropriate. But I am inclined to take this unclarity as itself philosophically important in precisely the way explained above.

19. See, for example, the discussion of Wittgenstein and Kierkegaard in James Conant, "Must We Show What We Cannot Say?" in *The Senses of Stanley Cavell*, ed. R. Flem-

ing and M. Payne (Lewisburg, Pa.: Bucknell University Press, 1989); and James Conant, "Kierkegaard, Wittgenstein and Nonsense," in *Pursuits of Reason,* ed. Ted Cohen, Paul Guyer, and Hilary Putnam (Lubbock: Texas Tech University Press, 1993).
20. See Wittgenstein, *Tractatus* 6.421 and 6.521.
21. I would suggest that use of this term in the early Heidegger is not unrelated.
22. It may also not carry the individualist or introspectionist connotations that the label might conceivably suggest. Instead it is a reflection on how we live, on how what we say relates to what we do.
23. My suspicion is that we may learn more by reflecting on examples of the work of the artists, scientists, and philosophers who seem to have revealed to us these forms of folly. Examples range from *The Interpretation of Dreams, The Genealogy of Morals, 1984,* and *Hard Times* to *Dilbert* (the cartoon series spoofing modern managerialism and bureaucracy in business) and *Yes Minister* (the satirical British TV series parodying governmental bureaucracy and spin-doctoring). This suggestion, along with others offered in this concluding section may sound similar to views propounded by Richard Rorty. It would require further work to determine whether that similarity runs deep.
24. For comments on earlier versions of some of the material presented here, I would like to thank John Divers, Cressida Heyes, Joanna Hilken, and David Owen, along with audiences at the conference on Peter Winch and the Idea of a Social Science held at the University of Bristol in September 2000 and the conference on Scepticism and Interpretation held at the University of Amsterdam in June 2000.

4. GENEALOGY AS PERSPICUOUS REPRESENTATION

1. Note that this is to say nothing against pictures *per se;* on the contrary, it points to the centrality of pictures to the activity of philosophy and, indeed, the activity of thought.
2. For an analysis of this issue, see Robert Fogelin, "Wittgenstein's Critique of Philosophy," in *The Cambridge Companion to Wittgenstein,* ed. Hans Sluga and David Stern (New York: Cambridge University Press, 1996), 34–58.
3. Ludwig Wittgenstein, "Remarks on Frazer's *Golden Bough,*" in *Philosophical Occasions 1912–1951,* ed. James Klagge and Alfred Nordmann (Indianapolis: Hackett, 1993), 118–55.
4. This does not mean that those things that "stand unshakeably fast" now cannot shift (OC §§ 95–99); there is no fixed Background in that sense captured by Collingwood's notion of "absolute presuppositions," rather the background is relative to the practices in which we engage. See David Stern, *Wittgenstein on Mind and Language* (Oxford: Oxford University Press, 1995).
5. Quentin Skinner, *Liberty before Liberalism* (Cambridge: Cambridge University Press, 1998), 116.
6. Gordon Baker, "*Philosophical Investigations* Section 122: Neglected Aspects," in *Wittgenstein's Philosophical Investigations,* ed. Robert L. Arrington and Hans-Johann Glock (London: Routledge, 1991), 48–49.
7. Skinner, *Liberty before Liberalism,* 116–17.
8. Ibid.; James Tully, *Strange Multiplicity: Constitutionalism in an Age of Diversity* (Cambridge: Cambridge University Press, 1995); see also David Owen, "Political Philosophy in a Post-Imperial Voice," *Economy and Society* 28, no. 4 (1999).

9. Raymond Geuss, *The Idea of a Critical Theory: Habermas and the Frankfurt School* (Cambridge: Cambridge University Press, 1981), 60.
10. Ibid., 58.
11. Michel Foucault, *The Use of Pleasure*, trans. R. Hurley (New York: Pantheon, 1985), 7.
12. Wittgenstein, "Remarks on Frazer's *Golden Bough*," 119.
13. Geuss, *Idea of a Critical Theory*, 58.
14. Ibid., 68.
15. James Tully, "To Think and Act Differently: Foucault's Four Reciprocal Objections to Habermas' Theory," in *Foucault contra Habermas: Recasting the Dialogue between Genealogy and Critical Theory*, ed. Samantha Ashenden and David Owen (London: Sage Publications, 1999), 94.
16. James Conant, "Nietzsche, Kierkegaard and Anscombe on Moral Unintelligibility," in *Morality and Religion*, ed. Timothy Tessin and Marion von der Ruhr (New York: St. Martin's), 250–98.
17. Michel Foucault, *History of Sexuality*, vol. 1, trans. R. Hurley (Harmondsworth, England: Penguin, 1978), 88–89; emphasis added.
18. Michel Foucault, "The Ethics of the Concern for the Self as a Practice of Freedom," in *Michel Foucault: Ethics, Subjectivity and Truth*, ed. Paul Rabinow (New York: The New Press, 1997), 298–99.
19. Foucault, "What Is Enlightenment?" 315–16.
20. We should note that the historical or comparative dimension in question may be imaginary—as in the case of imaginary histories or utopias.

5. NOTES ON THE NATURAL HISTORY OF POLITICS

1. See Pierre Aubenque, *La prudence chez Aristôte* (Paris: Presses Universitaires de France, 1986), 155–78.
2. See Ludwig Hänsel, *Ludwig Wittgenstein: Eine Freundschaft*, ed. Ilse Somavilla et al., Brenner Studien, vol. 14 (Innsbruck: Haymon, 1994), 117; O. K. Bouwsma, *Wittgenstein: Conversations 1949–1951*, ed. J. L. Craft and Ronald Hustwit (Indianapolis: Hackett, 1986), 47; *Ludwig Wittgenstein: Personal Recollections*, ed. Rush Rhees (Totowa, N.J.: Rowman and Littlefield, 1981), 229 and passim.
3. See Allan Janik, *Style, Politics and the Future of Philosophy* (Dordrecht: Kluwer, 1989), 40–80.
4. See Hanna Fenichel Pitkin, *Wittgenstein and Justice: On the Significance of Ludwig Wittgenstein for Social and Political Thought* (Berkeley: University of California Press, 1972), 338–39; J. C. Nyíri, "Wittgenstein's Later Work in Relation to Conservatism," in *Wittgenstein and His Time*, ed. B. McGuiness (Oxford: Blackwell, 1981), 44–68; Feruccio Rossi-Landi, "Towards a Marxist Use of Wittgenstein," in *Austrian Philosophy: Studies and Texts*, ed. J. C. Nyíri (Munich: Philosophia Verlag, 1981), 113–52; David Rubinstein, *Marx and Wittgenstein: Social Praxis and Social Explanation* (London: Routledge and Kegan Paul, 1981); David Bloor, *Wittgenstein, Rules and Institutions* (New York: Columbia University Press, 1983); Charles Taylor, "To Follow a Rule," in *Rules and Conventions: Literature, Philosophy, Social Theory*, ed. Mette Hjort (Baltimore: Johns Hopkins University Press, 1992); and Theodore Schatzki, *Social Practices: A Wittgensteinian Approach to Human Activity and the Social* (Cambridge: Cambridge University Press, 1996).

5. The text in *Zettel* and the conversation about politics and membership in a party with Rhees (note 2) should be read together.
6. "My formula for greatness in a human being is *amor fati*. That one wants nothing to be different, not forward, not backward, not in all eternity. Not merely bear what is necessary, still less conceal it—all idealism is mendaciousness in the face of what is necessary—but *love* it." Friedrich Nietzsche, *Ecce Homo*, trans. Walter Kaufmann, in *The Basic Writings of Nietzsche*, ed. Walter Kaufmann (New York: Modern Library, 1968), "Why I Am So Clever," § 10, p. 714.
7. Ludwig Wittgenstein, *Geheime Tagebücher*, ed. Wilhelm Baum (Vienna: Turia and Kant, 1992), 26.XI.1914.
8. Cf. OC § 501: "Am I not getting closer and closer to saying that logic in the end cannot be described? You must look at the practice of language, then you will see it." I am indebted to Kjell S. Johannessen for innumerable discussions of Wittgenstein's later philosophy during the period when the ideas presented here were developed.
9. William Connolly, *The Terms of Political Discourse*, 2d ed. (Princeton, N.J.: Princeton University Press, 1983).
10. W.B. Gallie, "Essentially Contested Concepts," *Proceedings of the Aristotelian Society* 1955/6, reprinted in *The Importance of Language*, ed. Max Black (Englewood Cliffs, N.J.: Prentice-Hall, 1962).
11. Karl Marx, "The Critique of the Gotha Program," in *The Marx-Engels Reader*, ed. Robert Tucker (New York: Norton, 1972), 385.
12. Connolly, *Terms of Political Discourse*, 40.
13. See Taylor's brilliant article "The Opening Arguments of the Phenomenology," in *Hegel: A Collection of Critical Essays*, ed. Alasdair MacIntyre (Garden City, N.Y.: Doubleday, 1972), 151–88. See also Taylor's "To Follow a Rule."

6. WITTGENSTEIN AND THE CONVERSATION OF JUSTICE

1. Plato, *Republic*, trans. G.M.A. Grube (Indianapolis: Hackett, 1974), IX, 592b, 238.
2. Plato, *Republic*, IX, 586e, 233.
3. Thomas Hobbes, *Leviathan*, ed. C.B. Macpherson (London: Penguin Books, 1981), bk. I, chap. XI, 160–61.
4. Ibid., 161, 162.
5. Ronald Dworkin, *Law's Empire* (Cambridge: Harvard University Press, 1986), 5.
6. Ibid., 410.
7. Ibid., 225, 397–98, 413.
8. Ibid., 398.
9. Ibid., 412.
10. This reading of *Philosophical Investigations* as the ongoing reenactment of a condition—rather than as the conclusive establishment via (deductive or quasi-deductive) argumentation of theses about the nature of meaning or understanding—is the main theme of Richard Eldridge, *Leading a Human Life: Wittgenstein, Intentionality, and Romanticism* (Chicago: University of Chicago Press, 1997).
11. Stanley Cavell, *The Claim of Reason: Wittgenstein, Skepticism, Morality, and Tragedy* (Oxford: Oxford University Press, 1979), 207, emphasis added.
12. Ibid.

13. Stanley Cavell, *Conditions Handsome and Unhandsome: The Constitution of Emersonian Perfectionism* (Chicago: University of Chicago Press, 1990), 83.
14. Plato, *Republic*, VII, 517c, 170.
15. Cavell, *Conditions Handsome and Unhandsome*, 86.
16. Stanley Cavell, "Being Odd, Getting Even," in *In Quest of the Ordinary: Lines of Skepticism and Romanticism* (Chicago: University of Chicago Press, 1988), 135.
17. Cavell, *Conditions Handsome and Unhandsome*, 92.
18. Cavell, "Being Odd, Getting Even," 119.
19. Cavell, *Conditions Handsome and Unhandsome*, xxxii.
20. Pierre Bourdieu, *Homo Academicus*, trans. Peter Collier (Cambridge: Cambridge University Press, 1988), 57.
21. Stanley Cavell, *A Pitch of Philosophy: Autobiographical Exercises* (Cambridge: Harvard University Press, 1994), 22.
22. See Joseph Raz, *The Morality of Freedom* (Oxford: Clarendon Press, 1986).
23. See Richard Eldridge, *On Moral Personhood: Philosophy, Literature, Criticism, and Self-Understanding* (Chicago: University of Chicago Press, 1989), 7–9, for a development of this (Hegelian) criticism in reference to Rawls.
24. Here I am alluding to and drawing on Hans Oberiek's account of tolerance as a virtue of character to be developed and practiced affirmatively. See Oberiek, *Tolerance: Between Forbearance and Acceptance* (Lanham, Md.: Rowman and Littlefield, 2001).
25. See Hans Oberiek's discussion of personal autonomy in *Tolerance*, 117–29, drawing on the work of Raz. See also Charles Larmore, "The Moral Basis of Political Liberalism," *Journal of Philosophy* 96, no. 12 (December 1999), 608–9: "the idea of respect is what directs us to seek the principles of our political life in the area of reasonable agreement.... [The principle of respect] must instead be understood as having more than just political authority. We must consider respect for persons as a norm binding on us independent of our will as citizens, enjoying a moral authority that we have not fashioned ourselves. For only so can we make sense of why we are moved to give our political life the consensual shape it has." Whence, then, our commitment to the principle of respect? Perhaps it is like our commitment to the integers: at a certain point in historical life—for example, when interest developed in keeping track of profits and losses during a production cycle—it became evident that the operation of subtraction could be extended to yield an answer to the question, What is seven minus nine? Presumably human beings always could have extended this operation in this way, and once it is thus extended the usefulness of the integers is apparent to nearly everyone. Yet this extension of *our* operation emerged at a historical moment.
26. Conversation with Suzanna Sherry helped me to formulate the problems of Dworkin's interpretivism as a method. Cressida Heyes commented helpfully on an earlier draft of this chapter. Discussion at Northwestern University prompted some final revisions. I am grateful to all these interlocutors.

7. DOING WITHOUT KNOWING

1. Martine Aliana Rothblatt, *The Apartheid of Sex: A Manifesto on the Freedom of Gender* (New York: Crown Publishers, 1995). Like Anne Fausto-Sterling (cited below), Rothblatt (vice-chair of the Bioethics Subcommittee of the International Bar Associ-

ation and herself a transsexual) argues that our two-sex system is too simplistic to accommodate the plurality of sexes and genders. She contests standard criteria for sex difference like chromosomal differentiation and genitals, which she finds as irrelevant to one's place in society as skin tone. The book argues for fundamental changes in our language and concludes with an International Gender Bill of Rights.

2. Anne Fausto Sterling, "The Five Sexes: Why Male and Female Are Not Enough," *The Sciences* 33 (March/April 1993): 20–25.

3. "But can't it be imagined that there should be no physical objects? I don't know. And yet 'There are physical objects' is nonsense. Is it supposed to be an empirical proposition?—" (OC § 35).

4. This includes a complex thinker like Judith Butler, who explicitly states that she is not making antifoundationalist claims, for that would be to remain within "foundationalism and the skeptical problematic it engenders." What she wants to interrogate, rather, is "what the theoretical move that establishes foundations *authorizes*, and what precisely it excludes or forecloses." Butler, "Contingent Foundations," in *Feminists Theorize the Political*, ed. Judith Butler and Joan Scott (New York: Routledge, 1992), 9. My argument is not that Butler is indeed making such claims but, rather, that her epistemic commitments are an obstacle to her political analysis. As I argue below, those commitments turn on the notion of certainty as a knowledge claim that can and must be put into doubt.

5. Linda Nicholson calls this the "coat-rack view of self-identity," in "Interpreting Gender," in *Social Postmodernism: Beyond Identity Politics*, ed. Linda Nicholson and Steven Seidman (Cambridge: Cambridge University Press), 39–69, 41. For a powerful critique of "the ostensibly natural facts of sex" that underwrite the sex/gender distinction, see Judith Butler, *Gender Trouble: Feminism and the Subversion of Identity* (New York: Routledge, 1990), 7.

6. Butler, *Gender Trouble*, 4–5.

7. As Michael Williams observes, there is a difference in "emotional tone" between *An Enquiry concerning Human Understanding* and *A Treatise of Human Nature*. In the former (earlier) text, Hume views skepticism in its "academic guise as a theoretical insight, the recognition that our ordinary beliefs never really amount to knowledge"—an insight that is disappointing but not necessarily threatening. Skepticism is seen as "an epistemological thesis, not a state of mind." In the latter (later) work, however, Humean skepticism reveals its more "Pyrrhonian" side. Now it is not simply a matter of our beliefs amounting to less than knowledge but also our sense that we no longer know what to believe. "For Hume, then, skepticism manifests itself as both a surprising epistemological thesis and a disturbing epoche. If Hume is more relaxed in the *Enquiry*, this is because academic skepticism is in the ascendant and it is easier to be ironic about an epistemological thesis than about chronic instability in one's beliefs." I would say that the state of feminism after identity politics looks more like this chronic instability. Michael Williams, *Unnatural Doubts: Epistemological Realism and the Basis of Skepticism* (Princeton, N.J.: Princeton University Press, 1996), 356.

8. Stanley Cavell, *The Claim of Reason: Wittgenstein, Skepticism, Morality, and Tragedy* (Oxford: Oxford University Press, 1979), 52. See also 136–38.

9. Simone de Beauvoir, "Introduction to Part II," in *The Second Sex*, trans. H. M. Parshley (New York: Vintage, 1974), xxxv.

10. The translator of *The Second Sex*, H.M. Parshley, rendered the French title of Book II, "L'expérience vécue," as "Woman's Life Today," thereby setting the stage for massive misinterpretations of Beauvoir's project.

11. Teresa de Lauretis, *Technologies of Gender: Essays on Theory, Film, and Fiction* (Bloomington: Indiana University Press, 1987), 20.
12. Beauvoir, *Second Sex*, xvii.
13. Ibid., xvi, xvii.
14. Beauvoir adds: "But I know that my only defense is to reply: 'I think thus and so because it is true,' thereby removing myself from the argument. It would be out of the question to reply: 'And you think the contrary because you are a man,' for it is understood that the fact of being a man is no peculiarity. A man is in the right in being a man; it is the woman who is in the wrong" (ibid., xviii). In contrast to the woman, Beauvoir writes, "a man never begins by presenting himself as an individual of a certain sex; it goes without saying that he is a man," where the "goes without saying" refers to his unquestioned enunciative authority (xvii).
15. Luce Irigaray, "Questions," in *This Sex Which Is Not One*, trans. Catherine Porter (Ithaca, N.Y.: Cornell University Press, 1985), 120, 122. Like Beauvoir, Irigaray recognizes that no one would ask a speaker: "Are you a man? In a way that goes without saying" (121).
16. Ibid., 148–49.
17. Hans-Johann Glock, *A Wittgenstein Dictionary* (Cambridge, Mass.: Basil Blackwell, 1996), 153.
18. Irigaray, *This Sex Which Is Not One*, 143.
19. Lucy Sargisson, *Contemporary Feminist Utopianism* (New York: Routledge, 1996), 63.
20. As Richard Flathman interprets Wittgenstein on this point, "we must not 'sublime' rules," as if they were " 'strict calculi,' calculi that, by themselves or of their own accord as it were, do, could or should fully determine our actions." To act as a standard, a rule has to be applied; and in the application are already decisions and choices. Richard Flathman, *Reflections of a Would-Be Anarchist* (Minneapolis: Minnesota University Press, 1998), 66.
21. Irigaray, *This Sex Which Is Not One*, 161, 163.
22. Jacques Bouveresse, *Wittgenstein Reads Freud: The Myth of the Unconscious*, trans. Carol Cosman (Princeton, N.J.: Princeton University Press, 1995), 52.
23. Wittgenstein does not take it for granted that "reasonable" *must* mean I do not doubt the existence of my hands or my body. Rather he shows how what counts as reasonable, and as a reasonable person, will include not subjecting this sort of thing to doubt. Like doubting, acting reasonably is a language-game with certain conventions.
24. "I can imagine a man who had grown up in quite special circumstances and been taught that the earth came into being 50 years ago, and therefore believed this. We might instruct him: the earth has long ... etc.—We should be trying to give him our picture of the world. This would happen through a kind of *persuasion*" (OC § 262).
25. According to Avrum Stroll, "Wittgenstein's genius consisted in constructing an account of human knowledge whose foundations, whose supporting presuppositions, were in no ways like knowledge. Knowledge belongs to the language-game, and certitude does not." *Moore and Wittgenstein on Certainty* (New York: Oxford University Press, 1994), 145. Thus Stroll reads Wittgenstein as "a foundationalist of sorts," but not the traditional sort for whom everything is knowledge, and knowledge of two kinds: noninferential (foundational) and inferential (nonfoundational). Although I agree with Stroll's fascinating interpretation of the substance of Wittgenstein's intervention into the debate over epistemic justification, I am wary of taking Wittgenstein too far in the direction of what Stroll calls an "absolutistic" view

of certainty. As I explain below, Stroll is right to argue that Wittgenstein develops an account of certainty in which what stands fast is the product not of intellect but of rote training. But one should guard against turning Wittgenstein's river metaphor, cited below, into all hard rock and little sand or water.

26. David Stern offers an interesting reading of this metaphor as a way to make sense of the change in Wittgenstein's thinking from the *Tractatus* to the *Philosophical Investigations*. See *Wittgenstein on Mind and Language* (New York: Oxford University Press, 1995), especially chap. 6.

27. A mistake belongs to the language-game. If I add up a list of numbers whose total is 1,253 but I give a calculation of 1,251, that is a mistake. If I give a calculation of 14, that is something altogether different. Likewise, if someone were to say that the earth is 2.5 billion years old and authorities on the matter say that it is 2.7 billion years old, that is a mistake. But if that person were to say that the earth is five years old, she or he is making no mistake but is outside the language-game. See Stroll, *Moore and Wittgenstein on Certainty*, 150.

28. Sigmund Freud, "Femininity," in *New Introductory Lectures on Psychoanalysis*, ed. and trans. James Strachey (New York: Norton, 1965), 100.

29. Bouveresse, *Wittgenstein Reads Freud*, 17.

30. I think the German gives a somewhat different meaning, in which the temporality of the passionate decision does not take the form of a "before" and "after" (as is suggested in the translation: "It would be as though someone were first to let me see the hopelessness of my situation and then show me the means of rescue"). The German text, "Es wäre, als ließe mich jemand auf der einen Seite meine hoffnungslose Lage sehen, und auf der andern stellte er mir das Rettungswerkzeug dar," is better understood as saying, "It would be as though someone were to let me see the hopelessness of my situation, on the one side, and, on the other, show me the means of rescue." I think the notion of before and after ("first . . . and then") both gives the wrong sense of how one makes this sort of decision for a frame of reference and eliminates what for Wittgenstein is the crucial element of struggle. ("If you want to stay within the religious sphere you must *struggle*" [CV 86e]). It is as problematic as Freud's comment about the difference between the little boy's and little girl's passionate decision in favor of the system of reference that goes under the name of the phallus: the boy is initially uninterested in the girl's lack of a penis until, under the threat of castration (let's call it "the hopelessness of his situation"), he comes to "believe in the reality of the threat" (i.e., that he too could lose what she must once have had), and, we could say, grasps hold of "the means of rescue" which is the Name of the Father. "The little girl behaves differently. She makes her judgment and her decision in a flash. She has seen it and knows that she is without it and wants to have it" (Sigmund Freud, "Some Psychological Consequences of the Anatomical Distinction between the Sexes," in *Sexuality and the Psychology of Love* [New York: Collier, 1963], 187–88). I think that a reading of these well-known passages about sexual development would profit from considering them in relation to Wittgenstein's remarks about how one comes to religion. What does it mean to take up a position as a man or as a woman if not passionately to seize hold of, or commit oneself to, a system of reference?

31. The issue here is not whether hinge propositions can be stated but rather that they are, by and large, not stated. If stated, they are not posed as questions. There is nothing in Wittgenstein's account of these propositions that suggests that they are ineffable.

32. Judith Butler, "The Force of Fantasy: Feminism, Mapplethorpe, and Discursive Excess," *differences: A Journal of Feminist Cultural Studies* 2, no. 2 (1990): 106.
33. Once again I think that the English translation leads us astray here. The German reads: "Die Schwierigkeit ist, die Grundlosigkeit unseres Glaubens einzusehen." The verb *"einsehen"* is translated as "to realize." Although *einsehen* can mean "understand" or "recognize," it also means "to see" (something) or "look into" (e.g., files) or "look at" (e.g., books). But "realize" is closer to the German *begreifen, erkennen*, or *(sich) klarwerden* than to *einsehen*. It is perfectly possible for me to realize something without being able to see it or look at it. What one looks at, when one tries to look, is precisely the "picture" that, according to Wittgenstein, holds us "captive" and that lies in our language: the picture of a correspondence between the underlying structure of reality and our language, beliefs, and knowledge.
34. An important issue that I cannot address here is the way in which Wittgenstein resists both communitarian and transcendental notions of rule-following. The definition of correct rule-following is not what the community agrees to, but neither is it metaphysically guaranteed from above. Rules are our standards of correctness; still, if they were dependent on communal agreement, whatever the community agreed upon could count as following a rule. Likewise, if rules did not elicit our agreement, they would have no point: we would not follow them.
35. Butler, "Contingent Foundations," 7.
36. Although Monique Wittig offers a powerful critique of what she calls the political "category of sex," she also recognizes that "sex" belongs to the "what-goes-without-saying" of the straight mind, and that what sustains it is not, finally, a matter of knowledge. Sex is more like a "fetish," as Wittig herself says, in that it is not in any way accountable to reality. See Wittig, *The Straight Mind and Other Essays* (Boston: Beacon, 1992). What undoes "sex" is not a feminist theory but an act of radical imagination. Hence the power and the necessity of Wittig's utopic fiction (e.g., *Les Guérillères*, trans. David LeVay [Boston: Beacon, 1985]; and *Le Corps lesbien* [New York: William Morrow, 1975]).
37. On a related point, see PI §§ 139–40.

8. ON SEEING LIBERTY AS

1. Ray Monk, *Ludwig Wittgenstein: The Duty of Genius* (London: Jonathan Cape, 1990), 508.
2. Ibid., 514.
3. Stephen Mulhall, *On Being in the World: Wittgenstein and Heidegger on Seeing Aspects* (London: Routledge, 1990), 8.
4. Ibid., 11–12.
5. Ibid., 17.
6. Ibid., 20.
7. Ibid., 18.
8. Ibid., 23.
9. The distinction between the activities of political theory and political philosophy was pointed out to me by James Tully.
10. Berlin's move here is symptomatic of a different kind of meaning-blindness (not discussed by Wittgenstein): that there are competing concepts. This form of meaning-blindness arises when the theorist believes that the purpose of political

theory is to separate out competing concepts and decide which one is the best concept.
11. Isaiah Berlin, "Two Concepts of Liberty," in *Four Essays on Liberty* (Oxford: Oxford University Press, 1969), 133.
12. Charles Taylor, "What's Wrong with Negative Liberty," in *Philosophy and the Human Sciences: Philosophical Papers,* vol. 2 (Cambridge: Cambridge University Press, 1985), 213.
13. Ibid., 213.
14. Ibid., 218–19.
15. Ibid., 227.
16. Skinner, *Liberty before Liberalism* (Cambridge: Cambridge University Press, 1998), 205.
17. Ibid., 205, 206.
18. The classic survey of Machiavelli's influence on European political thought up to the American revolution is J. G. A. Pocock, *The Machiavellian Moment* (Princeton, N.J.: Princeton University Press, 1975). Skinner also offers a survey of republicanism during the English Civil War in *Liberty before Liberalism.*
19. Skinner, *Liberty before Liberalism,* 301.
20. Ibid., 303.
21. Stephen Toulmin, *Cosmopolis: The Hidden Agenda of Modernity* (Chicago: University of Chicago Press, 1990), 36–44.
22. The point here is *not* to place those who identify themselves as political philosophers in competition with those who identify themselves as political theorists; rather, it is to use these two different terms (theory and philosophy) to underscore the differences between the two different ways of studying political concepts.
23. James Tully, "Political Philosophy as a Critical Activity," *Political Theory* 30, no.4 (August 2002).
24. An excellent account of this shift is offered in Toulmin, *Cosmopolis.*
25. Toulmin, *Cosmopolis,* 11.
26. Tully, "To Think and Act Differently: Foucault's Four Reciprocal Objections to Habermas' Theory," in *Foucault contra Habermas: Recasting the Dialogue between Genealogy and Critical Theory,* ed. Samantha Ashenden and David Owen (London: Sage Publications, 1999), 1.
27. Thanks to Michael Blackburn, Cressida Heyes, Jeffery Lomonaco, and James Tully for their valuable comments on earlier drafts of this chapter.

9. "BUT ONE DAY MAN OPENS HIS SEEING EYE"

1. Carol Adams, *Neither Man Nor Beast: Feminism and the Defense of Animals* (New York: Continuum, 1995), 73–74.
2. Ibid., 74–75.
3. Wendy Lee-Lampshire (Wendy Lynne Lee), "Anthropomorphism without Anthropocentrism: A Wittgensteinian Ecofeminist Alternative to Deep Ecology," *Ethics and the Environment* 1, no. 2 (fall 1996). Also see Wendy Lee-Lampshire, "Women-Animals-Machines: A Grammar for a Wittgensteinian Ecofeminism," in *Ecofeminism: Woman, Culture, Nature,* ed. Karen Warren (Bloomington: Indiana University Press, 1997).

4. Toni Morrison, *Beloved* (New York: Alfred Knopf, 1987), 193.

5. Daniel Dennett, *The Intentional Stance* (Cambridge: MIT Press, 1987), 20. Wittgenstein suggests a similar view when he remarks that "nothing is more wrongheaded than calling meaning a mental activity" (PI § 693). For we attribute meaning or intending on the basis of a particular interpretation of a thing's behavior, a particular use of that interpretation. "It would ... be possible to speak of an activity of butter when it rises in price," remarks Wittgenstein, but nothing in this way of speaking need move us to postulate a mental state such as "thinking" to the butter (PI § 693). Similarly, nothing in recognizing that we are not positing such a state makes anthropomorphizing a useless activity. Indeed, we not only do say such things but can gain significant explanatory value when we speak, for example, of the attractions of magnets or the flower warming its "face" in the sun, or the leaf taking its sweet time wafting toward the forest floor.

6. Dennett, *Intentional Stance*, 22–23.

7. Ibid., 23.

8. Ibid.

9. It is important to note here that I have translated the German *Mensch* as "man." While some more contemporary translations may render *Mensch* as "person," I would argue that the translation that makes best sense of both the grammar and the meaning of Wittgenstein's example is "man." This interpretation is, of course, just the point of my analysis. For a more extended analysis of Wittgenstein's use of "Mensch" as "man," see Wendy Lee-Lampshire, "Wittgensteinian Visions: A Queer Context for a Situated Episteme," in *Rereading the Canon: Feminist Interpretations of Ludwig Wittgenstein*, ed. Naomi Scheman (University Park: Pennsylvania State University Press, 2002).

10. Naomi Scheman, *Engenderings: Constructions of Knowledge, Authority, and Privilege* (New York: Routledge, 1993), 76.

11. bell hooks, *Wounds of Passion: A Writing Life* (New York: Henry Holt, 1999), 41.

12. Morrison, *Beloved*, 163–64.

13. Ibid. See Wendy Lee-Lampshire, "The Sound of Little Hummingbird Wings: A Wittgensteinian Investigation of Forms of Life as Forms of Power," *Feminist Studies* 25, no. 2 (1999).

14. hooks, *Wounds of Passion*, 64, 65.

15. A typical representation of this perspective is represented in the work of the philosopher Val Plumwood. See, for example, "Nature, Self, and Gender: Feminism, Environmental Philosophy, and the Critique of Rationalism," *Hypatia* 6, no. 1 (1991): 3–27; and "Ecosocial Feminism as a General Theory of Oppression" in *Ecopolitics V Proceedings* (Centre for Liberal and General Studies, University of New South Wales: Kensington, N.S.W., Australia, 1992), 63–72. I would also like to express gratitude for the opportunity to engage Plumwood on the issue of whether anthropocentrism forms a ubiquitous feature of our human-all-too-human epistemic situations; I believe it does, and my exchange with Plumwood has proved invaluable to my endeavor to sharpen my case. Thanks both to Plumwood and to the organizers of the Simposio Internacional Feminismo y Ecologia: Perspectivas Historico-Filosoficas, Universidad Complutense de Madrid, March 23–24, 2001.

16. See also Wendy Lynne Lee and Laura Dow, "Queering Ecofeminism: Erotophobia, Commodification, Art, and Lesbian Identity," *Ethics and the Environment* 6, no. 2 (2001).

17. Earlier drafts of this chapter were presented at the annual meeting of the American Political Science Association, Washington, D.C., August 31–September 3, 2000; at Wissen, Macht, Geschlecht: The International Association of Women Philosophers (IaPh), IX Symposium, Zurich, Switzerland, October 11–14, 2000; and at the Simposio Internacional Feminismo y Ecologia: Perspectivas Historico-Filosoficas, Universidad Complutense de Madrid, March 23–24, 2001. A Spanish-language version is scheduled to appear in the conference proceedings of the Simposio Internacional Feminismo.

10. DOES YOUR PATIENT HAVE A BEETLE IN HIS BOX?

1. David Healy, *The Antidepressant Era* (Cambridge: Harvard University Press, 1998).
2. Herb Kutchins and Stuart A. Kirk, *Making Us Crazy: DSM: The Psychiatric Bible and the Creation of Mental Disorders* (New York: The Free Press, 1997).
3. Lawrie Reznek, *The Philosophical Defense of Psychiatry* (London: Routledge, 1991), 163.
4. Ian Hacking, *Rewriting the Soul* (Princeton, N.J.: Princeton University Press, 1995); *Mad Travelers* (Charlottesville: University Presses of Virginia, 1998); *The Social Construction of What?* (Cambridge: Harvard University Press, 2000).
5. Hacking, *Mad Travelers*.
6. Willard Gaylin, "Faulty Diagnosis," *Harper's*, October 1993, 57–64.
7. Healy, *Antidepressant Era*.
8. M.B. Stein et al., "Paroxetine Treatment of Generalized Social Phobia (Social Anxiety Disorder): A Randomized Controlled Trial," *Journal of the American Medical Association* 280:8 (1998): 708–13; R.C. Kessler, K.A. McGonagle, and S. Zhao, "Lifetime and 12-Month Prevalence of DSM-III-R Psychiatric Disorders in the United States: Results from the National Comorbidity Survey," *Archives of General Psychiatry* 51 (1998): 4–19; W.J. Magee et al., "Agoraphobia, Simple Phobia, and Social Phobia in the National Comorbidity Survey," *Archives of General Psychiatry* 53 (1996): 159–68.
9. M.R. Liebowitz et al., "Phenelzine in Social Phobia," *Journal of Clinical Psychopharmacology* 6:2 (1986): 93–98; M.R. Liebowitz et al., "Pharmacotherapy of Social Phobia: An Interim Report of a Placebo-Controlled Comparison of Phenelzine and Atenolol," *Journal of Clinical Psychiatry* 49, no. 7 (1988): 252–57; M.R. Liebowitz et al., "Phenelzine and Atenolol in Social Phobia," *Psychopharmacology Bulletin* 26, no. 1 (1990): 123–25.
10. M.B. Stein et al., "Paroxetine Treatment of Generalized Social Phobia (Social Anxiety Disorder): A Randomized Controlled Trial,"*Journal of the American Medical Association* 280:8 (1998): 708–13; D. Baldwin et al., "Paroxetine in Social Phobia/Social Anxiety Disorder: Randomised, Double-Blind, Placebo-Controlled Study," *British Journal of Psychiatry* 175 (1999): 120–26.
11. Healy, *Antidepressant Era*. See also David Healy, "Good Science or Good Business," *The Hastings Center Report* 30, no. 2 (March–April 2000): 19–23.
12. Victor Turner, *The Drums of Affliction: A Study of Religious Processes among the Ndembu of Zambia* (Oxford: Clarendon Press, 1968).
13. Paul Brodwin, personal conversation; see also Paul Rabinow, "Artificiality and Enlightenment: From Sociobiology to Biosociality," in *Essays on the Anthropology of Reason* (Princeton, N.J.: Princeton University Press, 1996), 81–111.

14. Erving Goffman, *Stigma: Notes on the Management of Spoiled Identity* (1963; New York: Simon and Schuster, 1986).

15. James Nelson, "The Silence of the Bioethicists: Ethical and Political Aspects of Managing Gender Dysphoria," *GLQ* 4, no. 2 (1998): 213–30.

11. WITTGENSTEIN ON BODILY FEELINGS

1. In quoting *Culture and Value* I will occasionally provide my own translation from the German when it seems clearer or more accurate. Some of the problematic translations have been corrected in the revised edition of the book, but I prefer to cite from the earlier, more familiar edition that is less encumbered with scholarly notations.

2. See, for example, "Somaesthetics: A Disciplinary Proposal," in *Journal of Aesthetics and Art Criticism* 57 (1999): 299–313; revised in *Pragmatist Aesthetics: Living Beauty, Rethinking Art*, 2d ed. (New York: Rowman and Littlefield, 2000), chap. 10; and *Performing Live* (Ithaca, N.Y.: Cornell University Press, 2000), chaps. 7, 8.

3. For my account of philosophy as a way of life and of how Wittgenstein so conceived and practiced it, see Shusterman, *Practicing Philosophy: Pragmatism and the Philosophical Life* (New York: Routledge, 1997), chap. 1.

4. Friedrich Schiller, *On the Aesthetic Education of Man*, trans. E. M. Wilkinson and L. A. Willoughby (Oxford: Clarendon, 1982), 55–57, 79–81, 97, 215–17.

5. See B. McGuinness and G. H. von Wright, eds., *Ludwig Wittgenstein: Cambridge Letters* (Oxford: Blackwell, 1996), 14, 140.

6. William James, *Principles of Psychology* (Cambridge: Harvard University Press, 1983), 1065–66.

7. Ibid., 1100–1104.

8. Ibid., 1104, 1107.

9. Wittgenstein adds that "James' introspection shewed, not the meaning of the word 'self' (so far as it means something like 'person,' 'human being,' 'he himself,' 'I myself'), nor any analysis of such a thing, but the state of a philosopher's attention when he says the word 'self' to himself and tries to analyse its meaning. (And a good deal could be learned from this.)" (PI § 413).

10. James, *Principles of Psychology*, 288–89.

11. Out of fairness to James, we should recall that he, too, insisted that we typically perform our ordinary bodily actions through unreflective habit without any explicit attention to our body feelings or any thematized awareness of the location of our body parts. See his discussion of habits in *Principles of Psychology*, 109–31.

12. I provide a detailed argument for this claim in *Practicing Philosophy*, chap. 1.

13. Ludwig Wittgenstein, *Lectures and Conversations on Aesthetics, Psychology, and Religious Belief* (Oxford: Blackwell, 1970), 17, 33.

14. Ibid., 37–40.

15. It may be that Wittgenstein's habits as a clarinet player had something to do with these somaesthetic feelings, since playing this instrument involves holding the teeth together.

16. The parenthetical term "foreground" refers to the German *Vordergrund*, which was a textual variant to "surface" *(Oberfläche)* in the manuscripts.

17. Ludwig Wittgenstein, *Denkebewegung: Tagebücher 1930–1932, 1936–1937* (Innsbruck: Haymon, 1997), 63.

18. Ibid., 139–40, my translation.

19. It is a common experience of negotiations between extremely hostile groups that mutual understanding is greatly improved once the negotiators actually spend enough agreeable time together to get somaesthetically comfortable with each other, which is why the sharing of meals and entertainment can be a fruitful part of the negotiating process. This was quite evident, for example, in negotiations between Israel and its Arab enemies.

20. Though Foucault sometimes promisingly advocates a creative "desexualization of pleasure" to achieve "a general economy of pleasure that would not be sexually normed," the program he actually elaborates is narrowly focused on "intensifying sexual relations" rather than enlarging our range of pleasures beyond the sexual. See Michel Foucault's interviews in *Foucault Live: Collected Interviews 1961–1984*, ed. S. Lotringer (New York: Semiotext(e), 1996), 212–19, 330–31. For a more detailed critique of this problem, see Richard Shusterman, "Somaesthetics and Care of the Self: The Case of Foucault," *Monist* 83, no. 4 (2000): 530–51; and "The Self as a Work of Art," *Nation*, June 30, 1997, 25–28.

21. See "The Foundations of Mindfulness," in *A Sourcebook of Asian Philosophy*, ed. John Koller and Patricia Koller (Upper Saddle River, N.J.: Prentice-Hall, 1991), 206.

22. Some of the methods are treated in *Performing Live*, chap. 8.

23. Memoirs of Wittgenstein often attest to this. See, for example, Fania Pascal, "Wittgenstein: A Personal Memoir," in *Recollections of Wittgenstein*, ed. Rush Rhees (Oxford: Oxford University Press, 1984), 18; and Norman Malcolm, *Wittgenstein: A Memoir*, 2d ed. (Oxford: Oxford University Press, 1985), 29.

Bibliography

Bloor, David. *Wittgenstein: A Social Theory of Knowledge.* New York: Columbia University Press, 1983.
——. *Wittgenstein, Rules, and Institutions.* London: Routledge, 1997.
Bogen, David. "Order without Rules: Wittgenstein and the Communicative Ethics Controversy." *Sociological Theory* 11, no. 1 (1993): 55–71.
Botwinick, Aryeh. *Wittgenstein, Skepticism, and Political Participation: An Essay in the Epistemology of Democratic Theory.* Lanham, Md.: University Press of America, 1985.
Bowden, Peta. *Caring: Gender-Sensitive Ethics.* New York: Routledge, 1998.
Brill, Susan B. *Wittgenstein and Critical Theory: Beyond Postmodernism and Toward Descriptive Investigations.* Athens: Ohio University Press, 1995.
Cavell, Stanley. "The Availability of Wittgenstein's Later Philosophy." In *Must We Mean What We Say?* Cambridge: Cambridge University Press, 1976.
——. *The Claim of Reason: Wittgenstein, Skepticism, Morality and Tragedy.* Oxford: Oxford University Press, 1979.
——. *In Quest of the Ordinary: Lines of Skepticism and Romanticism.* Chicago: University of Chicago Press, 1988.
——. *This New Yet Unapproachable America: Lectures after Emerson after Wittgenstein.* Albuquerque: Living Batch Press, 1989.
——. *Conditions Handsome and Unhandsome: The Constitution of Emersonian Perfectionism.* Chicago: University of Chicago Press, 1990.
——. *A Pitch of Philosophy: Autobiographical Exercises.* Cambridge: Harvard University Press, 1994.
——. *Philosophical Passages: Wittgenstein, Emerson, Austin, Derrida.* Oxford: Blackwell, 1995.
Cavell, Stanley, et al. "On Wittgenstein." *Philosophical Investigations* 24, no. 2 (April 2001).
Cerbone, David. "Don't Think But Look: Imaginary Scenarios in Wittgenstein's Later Philosophy." *Inquiry* 37, no. 2 (1994): 159–83.
Cohen, Ted, Paul Guyer, and Hilary Putnam. *Pursuits of Reason: Essays in Honor of Stanley Cavell.* Lubbock: Texas Tech University Press, 1993.
Colby, Mark. "The Epistemological Foundations of Practical Reason." *Inquiry* 42, no. 1 (1999): 25–48.

Connolly, William E. *The Terms of Political Discourse.* 2d ed. Princeton, N.J.: Princeton University Press, 1983.
Crary, Alice, and Rupert Read, eds. *The New Wittgenstein.* New York: Routledge, 2000.
Danford, John. *Wittgenstein and Political Philosophy.* Chicago: University of Chicago Press, 1978.
Das, Veena. "Wittgenstein and Anthropology." *Annual Review of Anthropology* 27 (1998): 171–95.
Davidson, Joyce, and Mick Smith. "Wittgenstein and Irigaray: Gender and Philosophy in a Language (Game) of Difference." *Hypatia* 14, no. 2 (1999): 72–96.
Diamond, Cora. *The Realistic Spirit: Wittgenstein, Philosophy, and the Mind.* Cambridge: MIT Press, 1991.
Eagleton, Terry. "Wittgenstein's Friends." *New Left Review* 135 (1982): 64–90.
Eagleton Terry, and Derek Jarman. *Wittgenstein: The Terry Eagleton Script/The Derek Jarman Film.* London: British Film Institute, 1993.
Edwards, James C. *Ethics without Philosophy: Wittgenstein and the Moral Life.* Tampa: University Press of Florida, 1982.
———. *The Authority of Language: Heidegger, Wittgenstein, and the Threat of Philosophical Nihilism.* Gainesville: University of South Florida Press, 1990.
Eldridge, Richard. "The Normal and the Normative: Wittgenstein's Legacy, Kripke, and Cavell." *Philosophy and Phenomenological Research* 46 (1986): 555–75.
———. *Leading a Human Life: Wittgenstein, Intentionality, and Romanticism.* Chicago: University of Chicago Press, 1997.
Elliott, Carl, ed. *Slow Cures and Bad Philosophers: Essays on Wittgenstein, Medicine, and Bioethics.* Durham, N.C.: Duke University Press, 2001.
Flathman, Richard E. *The Practice of Political Authority: Authority and the Authoritative.* Chicago: University of Chicago Press, 1980.
———. "Convention, Contractarianism, and Freedom." *Ethics* 98 (1987): 91–103.
———. *Reflections of a Would-Be Anarchist: Ideals and Institutions of Liberalism.* Minneapolis: Minnesota University Press, 1998.
Garver, Newton. *Derrida and Wittgenstein.* Philadelphia: Temple University Press, 1994.
Genova, Judith. *Wittgenstein: A Way of Seeing.* New York: Routledge, 1995.
Hekman, Susan J. "Some Notes on the Universal and Conventional in Social Theory: Wittgenstein and Habermas." *The Social Science Journal* 20, no. 2 (1983): 1–15.
———. *Moral Voices, Moral Selves: Carol Gilligan and Feminist Moral Theory.* University Park: Pennsylvania State University Press, 1995.
———. *The Future of Differences: Truth and Method in Feminist Theory.* New York: Blackwell, 1999.
Heyes, Cressida J. *Line Drawings: Defining Women through Feminist Practice.* Ithaca, N.Y.: Cornell University Press, 2000.
Hill, Greg. "Solidarity, Objectivity, and the Human Form of Life: Wittgenstein vs. Rorty." *Critical Review* 11, no. 4 (1997): 555–80.
Holt, Robin. *Wittgenstein, Politics, and Human Rights.* New York: Routledge, 1997.
Hurley, Susan. *Natural Reasons: Personality and Polity.* New York: Oxford University Press, 1987.
Hymers, Michael. "Wittgenstein, Pessimism and Politics." *Dalhousie Review* 80, no. 2 (2000): 187–216.

Janik, Allan. *Style, Politics, and the Future of Philosophy.* Norwell, Mass.: Kluwer, 1989.
Johansen, Kjell. "The Concept of Practice in Wittgenstein's Later Philosophy." *Inquiry* 31 (1988): 357–69.
Jones, K. "Is Wittgenstein a Conservative Philosopher?" *Philosophical Investigations* 9, no. 4 (1986): 274–87.
Kitching, Gavin. *Marxism and Science: Analysis of an Obsession.* University Park: Pennsylvania State University Press, 1994.
Kitching, Gavin, and Nigel Pleasants, eds. *Marx and Wittgenstein: Knowledge, Morality and Politics.* New York: Routledge, 2002.
Lamb, David. "The Philosophy of Praxis in Marx and Wittgenstein." *Philosophical Forum* 11 (1980): 273–98.
Landers, Scott. "Wittgenstein, Realism, and CLS: Undermining Rule Scepticism." *Law and Philosophy* 9, no. 2 (1990): 177–203.
Lear, Jonathan. "Leaving the World Alone." *Journal of Philosophy* 79 (1982): 382–402.
———. "The Disappearing 'We'." *Proceedings of the Aristotelian Society*, supp. 58 (1984): 219–42.
Lee-Lampshire, Wendy. "Women-Animals-Machines: A Grammar for a Wittgensteinian Ecofeminism." *Journal of Value Inquiry* 29, no. 1 (1995): 89–101.
———. "The Sound of Little Hummingbird Wings: A Wittgensteinian Investigation of Forms of Life as Forms of Power." *Feminist Studies* 25, no. 2 (1999): 409–26.
———. "Spilling All Over the 'Wide Fields of Our Passions': Frye, Butler, Wittgenstein and the Context(s) of Attention, Intention and Identity (Or: From Arm Wrestling Duck to Abject Being to Lesbian Feminist)." *Hypatia* 14, no. 3 (1999): 1–16.
Lovibond, Sabina. *Realism and Imagination in Ethics.* Minneapolis: University of Minnesota Press, 1983.
Lugg, Andrew. "Was Wittgenstein a Conservative Thinker?" *Southern Journal of Philosophy* 23, no. 4 (1985): 465–74.
———. "Wittgenstein on Politics: Not Left, Right, or Center." *International Studies in Philosophy* (forthcoming).
Minar, Edward. "Wittgenstein and the 'Contingency' of Community." *Pacific Philosophical Quarterly* 72:3 (1991): 203–34.
Moi, Toril. *What Is a Woman? and Other Essays.* Oxford: Oxford University Press, 1999.
Monk, Ray. *Ludwig Wittgenstein: The Duty of Genius.* London: Jonathan Cape, 1990.
Mouffe, Chantal. "Politics, Democratic Action, and Solidarity." *Inquiry* 38, nos. 1–2 (1995): 99–108.
———. *The Democratic Paradox.* New York: Verso, 2000.
Mulhall, Stephen. *Stanley Cavell: Philosophy's Recounting of the Ordinary.* Oxford: Clarendon Press, 1994.
———. "Promising, Consent, and Citizenship." *Political Theory* 25, no. 2 (1997): 171–92.
Nagel, Ludwig, and Chantal Mouffe, eds. *The Legacy of Wittgenstein: Pragmatism or Deconstruction.* Frankfurt: Peter Lang, 2001.
Nyíri, J. C. "Wittgenstein's Later Work in Relation to Conservatism." In *Wittgenstein and His Time*, edited by B. McGuiness. Oxford: Blackwell, 1981.
O'Connor, Peg. *Oppression and Responsibility: A Wittgensteinian Approach to Social Practices and Moral Theory.* University Park: Pennsylvania State University Press, 2002.

O'Donovan-Anderson, Michael. "Wittgenstein and Rousseau on the Context of Justification." *Philosophy and Social Criticism* 22, no. 3 (1996): 75–92.

Owen, David. "Cultural Diversity and the Conversation of Justice: Reading Cavell on Political Voice and the Expression of Consent." *Political Theory* 27, no. 5 (1999): 579–96.

———. "Political Philosophy in a Post-Imperial Voice: James Tully and the Politics of Cultural Recognition." *Economy and Society* 28, no. 4 (1999): 520–49.

Patterson, Dennis. "Postmodernism/Feminism/Law." *Cornell Law Review* 77, no. 2 (1992): 254–317.

———. *Law and Truth*. Oxford: Oxford University Press, 1999.

———, ed. *Wittgenstein and Legal Theory*. Boulder: Westview, 1992.

Peterman, James F. *Philosophy as Therapy: An Interpretation and Defense of Wittgenstein's Later Philosophical Project*. Albany: State University of New York Press, 1992.

Pitkin, Hanna Fenichel. *Wittgenstein and Justice: On the Significance of Ludwig Wittgenstein for Social and Political Thought*. Berkeley: University of California Press, 1972.

Pleasants, Nigel. "Nothing Is Concealed: De-centring Tacit Knowledge and Rules from Social Theory." *Journal for the Theory of Social Behaviour* 26, no. 3 (1996): 233–55.

———. "The Epistemological Argument against Socialism: A Wittgensteinian Critique of Hayek and Giddens." *Inquiry* 40, no. 1 (1997): 23–45.

———. "Free to Act Otherwise? A Wittgensteinian Deconstruction of the Concept of Agency in Contemporary Social and Political Theory." *History of the Human Sciences* 10, no. 4 (1997): 1–28.

———. *Wittgenstein and the Idea of Critical Social Theory: Giddens, Habermas, and Bhaskar*. London: Routledge, 1999.

Polhaus, Gaile, and John Wright. "Using Wittgenstein Critically: A Political Approach to Philosophy." *Political Theory* 30, no. 6 (2002): 800–827.

Putnam, Hilary. *Renewing Philosophy*. Cambridge: Harvard University Press, 1992.

———. *Pragmatism: An Open Question*. Cambridge, Mass.: Blackwell, 1995.

Rossi-Landi, Ferrucio. "Towards a Marxist Use of Wittgenstein." In *Austrian Philosophy: Studies and Texts*, edited by J. C. Nyíri. Munich: Philosophia Verlag, 1981.

Rubenstein, David. *Marx and Wittgenstein: Social Praxis and Social Explanation*. New York: Routledge, 1981.

Schatzki, Theodore. *Social Practices: A Wittgensteinian Approach to Human Activity and the Social*. Cambridge: Cambridge University Press, 1996.

Scheman, Naomi. "Forms of Life: Mapping the Rough Ground." In *The Cambridge Companion to Wittgenstein*, edited by Hans Sluga and David Stern. New York: Cambridge University Press, 1996.

———. "Queering the Center by Centering the Queer: Reflections on Transsexuals and Secular Jews." In *Feminists Rethink the Self*, edited by Diana Meyers. Boulder: Westview, 1997.

Scheman, Naomi, and Peg O'Connor, eds. *Re-Reading the Canon: Feminist Interpretations of Ludwig Wittgenstein*. University Park: Pennsylvania State University Press, 2002.

Schulte, Joachim. "Wittgenstein and Conservatism." *Ratio* 25 (1983): 69–80.

Shapiro, Michael J. *Language and Political Understanding: The Politics of Discursive Practices*. New Haven: Yale University Press, 1981.

Shusterman, Richard. "Wittgenstein and Critical Reasoning." *Philosophy and Phenomenological Research* 46 (1986): 91–110.
———. *Practicing Philosophy: Pragmatism and the Philosophical Life*. New York: Routledge, 1997.
Sparti, Davide, ed. *Wittgenstein politico*. Milan: Feltrinelli, 2000.
Staten, Henry. *Wittgenstein and Derrida*. Lincoln: University of Nebraska Press, 1984.
Taylor, Charles. "To Follow a Rule." In *Rules and Conventions: Literature, Philosophy, Social Theory*, edited by Mette Hjort. Baltimore: Johns Hopkins University Press, 1992.
Toulmin, Stephen. *Return to Reason*. Cambridge: Harvard University Press, 2001.
Tully, James. "Wittgenstein and Political Philosophy: Understanding Practices of Critical Reflection." *Political Theory* 17, no. 2 (1989): 172–204.
———. *Strange Multiplicity: Constitutionalism in an Age of Diversity*. Cambridge: Cambridge University Press, 1995.
———. "The Agonic Freedom of Citizens." *Economy and Society* 28, no. 2 (1999): 161–82.
———. "Political Philosophy as a Critical Activity." *Political Theory* 30, no. 4 (2002): 533–555.
von Wright, G. H. "Wittgenstein in Relation to His Times." In *Wittgenstein and His Time*, edited by B. McGuiness. Oxford: Blackwell, 1981.
Whitaker, Mark. "Ethnography as Learning: A Wittgensteinian Approach to Writing Ethnographic Accounts." *Anthropological Quarterly* 69, no. 1 (1996): 1–13.
Williams, Bernard. "Left-Wing Wittgenstein, Right-Wing Marx." *Common Knowledge* 1, no. 1 (1992): 33–42.
Winch, Peter. *The Idea of a Social Science and Its Relation to Philosophy*. London: Routledge and Kegan Paul, 1958.
———. "Understanding a Primitive Society." In *Ethics and Action*. London: Routledge and Kegan Paul, 1972.
———. "Certainty and Authority." In *Wittgenstein: Centenary Essays*, edited by A. Phillips Griffiths. Cambridge: Cambridge University Press, 1991.

About the Contributors

DAVID R. CERBONE is Assistant Professor of Philosophy at West Virginia University. He has published articles on Wittgenstein, Heidegger, and the analytic and phenomenological traditions more generally.

RICHARD ELDRIDGE is the author of *On Moral Personhood: Philosophy, Literature, Criticism, and Self-Understanding; Leading a Human Life: Wittgenstein, Intentionality, and Romanticism;* and *The Persistence of Romanticism.* He is the editor of *Beyond Representation: Philosophy and Poetic Imagination* and *Stanley Cavell.* He is Professor of Philosophy and Chair of the Department of Philosophy at Swarthmore College.

CARL ELLIOTT is Associate Professor of Pediatrics and Philosophy at the University of Minnesota. He is the author of *A Philosophical Disease: Bioethics, Culture and Identity* and *Better Than Well: American Medicine Meets the American Dream.* He is the editor of *Slow Cures and Bad Philosophers: Essays on Wittgenstein, Medicine and Bioethics* and coeditor with Tod Chambers of *Prozac as a Way of Life.*

JONATHAN HAVERCROFT is a Ph.D. student in political science at the University of Minnesota. He received his M.A. in political science from the University of Victoria in 2000. His current research interest is in the history of sovereignty in Western political thought.

CRESSIDA J. HEYES is Associate Professor of Philosophy at the University of Alberta. She is the author of *Line Drawings: Defining Women through Feminist Practice* and of "Back to the Rough Ground! Wittgenstein, Essentialism, and Feminist Methods," in *Feminist Interpretations of Ludwig Wittgenstein,* edited by Naomi Scheman and Peg O'Connor.

ALLAN JANIK received his A.B. in philosophy from St. Anselm College, his M.A. from Villanova University, and his Ph.D. from Brandeis University. He is currently Research Fellow at the Brenner Archives Research Institute. He is also Adjunct Professor for the Philosophy of Culture at the University of Vienna and has held visiting professorships at the University of Graz, University of Innsbruck, University of Bergen, University of Mexico City, Northwestern University, and Stockholm School of Economics and the Royal Institute of Technology, Stockholm.

WENDY LYNNE LEE (formerly Lee-Lampshire) is Professor of Philosophy at Bloomsburg University in Pennsylvania. Her areas of interest include the philosophy of language and mind, feminist philosophy, and ecological philosophy. Her work can be found in journals such as *Hypatia, Feminist Studies, The Journal of Mind and Behavior, Ethics and the Environment,* and *Apieron,* and she is the author of *On Marx: A Critical Introduction.*

DENIS MCMANUS studied philosophy at Oxford, Cambridge, and Harvard. He teaches at the University of Southampton. He has published on the philosophy of mind, the philosophy of language, and the work of Wittgenstein and Heidegger. He is presently completing a book provisionally titled *Logic, Meaning, Life and Madness: The Philosophy of Wittgenstein.*

DAVID OWEN is Senior Lecturer in Political Theory and Assistant Director of the Centre for Post-Analytic Philosophy, University of Southampton. He is the author of *Maturity and Modernity* and *Nietzsche, Politics and Modernity,* the editor of *Sociology after Postmodernism,* and the coeditor of *Foucault contra Habermas* and *Inhuman Reflections.* He is currently working on perfectionism and democratic theory.

RICHARD SHUSTERMAN was educated at Jerusalem and Oxford and is Chair of Philosophy at Temple University and Directeur de Programme at the Collège International de Philosophie, Paris. He is the author of *The Object of Literary Criticism, T. S. Eliot and the Philosophy of Criticism, Pragmatist Aesthetics, Practicing Philosophy, Performing Live,* and *Surface and Depth* and the editor of *Analytic Aesthetics* and *Bourdieu: A Critical Reader.*

JAMES TULLY is the Henry N. R. Jackman Distinguished Professor of Philosophical Studies, University of Toronto. He has held positions at McGill University and the University of Victoria. Recent publications include *Strange Multiplicity: Constitutionalism in an Age of Diversity; Multinational Democracies,* coedited with A.-G. Gagnon and C. Taylor; "Democracy and Globalisation," in *Canadian Political Philosophy,* edited by R. Beiner and W. Norman; "The Unfreedom of the Moderns," *Modern Law Review* 65, no. 2

(2002); and "Political Philosophy as a Critical Activity," *Political Theory* 30, no. 4 (2002).

LINDA M. G. ZERILLI is Professor of Political Science at Northwestern University. She is the author of *Signifying Woman: Culture and Chaos in Rousseau, Burke, and Mill* and *Feminism and the Abyss of Freedom*.

Index

Adams, Carol, 167–69, 180, 183
Aesthetics, 203–5, 211–13
Agreement. *See Einverständnis;*
 Verständigung
 in judgment, 67, 84–6, 144
Androcentrism, 169–74, 178, 184
Animalizing, 167–85
Anscombe, G.E.M., 221 n. 5
Anthropocentrism, 169–176, 184
Anthropomorphizing, 167–85, 242 n. 5
Anti-metaphysical, 63
Anti-Semitism, 2, 214
Argument of the ordinary, 10, 123–27
Aristotle, 99
Arithmetic, 69–73, 231 n. 7
Art, 211–13
Aspect-blindness, 155–58, 162–63
Aspect-changes, 150–152
Aspect-dawning, 150–52, 155–62
Aspect-perception, 151–157, 162
Aspectival captivity, 82–92, 96
Aspectival concept, 150
Augustine, 35, 83, 99, 144
Äußerung, 152, 162

Baldwin, James, 59–62, 231 n. 34
Beauvoir, Simone de, 131, 133–35, 137, 147, 238 n. 14
Beetle in a box, 188–91, 201
Behaviorism, 71
Belief, 137, 141–42
Benhabib, Seyla, 225 n. 39
Berlin, Isaiah, 150, 157–61, 240 n. 10
Bloor, David, 4, 45–7, 52–3, 103, 229 n. 12
Bodily feelings, 204–209
Body, 214–17
Boundaries, 31–2, 44, 226 n. 42. *See also*
 Limit; Constraint

Bourdieu, Pierre, 126
Bouveresse, Jacques, 137, 141
Butler, Judith, 237 n. 4

Cavell, Stanley, 7, 13, 82, 122–28, 133, 144, 222 n. 26, 231 n. 34
Certainty, 138–44, 237 n. 4, 238–39 n. 25
Chambers, Simone, 225 n. 39
Concepts, 45–59, 65–8, 105–16, 121, 202–3
Connolly, William, 103–12
Consensus, 34. *See also Einverständnis*
Conservatism, 2–7, 18, 43–62, 66, 103, 122, 228 n. 2, 230 n. 19, 231 n. 34
Constraint, 44, 53. *See also* Boundaries; Limit
Conversation of justice, 10, 125–8
Correspondence, 56–7, 140, 176
Crary, Alice, 228 n. 2
Critical reflection, 17–42, 63
 interpretive/ hermeneutic, 35–6
 justificational/ validational, 18–23
Critical theory, 9, 89
Culture and Value, 223 n. 57–64, 224 n. 1

de Lauretis, Teresa, 134, 148
Dennett, Daniel, 172–74, 183
Descartes, René, 6
Diamond, Cora, 7, 43, 230 n. 26
Direct expression. *See Äußerung*
DSM, 186, 191, 194, 195
Dworkin, Ronald, 119–20, 125–27

Eagleton, Terry, 4
Ecological niche, 192–93
Einverständnis, 21–4
Emotions, 205–19
Essence, 121, 133, 136
Essential contestability, 105, 108–12

Essentialism, 132
Ethics, 2, 80, 102, 203, 214

Facts, 54–8, 64, 138
Family resemblance, 4, 103–16, 191
Fausto-Sterling, Anne, 129–30
Feminism, 8, 130–48, 174, 184, 237n. 7
Fetishism, 73–80, 232n. 15
Form of life, 3–7, 34, 44, 48–9, 84, 144, 191–93, 201
Foucault, Michel, 32, 82–3, 89–96, 164, 217, 227n. 68, 245n. 20
Foundationalism, 131–32, 138–39, 142–43, 238n. 25
Freedom, 23, 31, 32, 159–61. *See also* Liberty
Frege, Gottlob, 46–7

Galileo, 75, 232n. 11
Gellner, Ernest, 4–5, 48–50, 58, 229n. 5, 230n. 21
Genealogy, 32, 82, 88–96
Generic, masculine as, 175–83
Generic object, 133–34, 147
Gender, 145–46
Gestalt, 149, 155–56, 162
Geuss, Raymond, 89, 91–2
Goffman, Irving, 198
Gordon, Scott, 66
Grammar, 3, 54, 135–36, 188–89
Ground, 26–7, 213

Habermas, Jürgen, 6, 17–8, 26–36, 223n. 6–8, 224n. 17, 24, 225n. 36
  on justificational critical reflection, 18–23
  practice of validation, 23–4
Hacking, Ian, 192–93
Hegel, G. W. F., 31, 112, 172
Heidegger, Martin, 17, 154–55, 232n. 10
Hermeneutic, 35–6
Heteropatriarchal, 178, 180
Heterosexism, 169, 174, 184
Hinge propositions, 34, 138–46, 239n. 31
Hobbes, Thomas, 118
Homophobia, 167
hooks, bell, 179–84
Hume, David, 132–33, 237n. 7

Idealism, 43–4, 48, 57
Ideological captivity, 88–92
Ideology-critique, 90–93
Inner copies, 151–53
Instrumental worth, 173–74, 182–84
Interpretation, 35–41, 169, 227n. 59
Interpretivism, 119–20, 125–26
Intrinsic worth, 173–74, 182–84
Irigaray, Luce, 135–37

James, William, 205–7, 244n. 9, n. 11
Janik, Allan, 4
Jastrow, Joseph, 149, 155–57, 162
Judgments, 84–91, 120. *See also* Agreement in judgment
  aesthetic, 211
Justice, 204
Justification, 23–5

Kant, Immanuel, 6, 93
Kinaesthetic feelings, 206–8, 211–12
Knowledge, 137–39, 153–58, 237n. 4, 238n. 25
Körpergefühl. *See* Bodily feelings

Language, 5, 35, 56–8, 65, 102–8, 115, 121, 168, 178, 183, 191–92, 218, 231n. 1
Language-games, 5, 8, 18, 21, 26–8, 40, 99, 139–40, 147, 156, 188–91, 218, 239n. 27
  of gender, 134–35
Last Writings on the Philosophy of Psychology, 200
Liberty, 150, 156–64. *See also* Freedom
Limit, 6, 44, 51, 83. *See also* Boundaries; Constraint
Logic, 3, 46–7
Logic of domination, 170–75, 180–85
Lovibond, Sabina, 7

Machiavelli, Niccolò, 160
Marx, Karl, 73–4, 103–5, 112
Mathematics, 46–7, 69–73
Meaning, 188–89
Mensch, problems of translating, 242n. 9
Mental illness. *See* Psychopathology
Monk, Ray, 2
Moore, G. E., 138
Morrison, Toni, 171–74, 181–83
Mulhall, Stephen, 7, 151, 153–54

Nagel, Thomas, 48–9
Natural history, 40, 44, 47, 54, 101, 106, 111, 229n. 13
Naturalism, empiricist, 124
Nietzsche, Friedrich, 40, 72, 80, 82, 90, 93–5, 103, 235n. 6
Nonsense, 25, 80–1
Nyíri, J.C., 4–5, 48–51, 103, 222n. 57–64

Oakeshott, Michael, 4
On Certainty, 5, 26, 28, 83–4, 138
Oppression, 60–2, 167–69, 178, 184–85
Ordinary practice, 121–25

Perfectionism, 125, 127

Perspective, 229 n. 12
Perspicuous representation, 8, 86–8, 95–6, 153, 163, 223 n. 5. *See also Übersicht*
Philosophical Investigations, 3, 25, 82–3, 88, 99, 120–7, 226 n. 50, 235 n. 10
Philosophy, 1, 27, 112–14, 187, 203, 211
   of language, 3
   of mind, 203, 208, 211, 213
   political, 3, 82, 157, 162–64, 240 n. 9, 241 n. 22
Picture, 3, 18, 83–90, 96, 143, 154, 169, 175–77, 233 n. 1
Pitkin, Hanna, 7, 103, 222 n. 25
Plato, 117. *See also Republic*
Political judgment, 125
Political science, 105–6, 118, 125–27
Political theory, 117–18, 124–27, 157, 163, 203–4
Politics, 1, 148, 203, 213
   as rule-following, 99–116
Power, 94, 150
Practice, 26, 34, 38, 40, 63, 65, 106, 202
   of justification, 27–8
   of reflection, 41
Private language, 106–7, 116
Psychopathology, 186–88, 192–93, 201
Putnam, Hilary, 229 n. 12

Quietism, 3, 101

Racism, 167–74, 184
Raz, Joseph, 127
Ready-to-hand, 154–56, 159–61
Reasonable, 21, 24, 28, 31, 238 n. 23
Reasonable disagreement, 224 n. 22, 236 n. 25
Reich, Wilhelm, 217
Remarks on Colour, 45
Remarks on the Philosophy of Psychology, 52, 53, 150
Republic, 10, 203. *See also* Plato
Republicanism, 160–61
Reznik, Lawrie, 187
Rightness, validity claim of, 30–3
Rossi-Landi, Ferrucio, 103
Rothblatt, Martine, 129–30, 236–37 n. 1
Rubinstein, David, 103
Rule-following, 4, 27, 108–16
Rules, 37–8, 106–16, 136, 149, 188–89, 238 n. 20, 240 n. 34
Russell, Bertrand, 1–2

Sargisson, Lucy, 136
Sartre, Jean-Paul, 18
Schatzki, Theodore, 103

Scheman, Naomi, 7, 176, 222 n. 57–64
Schiller, Friedrich, 204
Science, 140–41
Scientific method, 87–8
Seeing-as, 149–63, 169, 227 n. 64
Self-government, 82–95
Self-improvement, 203
Self-knowledge, 203–9
Self-mastery, 211
Self-reflection, 90–5
Sex and Character, 2
Sex/gender system, 129–32, 143–6
Sexism, 167–74
Sign, 36–41
Skepticism, 115, 124, 131–34, 138, 237 n. 7
Skinner, Quentin, 8, 29, 225 n. 35, 232 n. 15
   on aspectival captivity, 86–7, 96
   on liberty, 150, 157–61
Socialism, 2
Social phobia, 193–97, 201
Somaesthetics, 202–19, 245 n. 19
Stroll, Avrum, 238 n. 25
Survey, 18, 223 n. 5
Synoptic view. *See Übersicht*
System of reference, 141–46, 239 n. 30

Taylor, Charles, 8–9, 17–8, 103, 112, 226 n. 52
   on interpretation as critical reflection, 35–6
   on liberty, 150, 157–61
Tolerance, 236 n. 24, 25
Toulmin, Stephen, 4
Tractatus, 102
Tully, James, 8–9, 87, 93, 96, 164
Turner, Victor, 197–99

Übersicht, 149–50
Uncle Tom's Cabin, 59–62, 230 n. 28
Understanding, 36–41, 227 n. 59

Verständigung, 18–39, 224 n. 23

Warren, Karen, 170
Weininger, Otto, 2, 221 n. 7
Weltanschauung, 149
Winch, Peter, 5, 65–6
Wittig, Monique, 130, 146, 240 n. 36
Women,
   in feminist philosophy, 131–7, 140–3, 146–8
   Wittgenstein's views on, 2, 221 n. 7

Zettel, 25, 235 n. 5

www.ingramcontent.com/pod-product-compliance
Lightning Source LLC
Chambersburg PA
CBHW052058300426
44117CB00013B/2184